A HISTORY OF THE ISRAELI ARMY

A HISTORY OF
THE ISRAELI ARMY

1874 TO THE PRESENT

Ze'ev Schiff

MACMILLAN PUBLISHING COMPANY

New York

Macmillan Publishing Company
866 Third Avenue, New York, N.Y. 10022
Collier Macmillan Canada, Inc.

Library of Congress Cataloging-in-Publication Data
Schiff, Ze'ev, 1932–
A history of the Israeli Army, 1874 to the
present.
Includes index.
1. Israel—History, Military. 2. Israel—Armed
Forces—History. I. Title.
DS119.2.S3413 1986   355′.0095694   85-15392
ISBN 0-02-607140-1

Macmillan books are available at special discounts for bulk purchases
for sales promotions, premiums, fund-raising, or educational use.
For details, contact:

Special Sales Director
Macmillan Publishing Company
866 Third Avenue
New York, N.Y. 10022

10 9 8 7 6 5 4 3 2 1

Designed by Jack Meserole

Printed in the United States of America

Contents

Preface

The Israel Defense Forces (IDF) is a unique citizens army, a classic people's militia that was born with the State of Israel to defend the country and its independence. Ever since its creation the IDF has been fighting a long war that has assumed a number of forms and been conducted on a variety of fronts. It has ranged from a series of punishing, full-blown clashes with regular armies to an insidious guerrilla war, a public campaign against terrorism to a secret war. It is impossible to appreciate the accomplishments of Israel or the earlier Zionist movement in Palestine without an understanding of the IDF, the concepts that guide it, and the wars that have shaped it.

The need for a Jewish defense force arose almost immediately upon the renewal of Jewish settlement in Palestine more than a century ago. As the Jewish community extended its gains in the country the need to defend its achievements naturally became all the greater. What's more the Jews of Palestine were quick to learn that they could not rely on outside elements to guarantee their security; only an independent Jewish force could be so entrusted. It was out of such a force that the IDF emerged—farmers, builders, and their sons, who conquered the land by working the soil also turned to soldiering and became experts in combat doctrine and strategy. When Israel attained her independence her people knew that without a strong army the state would be destroyed by its enemies, and the Jewish national movement would come to naught. At the same time the IDF served as the melting pot for the hundreds of thousands of immigrants coming in from the ends of the earth and speaking a babel of languages. Little wonder that the people of Israel took pride in their army—a pride shared by Jews the world over.

It was for these reasons that the IDF sometimes came above

everything, including criticism. Yet its founder, David Ben-Gurion—Israel's first Prime Minister and Minister of Defense—stated repeatedly that military might was not enough; the State of Israel required an army that could draw on both military and moral strength. Thus in addition to maintaining high standards of combat the IDF was to stand out for its commitment to combat ethics.

Such is the army to which this volume is devoted. Since the subject is far too broad to be covered in detail in any one book, I have chosen to approach it from two vantages—the IDF's performance in Israel's wars, and the professional side of the army—to provide a sharper portrait of how the Israeli Army works and the problems with which it must deal. The IDF's achievements are many, but it has also known painful reversals and setbacks and they too are a part of the story told here.

The original edition of this book, published in a different format by Straight Arrow Books in 1974, was skillfully edited and translated by Raphael Rothstein, who was also the prime mover behind the reissue of this book. Since then the IDF has fought yet another war, struggled against terrorism and guerrilla warfare, and faced a number of grave internal problems. In light of these developments Macmillan proposed that I revise the book, which entailed adding a number of completely new chapters and rewriting others. Assisting me in her practiced and professional way was editor and translator Ina Friedman, who has my gratitude.

ZE'EV SCHIFF

Tel Aviv
January 1985

A HISTORY OF THE ISRAELI ARMY

Fathers of the Israeli
Defense Forces

THE ROOTS of the modern Israeli Army go back to the 1880s when the Jewish settlers in Palestine first grappled with the problem of self-defense. From the moment Jews decided to return to Palestine and cultivate their own lands the need to protect life and property became a major concern. The first Jewish settlement, Mikveh Israel, was founded in 1870, when there were only 25,000 Jews in the whole of the country. It was followed by Petach Tikvah, Rehovot, Gedera, Hadera, and similar villages. Known as *moshavot,* these settlements were built for all-around defense, as though the houses were covered wagons making a stand against Indian attack. Yigal Allon, later a commander of the Palmach (the commando corps established in the 1940s) and himself a native of a moshavot, explained that the founders of these first settlements thought in nationalist terms and regarded their modest villages as forward positions that would someday play a role in determining the borders of a Jewish state.

In those days security was virtually nonexistent in Palestine, and Bedouin marauders regularly plundered the settlements and robbed travelers on the roads. Hardly a single Jewish settlement escaped attack by the Bedouin or by their more sedentary Arab neighbors. This first period of Jewish self-defense in Palestine was embodied by a group called the Shomrim (watchmen) whose leading members—such as Yehoshua Stamper, one of the founders of Petach Tikvah, and Yehuda Raab who had come to Palestine from a small village in Hungary—were pioneers in self-defense among the Jewish settlers. At first these Shomrim consisted of farmers, idealistic day workers, and socialist pioneers.

At the same time a new consciousness was evolving among European Jews as a consequence of the wave of pogroms that rumbled through czarist Russia in the 1880s. These massacres set the Jewish masses thinking about a future of national freedom and independence—thoughts that inspired the spontaneous organization of largely ad hoc defense groups. In 1903 an historic event took place in the town of Homel on the border of the Ukraine. Jewish youth affiliated with the Zionist Social Party organized into self-defense units and for three days repelled the rampaging mobs and the policemen who were among the organizers of a pogrom. Some of the men of the Homel socialist group immigrated to Palestine in the following year and joined in the establishment of the first real Jewish defense network there.

Bar-Giora was a secret association of watchmen founded in September 1907 by ten men who met in Jaffa and named their clandestine society after the Jewish warrior who had distinguished himself in the revolt against the Romans in A.D. 70. The organization adopted as its motto the biblical epigram that echoed through decades of blood-soaked history in Palestine: "In blood and fire Judea fell and in blood and fire Judea shall arise!" Yet sentiment in the Arab camp was running equally as strong: in their staunch opposition to Jewish settlement the Arabs of Palestine dubbed the Jews *walad el-mita* (the children of death). Nevertheless, the members of Bar-Giora hoped to change this disparaging attitude and they were encouraged by the example of the Circassian villages in Palestine. Although the Circassians were a minority group, the Arabs stood in awe of them and respected them as fierce fighters. Aspiring to a similar position of coexistence based on a healthy respect for their prowess, the members of Bar-Giora underwent training in the use of arms and then accepted their first assignment: guarding the *moshavah* of Sejera in the Galilee.

By 1909 the members of Bar-Giora had decided that a secret association of watchmen was not enough. If they wanted to become a force of national significance they would have to create a larger and at least partially open organization. Hence in April they held a general meeting and decided to establish a new defense organization to be known as Hashomer (the watchman). Although still a relatively primitive organization, Hashomer represented an important stage in the development of Jewish self-defense in Palestine: it assumed responsibility for protecting additional Jewish agricultural settlements and replaced the paid Arab watchmen who often worked in league with thieves for a share of the take.

Bar-Giora and Hashomer were founded and nurtured by the men of the Second Aliyah, the wave of immigration that began in 1904 and continued until the First World War. It brought to Palestine East European Jews who had been profoundly influenced by the 1905 Russian Revolution. Mostly young people who had turned their backs on the stagnation of ghetto life and believed they would fulfill themselves by pioneering work on the land, they were drawn by the Zionist vision and espoused a mixture of nationalist and socialist views. In establishing Hashomer they stressed the bond that united settlement on the land and military training—a motif that was to continue through the formation of the Haganah in the 1930s, the Palmach in the 1940s, and the Nahal units of the Israel Defense Forces. Members of Hashomer were among the founders of Degania, the first kibbutz, as well as other collective settlements. They were also involved in establishing a labor legion in which all young people were to dedicate two years to defense and labor on the land.

Although the people of Hashomer concentrated mainly on guard duties, they also undertook modest retaliatory actions against Arabs who had attacked Jewish settlers or their property, and many of their men were lost in clashes with Arab brigands. They also tried, albeit unsuccessfully, to manufacture arms and explosive devices. Yet despite such setbacks their bravery fired the imagination of Jews in the Diaspora, and a fund was set up in Russia to acquire arms, equipment, and horses for the watchmen, and to compensate their families in the event of their disablement or death.

Like the rest of the Jewish community of Palestine—known collectively as the Yishuv—Hashomer declined during World War I. Its leaders had hoped to use the hostilities to their advantage and proposed to the Ottoman authorities the establishment of a local Jewish militia. But the idea was summarily rejected and Hashomer was formally outlawed.

The next phase in the development of a Jewish fighting force began in Egypt in the refugee camps populated by Jews who had been exiled from Palestine by the Turks. It was here that two Russian Jews actively promoted the idea of establishing Jewish battalions to fight as part of the British Army in liberating Palestine from Ottoman rule.

Ze'ev Jabotinsky, a journalist and gifted orator from Odessa who was to go down in history as the head of the Revisionist wing of the Zionist movement, joined forces in advocating the establishment of these units with Joseph Trumpeldor, a former officer in the czar's army who had lost his left arm in the Russo-Japanese War. At first the British refused to consider the idea and agreed only to establish a battalion of mule drivers. Jabotinsky, entertaining visions of a Jewish legion, was sorely disappointed, but Trumpeldor enlisted in the battalion as one of its officers. Six hundred and fifty men of the Zion Mule Corps were transferred to the Gallipoli front, where they did yeoman's service transporting arms and supplies to the besieged British forces. When the campaign drew to a close the British, impressed by the corps' record and courage, wanted to transfer them to Ireland to quell the uprising there, but the men refused and the battalion was disbanded. Meanwhile Jabotinsky continued to lobby for a Jewish legion.

In 1917, after the publication of the Balfour Declaration—in which the British recognized the right of the Jews to establish a national home in Palestine—the idea of creating Jewish units was raised again and this time Jabotinsky and Trumpeldor were invited to the War Office in London to discuss the matter. After much deliberation Jabotinsky finally prevailed and three units of the Royal Fusiliers were combined to form the First Judean Regiment. As volunteers from England, the United States, and Canada swelled its ranks, the regiment became known as the Jewish Legion. Among the recruits were David Ben-Gurion and Yitzhak Ben-Zvi (second president of Israel), both of whom had been expelled from Palestine by the Turks.

In 1918 two battalions of the Jewish Legion reached the Palestinian front, while a third battalion was organized among the Palestinian exiles in Egypt. They were attached to General Edmund Allenby's forces that had been assigned to drive the Turks out of Palestine. The Judean Regiment was the largest Jewish military formation since antiquity, and many of its veterans would subsequently contribute to the development of a security force for the Yishuv.

While Jabotinsky enlisted as a private in the Jewish Legion, Joseph Trumpeldor returned to Russia with the idea of raising a Jewish army there in his dream of Jewish fighters invading Palestine via the Caucasus and Persia. But even though he did not take part in the conquest of Palestine, by 1917 Trumpeldor was considered without peer as the most outstanding military figure in the Yishuv. Trumpeldor had enlisted in the Russian Army in 1902 at the age of twenty-two and a year later was sent to the front at Port Authur, where he distinguished himself in battle. Although he had lost an arm he asked to be again sent to the front—a request that was granted. He returned from the war with many decorations and the unique distinction of being the only Jew to be commissioned as an officer in the czar's army. While a prisoner of war he organized other Jewish POWs planning to immigrate to Palestine into a group called B'nai Zion (the sons of Zion), and he himself reached Palestine in 1912 and joined the Degania kibbutz. As a Russian citizen, however, he was deported by the Turks during World War I.

Like Jabotinsky Trumpeldor traveled far and wide promoting the idea of a Jewish army. He was an unusual mixture of a man of war and a settler on the land. When the first Jewish soldier of the Zion Mule Corps was killed in Gallipoli, his men contended that it was a day for celebration for Trumpeldor because Jewish blood had been shed not in a pogrom but in battle. Tall, handsome, Nordic, he was keen on anything Hebrew—Hebrew labor, a Hebrew army, and the like—although he never really mastered the Hebrew language. When his plan to form a Jewish army failed to gain support in Russia he persuaded many Jewish youth to emigrate. Among his recruits to Palestine was Yitzhak Sadeh, who himself would become one of the fathers of the IDF.

When Trumpeldor returned to Palestine at the end of 1919 he found the atmosphere there charged. In the north of the country the Arabs were embroiled in a rebellion against the French who had been granted a mandate over Syria and Lebanon. Trumpeldor made his way to the northern border settlement of Tel Hai, where he took command of other small farming and shepherding settlements, and where he later met his death in an Arab attack. Thereafter Tel Hai became a symbol of Jewish self-defense and Trumpeldor a paragon of personal heroism for generations of Israeli youngsters. His legendary last words— "No matter, it is good to die for our country!"—were adopted as the motto of later Jewish underground organizations, although some historians suggest that in view of his shaky Hebrew and his penchant for salty language Trumpeldor probably died with a Russian curse on his lips.

At about the time Tel Hai fell and three other Jewish settlements in the north were abandoned riots in Jerusalem took a grim toll in Jewish lives. Jabotinsky, who headed the Jewish self-defense effort in the city, was arrested and deported by the British mandatory authorities. He never returned to the country again, though his influence was felt for many years to come.

In 1920 the Arab riots spread to Jaffa, the gateway to the country, claiming the lives of many new immigrants. Considering the Yishuv's upbeat mood with the advent of the British mandate, the Jews were stunned by the outbreak of violence and dismayed by the realization that their political situation had actually taken a turn for the worse because the British authorities were less than eager to honor the promise implied by the Balfour Declaration. The shock was all the greater because of the glaring failure of the Jewish defense organizations to cope with the assaults on Jews. The mounted watchmen were clearly not adequate to meet the challenge of the times; it would take a far more versatile and popular defense organization to deal with the security problem in the cities as well the countryside.

Hashomer, as a result, was voluntarily disbanded in May 1920, and a month later the Haganah was established at a conference of one of the major workers parties. (It was later transferred to the jurisdiction of the Histadrut, the General Federation of Labor.) In that the British forbade the Jews of Palestine to bear arms, the Haganah was from the start (and would always remain) a clandestine organization. It was clearly the creation of the Jewish Labor movement in Palestine, and even when more right-wing elements participated in its national command, Labor continued to set the tone.

Just as Hashomer can be categorized as a product of the Second Aliyah, the Haganah drew its impetus from the subsequent wave of immigration, the Third Aliyah, which began at the close of the world war and continued until 1924. Many of these immigrants were Russians and Poles who had been both displaced and profoundly influenced by the Bolshevik Revolution—at least to the degree that they were dedicated to the principle of settlement on a cooperative basis. During this period alone the Yishuv's population of 90,000 grew by more than a third, most of the newcomers being young, single, and eager to take on the challenges that Palestine had to offer.

One of these challenges was the effort to establish permanent armed units within the framework of the Haganah. The most promising way to do this was to convert the extant labor-and-defense battalion of a few hundred men into the nucleus of a permanent military structure. The unit was called the Trumpeldor Battalion, and its members did agricultural work, paved roads, and worked in quarries throughout the country. Its transformation into a standing unit was effectively an acknowledgment by the Jewish leadership that the tension between Arabs and Jews was growing increasingly volatile, fueled as it was by the Arabs' rejection of the Balfour Declaration or any program aimed at affording the Jews a national presence in Palestine. This reading was all too correct unfortunately, for between the two world wars Arab hostility was to erupt in three major outbreaks of terrorism: the disorders of 1921, 1929, and 1936–39.

In 1921 the Arab riots, as attacks on Jewish settlements and population centers came to be known, were aimed at both discouraging the Zionist enterprise and pressuring the British to alter what the Arabs perceived as a favorable attitude toward the establishment of a Jewish national home. Although hostility was initially confined to a small section of the Arab community, it was fanned by the Arab nationalist movement, which itself aspired to oust the mandatory powers and unify Syria and Palestine into an independent Arab kingdom. Thus in the course of the 1920s the anti-Zionist assaults took on the complexion of a political and religious struggle that fed on such slogans as *Itbahu al-yahud* (Slaughter the Jews) and *Falastin bladna wa-al-yahud clabna* (Palestine is our country and the Jews our dogs). The extremism of this enmity more than just astounding the Yishuv, it quickly dispelled the belief that the Arabs were willing to live peacefully with their Jewish neighbors.

The wave of terrorism spread from Jerusalem to Jaffa, the Arab port city south of Tel Aviv where both long-time Jewish residents and newcomers were massacred. From Jaffa the terror struck in Petach Tikvah, Hadera, Rehovot, and other Jewish settlements, and finally erupted again in Jerusalem. The Yishuv emerged from this first encounter with violent Arab opposition determined not only to protect itself against the recurrence of terror but also to develop autonomous economic institutions that would mitigate dependence on the Arabs. In this way Arab hostility, finally suppressed by authorities in 1921 after scores of people had been killed, was really the main impetus for expansion and development of both the Haganah and an independent Jewish economy.

In a bid to obtain the cooperation of foreign governments in training its men the Haganah sent emissaries abroad. Contact with the Soviet Union was established in 1925 through the Soviet ambassador in Berlin, and a year later a delegation of three men went to Russia, returning with the Kremlin's agreement to accept one Jewish youth from Palestine for flight training. The candidate completed the course successfully, but to the chagrin of Haganah he decided to remain in the Soviet Union.

The Haganah then decided to seek the assistance of Jews abroad in recruiting men, raising funds, and obtaining weapons. At the same time it began to smuggle weapons from Europe into Palestine in defiance of a British ban and drew up ambitious plans for equipping its men. But the relative calm of the late 1920s lulled the leaders of the Yishuv into a sense of complacency about security and the Haganah received little support for its procurement program.

The tranquility of the late 1920s came to an abrupt end in 1929 when the Yishuv was rocked by yet another wave of Arab violence. It began in Jerusalem as a religious dispute over prayer rights during High Holy Days at the Western Wall, a lodestone for Jewish worshippers adjoining the Haram a-Sharif compound of mosques sacred to Islam. In defiance of a prohibition issued by the Moslem religious authorities a group of Jews held prayers at the wall on August 23, 1929 and were attacked by a group of Arabs. A few days later an Arab mob rampaged through Hebron, murdering fifty-nine of the city's Jewish residents. An eyewitness account of the massacre published in the *The Times* of London on Friday August 30, 1929 reads as follows:

The first house attacked was a large Jewish house on the main road, and the occupants locked themselves in. For some unknown reason the gates were opened to allow two young boys to leave, and they were immediately killed. This inflamed the crowd, who entered the house and beat or stabbed the inmates to death. The local police force, which consisted of only a British officer, two Arab officers and 30 Arabs, made every effort to control the situation, but the crowd was out of hand, and attacked other Jewish homes, beating and stabbing the inhabitants—men, women and children. The police fired, but the situation was not definitely in hand until the arrival of 12 British police and 12 Royal Air Force personnel from Jerusalem.

The historic Jewish community of Safed in northern Palestine was also hard hit by Arab terrorists, and in the wake of the fevered violence the Jewish communities of Nablus, Gaza, Tulkarem, Jenin, and Beisan abandoned these overwhelmingly Arab cities and towns, having learned that their greatest security lay in banding together in exclusively Jewish settlements and neighborhoods.

While Yishuv was badly battered in 1929, the Arabs failed to bring about its complete collapse because British troops intervened to reestablish order. Even so the British were not always able to reach beleaguered areas and the Jews resolved to bolster their own defense arrangements. The Haganah's first step in this direction was to begin planning defense on a national scale. The settlements were organized into defense blocs, and the procurement of weapons gained momentum. In Vienna, for example, the Haganah was assisted by the underground defense organization of the Austrian socialists, the Schutzbund, while Antwerp, Belgium was also a base for purchasing weapons. At the same time a clandestine arms industry was inaugurated in Palestine to manufacture bombs, hand grenades, cartridges, even tear gas.

The lessons learned from past failures changed the Haganah for the better, but its commanders were still idealists rather than pragmatic military men, more preoccupied with ideological debates than strategic analysis. One source of repeated conflict in the 1930s was the principle of civilian control over the military force, to the point where a number of senior Hanagah commanders were dismissed for resisting orders from the Yishuv's political leadership. Along with the need to fight against pacifism, long prevalent in Jewish society, came a new need to fight the inclination toward militarism emerging among the Haganah's commanders. To maintain community control over the Haganah, a national command comprising representatives of all the political groups in the Yishuv was established—although this did not ameliorate the feeling on the Right that the Haganah was controlled by its rivals on the Left.

In 1943 the constitution of the Haganah was amended, speaking not of a popular militia but of an organization that was a stage in the development of a national defense force. The new constitution stipulated that men and women from the age of seventeen upward could be accepted into the Haganah. A period of six months was set aside for basic training, followed by a year and a half of active service; thereafter a member was transferred to the reserves. This was the embryonic structure of the IDF.

In April 1936 the Jewish community faced a severe test. Known today as the Arab Revolt, this third wave of Arab terrorism was directed against British authority as well as the Yishuv. A key figure in the three-year uprising was the pro-Nazi Grand Mufti of Jerusalem, Amin el-Husseini, who exploited the mounting antagonism toward the Jews as well as Moslem fanaticism to fan Arab emotions. The revolt began in the cities and spread to the countryside. However, urban Arabs soon abandoned the struggle to their less-educated rural brothers, who attacked vehicles on the roads and who formed into guerrilla bands whose favorite targets included the pipeline carrying British-owned petroleum from the Kirkuk fields in Iraq to Haifa port. The guerrillas were commanded in a rather loose and haphazard manner by a former Ottoman army officer named Fawzi Kaoukji, himself dispatched by Syrian nationalist extremists to step up the Arab terror actions in Palestine.

The British Army's initial response to these guerrilla bands was ambivalent. In fact, although the Jewish community suffered heavy casualties, His Majesty's forces were often conspicuously unwilling to suppress this latest wave of violence. The Foreign Office feared that drastic measures would turn the entire Arab Middle East against Britain at a crucial time (the Nazi threat was growing in Europe, and the last thing the British needed was unrest in its colonies and mandated territories overseas), and Whitehall was particularly mindful of the inroads Nazism had made among rightist Arab political groups in Egypt. Only later, when the Arab Revolt was well underway, did the British Army receive authorization to put down the rebellion.

The Haganah realized the danger to both life and property inherent in the new situation as well as the implicit political threat. It was clear that under the circumstances the neutrality of the British and their occasional indirect support of the Arabs would undermine the Jewish presence and might lead to a reversal of Britain's commitment to the Balfour Declaration.

At first the leaders of the Yishuv were in favor of defensive actions in response to the Arab hostility because it was assumed that the British would eventually intervene in the Jews' favor. Seventy percent of the Jewish community at that time lived in the three major cities of Tel Aviv, Haifa, and Jerusalem, the remainder in fortified agricultural settlements and villages. The nature of Jewish defense was static, as the settlers tended to garrison themselves, and large areas were abandoned to marauding Arabs.

The military initiative was in Arab hands, but despite this tactical advantage they made a number of serious errors during this period. Many of their commanders exaggerated the power of their own forces and underestimated the potential of the Jews. The clashes of 1936 were essentially between two national groups, and the Arabs erred in directing their hostility against the British too. The latter were preoccupied with the deteriorating international situation, making it natural for them to be in need of the Jewish community's cooperation, even if that meant military collaboration with the officially outlawed Haganah.

Faced with the prospect of civil chaos and alarmed by attacks on the Iraqi Petroleum Company's pipeline, the British finally embarked on an offensive to suppress the Arab guerrilla fighters. Severe punishment was imposed on terrorist gangs and the local Arab population; hardly a search of Arab communities was completed without several civilian casualties and the destruction of hundreds of homes, vineyards, and orchards by angry British troops and Palestine police, both as revenge and as deterrent measures. To prevent infiltration by Arabs from neighboring countries, the British set up Tegart police stations in frontier areas. The Haganah for its part was surprised by the ferocity of the clashes with the guerrillas and was not prepared for them. It seems that the Arab war potential had been underestimated: the Arabs had more fighters, more weapons, and were bolder than anticipated.

Recovery came slowly. While the Arabs almost succeeded in wresting control of large areas of land, the Jews responded by strengthening the Haganah. Losses were particularly heavy in these years: the Jewish population, which numbered 385,000 at the beginning of the disturbances and increased to 460,000 by the end, sustained 520 killed, some 2,500 wounded.

During the late 1930s *sabra*, sons of the generation of the Second Aliyah, began to reach the command levels of the Haganah. This generation was free of the psychological burden of its elders, who remembered the pogroms in Eastern European ghettos. Young men like Yigal Allon and Moshe Dayan stood out in this group and soon changes were made in planning and organization. In 1937 the Haganah prepared a plan to gain control over the entire country in the event that the British Army left Palestine. Known as Plan Avner, it included provisions for reorganizing the Haganah into divisions as well as the establishment of an army of 50,000 men, with an additional garrison force of 17,000. The ranks of the Haganah were clandestinely augmented by volunteers as well as professional men—doctors, engineers, scientists. In July 1938 Yohanan Rathner, a professor at the Haifa Technion, was appointed Chief of Staff of the Haganah. Until then it had been an underground army with management but not a command; now military problems moved from the jurisdiction of political leaders into the hands of professionals, and Jewish settlement was planned in accordance with strategic and political needs. The plan was to create regional concentrations to prevent settlements from being cut off in the event of partition. Stockade-and-watchtower settlements sprang up and access roads were paved. In the 1929 disturbances many settlements had been abandoned, but in this latest round of fighting fifty-two new ones were built. Many kibbutzim were transformed into paramilitary bases where agriculture was only one activity. As a result, the majority of top Haganah and later IDF commanders came primarily from kibbutzim.

A new mood made itself felt in the Haganah during the Arab Revolt, as a number of commanders criticized the weakening of defensive strength that could be expected to ensue if they sat waiting in prepared defensive positions and called on the Haganah to "move out beyond the perimeter," set ambushes, and mount preventive attacks. Outstanding among these activist commanders was Yitzhak Sadeh, a tough Russian Jew who had established a Jerusalem-based mobile patrol unit called "Nomad." Similarly mobile guard units were organized throughout the country and subsequently integrated into a new Jewish defense organization called the Supernumerary Police.

The British were reluctant to sanction a Jewish force, but the problem of quashing Arab terror made them acquiesce in Jewish demands for a legitimate peacekeeping force. The creation of the Supernumerary Police allowed for the training of thousands of Jews in the use of weapons and greatly strengthened the Haganah, since many of the police were secretly members of the Haganah. The Supernumeraries, or Settlement Police, as they were also known, became the basis of an incipient Jewish army. While the Jewish agency bore the burden of paying the Supernumeraries, the small arms came from the British.

The Supernumerary force reached its peak at the beginning of 1939, when it was reorganized into ten territorial battalions. In total, it encompassed some 22,000 members, or about five percent of the Yishuv, with somewhere around 8,000 rifles at their disposal. The Haganah had at the peak of the disturbances only 6,000 rifles, 24 machine guns, and 600 medium and submachine guns. By the time the Arab attacks subsided the Jewish community had come of age in the military sense and was well on its way to being prepared psychologically and physically for the possibility of an all-out confrontation with the Arabs of Palestine. It was thus that the Arab refusal to accommodate Jewish national rights served to increase the Yishuv's determination to develop the force needed to guarantee Jewish survival and defend Jewish nationhood.

Perhaps the most significant development for the Yishuv at this time was the arrival in Palestine of a slightly built, eccentric British officer named Orde Charles Wingate. He came to the country as a captain in 1936 and left his mark as the single most important influence on the military thinking of the Haganah. Born in India to a Scottish family with a long tradition of military service and religious dissent, Wingate was imbued with Puritanism and a deep love of the Bible. With the blazing eyes of a visionary he viewed the scores of Jewish settlements and kibbutzim as proof of biblical prophecies concerning the redemption of Zion.

Wingate's behavior was peculiar, his clothes slovenly, his manners crude. He could also be bad tempered and he consumed a steady diet of raw onions, as if to keep company at bay. But for all these eccentricities, within a short time he became an enthusiastic Zionist. As he wrote to his cousin, Sir Reginald Wingate, then British High Commissioner in Egypt: "When I was at school I was looked down on and made to feel that I was a failure and not wanted in the world. When I came to Palestine I found a whole people who had been treated like that through scores of generations, and yet at the end of it they were undefeated, were a great power in the world, building their country anew. I felt I belonged to such people."[1] And in another letter: "I have seen the young Jews in the kibbutzim. I tell you that the Jews will provide a soldiery better than ours. We have only to train it."[2]

Orde Wingate saw the Jewish people and their struggle to return to the land of Israel as a just and righteous cause and dedicated himself to making the Haganah an effective fighting instrument. He was a man of brilliance, reserve, and discipline. Fully conversant with and often quoting the Bible, he saw himself as a modern Gideon operating in the same terrain where the biblical Gideon fought the Midianites. He instilled in the men of the Haganah a sense of mission and professionalism. His word was law and he insisted on rigorous discipline. Although he prepared every operation thoroughly, he was gifted in improvisation and trained his men to respond with resourcefulness to changing battle conditions. As a military advisor, he set a personal example in courage and endurance and regarded the Haganah men in his command as partners in thinking and action. The members of the Haganah thought of him as a comrade, and he was known affectionately as *Hayedid* (the friend).

Wingate persuaded the British Army command in Palestine to allow him to train special Haganah night squads to fight bands of Arab terrorists. The British granted their grudging permission because they were worried over Arab sabotage of the major petroleum pipeline in northern Palestine. "The Arabs think the night is theirs. The British lock themselves up in their barracks at night. But we, the Jews, will teach them to fear the night more than the day,"[3] Wingate told his men. So it was that the initiative was slowly taken out of Arab hands. Wingate called for face-to-face combat and encouraged mobile ambush units, which roved the countryside. He handpicked his men, and needless to say the Haganah cooperated fully.

The nighttime raids and ambushes were carried out over wide areas of the Galilee on both sides of the pipeline. Dressed in blue shirts and Australian bush hats, the night fighters under Wingate's command helped drive Fawzi Kaoukji's guerrillas out of the Galilee, far from the petroleum pipeline.

Orde Wingate gave Yigal Allon, Moshe Dayan, and other future Israeli army commanders their first formal instruction in warfare, particularly counter-guerrilla tactics. Dayan greatly admired Wingate and throughout his career paid heed to the Englishman's emphasis on carrying the fight to the heart of the enemy's activity rather than assuming a static defense. Wingate's example inspired the Haganah to begin going on the offensive, instead of limiting itself to defensive guarding tactics. His maxim that offense is the best defense later became one of the primary combat doctrines of the Israel Defense Forces.

At kibbutz Ein Harod, night-squad training headquarters, Wingate would tell trainees in Hebrew: "We are creating the basis for the army of Zion here."[4] As his friendship for the Jews made him suspect in the eyes of the British Command, it was eventually decided to transfer him out of Palestine and disband the night squads. In his farewell speech, he told his men: "I promise you that I will come back, and if I cannot do it the regular way, I shall return as a refugee. The force has been disbanded but this does not mean that the dream of Jewish strength has been forsaken. It has only been delayed for a while, a short while I hope. I hope the vision of a free people of Israel in its homeland will be fulfilled soon."[5]

On the eve of his departure (May 1939), his commanders wrote in his personal file: "Orde Charles Wingate, DSO, is a good soldier, but so far as Palestine is concerned, he is a security risk. He cannot be trusted. He puts the interests of the Jews before those of his own country. He should not be allowed in Palestine again."

Wingate never returned. After fighting the Italians in Ethiopia he was transferred to Burma, where he fought in the jungle and lost his life in a plane crash in 1944.

A rival of the Haganah was another underground group, the *Irgun Tzvai Leumi* (National Military Organization), known in Palestine as the ETZEL and abroad as the Irgun. It was founded in April 1937 in reaction to the Haganah doctrine of *havlagah* (restraint) in the face of Arab terrorism. The ETZEL adopted many of Ze'ev Jabotinsky's ideas on the historic boundaries of the land of Israel and the importance of vigorous military action in defense of the Jewish community. The Yishuv's socialist leadership at the time endorsed restraint as a policy and even though the Haganah's commanders contended that only retaliation would silence Arab terror, the Haganah had to follow the Yishuv's civilian direction.

After publication of the White Paper by the British Government in 1939, with its severe restrictions on Jewish immigration to Palestine, the ETZEL moved against the British mandate authorities as well as the Arabs. The organization's emblem was a hand grasping a rifle over a map of the land of Israel, including Transjordan, and the words: *Rak Kach!* (Only Thus!)

As the Arabs found their activities to be increasingly costly in the face of British and Jewish counterattacks, their initiative gradually diminished until a relative peace was achieved in the spring of 1939. The Yishuv had survived, but the Arabs had scored political victories, particularly the White Paper of 1939, which implied a British realization that the mandate was untenable and that it could not be applied without the large-scale and constant use of force against the Arabs. On the other hand, the migration of German and Central European Jews to Palestine following Hitler's rise to power (by 1937 the Jewish population in Palestine was 400,000 as compared to 175,000 in 1932) made it equally difficult to reverse the moral-legal pledge to help establish a Jewish national homeland as implied in the Balfour Declaration.

Failing to achieve a settlement of the Palestine question through a special conference of Arabs and Jews, the British sought to retain Arab goodwill, which they believed was crucial to the war effort in the Middle East, and settled on the issuance of the White Paper. In effect it was a reversal of the Balfour Declaration since it severely restricted Jewish immigration and land purchase.

World War II:LEHI (The Stern Gang)

When World War II broke out the Haganah joined in the allies' war effort and the ETZEL suspended its activities against the British and was even prepared to cooperate with them. An ETZEL commander, David Raziel, was killed in Iraq, where he had been sent to assist in putting down the pro-Nazi Kilani rebellion. In opposition to the ETZEL's decision to cooperate with the British during the war, a group headed by Avraham Yair Stern broke away and established another military organization called *Lohamei Herut Yisrael* (Fighters for Israel's Freedom), known in Israel as LEHI and abroad as the Stern Gang. Stern and his men did not accept Ben-Gurion's dictum that Hitler should be fought as though the British White Paper did not exist and maintained that there was no cease-fire with the British. Their method consisted primarily of terrorism against the British. Stern was caught and killed by the British, but his comrades pressed on and in their most notorious action assassinated the British Minister for Middle Eastern Affairs, Lord Moyne, in Cairo.

The ETZEL also resumed its activities against the British at the beginning of 1944. Reports of the extermination of Jews in Europe filtered through to Palestine but the British refused to permit the refugees of the Nazi Holocaust to enter Palestine. The ETZEL's harassment steadily increased and there is no doubt that it had influence on the British government's decision to terminate its mandate over Palestine.

At its peak, the ETZEL numbered some 5,000 men operating in small units and was led by Menachem Begin, who often disguised himself as an orthodox rabbi to escape British arrest. It blew up the British High Command and Administrative Center in the King David Hotel in Jerusalem in the summer of 1946 and that same year engineered a prison break at Acre where many members of the Haganah and ETZEL were being held as political prisoners by the British. It also staged numerous attacks on British airfields in Palestine throughout the late forties. The ETZEL even acted against the British outside the country and blew up the British Embassy in Rome. Many ETZEL members were killed in battle and others were executed by the British.

During World War II, 28,000 men and 4,000 women of the Jewish community in Palestine volunteered for various units of the British Army, 450 of them attaining officer's rank. The percentage of volunteers was high (considering that the Yishuv numbered only 600,000 at the time). The volunteers acquired important military experience in infantry, commando, artillery, and engineering units, and in the air force, and with the outbreak of the War of Independence many senior IDF commanders were drawn from the ranks of these British Army veterans. Moreover, toward the end of the world war, the Jewish Brigade was established, and it participated in the allies' thrust through Italy.

Closer to home, as Rommel's forces approached Egypt and it became clear that the British intended to retreat from Palestine and establish their line of defense further to the north, the National Command of Haganah decided in 1941 to establish nine companies of commando troops—*Plugot Mahatz,* known as the Palmach—that would be a national reserve prepared for immediate action. The commandos were earmarked for the defense of the Yishuv against the Arabs in the event of a German invasion and for waging guerrilla war, with the agreement and cooperation of the British, against the Germans.

Yitzhak Sadeh, founder of the Nomad unit of the Haganah, was appointed first Commander of Palmach. He personally chose his company commanders, among them Allon and Dayan, and they in turn began to handpick the recruits. There was nobody in the Yishuv better suited to the job of organizing the Palmach than Sadeh, a fighter and a writer who by his courage and spirit became a symbol of the fighting spirit of the Jewish underground.

Sadeh was born in 1890 in Lublin, Poland, the son of a respected Jewish family. Grandson of the town rabbi, he attended a Russian gymnasium. In World War I he served as a sergeant in the czar's army, a rank which was generally the highest that a Jew could attain. He received the St. George Cross for distinction in battle and after the Revolution was appointed commander of a company in Petrograd. It was here that he first met Joseph Trumpeldor, who prevailed upon him to emigrate to Palestine. Before doing so, however, he went to the Crimea where he studied and earned money by wrestling. He was a burly, zestful man known for his Rabelaisian ways.

Sadeh was involved in every major defense enterprise in Palestine—the Labor Battalion, the defense of the Old City of Jerusalem in the disturbances of 1921, and the defense of Safed in the Arab Riots of 1929. In 1937 he had attempted to form a permanent Haganah field brigade. He had about a thousand men in this brigade, known as FOSH (Field Forces), but it was disbanded after a year and a half because the Haganah feared it would become a military elite.

Between these various tasks he was employed in a number of occupations, working as a newspaperman and a farmer, and for many years employed in a quarry, while writing articles, books, and plays. He attracted the young by both his bohemian spirit and his abilities as a commander. The Old Man, as his Palmach and IDF trainees called him, could take on the strongest among them. He set the free-wheeling, informal tone of the Palmach and played a key role in moving the Haganah from self-defense to an activist-defense policy. Sadeh was in strategic agreement with Wingate, although their personal styles varied greatly.

When the Haganah embarked upon its revolt against British authority, Sadeh was appointed its Chief of Staff, responsible for planning most of the Haganah and Palmach actions against the British. Later, when the IDF was founded, he was moved out of a senior position because of political rivalries within the Labor movement (his views were considered too "left-wing" for those in power). During the War of Independence, however, he was a brigade commander and the founder of the IDF's first armored units. Ironically, he found himself under the command of his former pupils who had in the course of time overtaken him in rank. Sadeh died three years after his release from the IDF at the age of sixty-two.

In 1941, the funds placed at the disposal of the Haganah by the British—one of the fruits of the new period of cooperation—600 men were recruited into the Palmach and began training in the forests around Kibbutz Mishmar Ha'Emek in the Jezreel Valley. A German-speaking platoon was set up for the purpose of carrying out actions behind German lines and an Arab-speaking platoon was organized to infiltrate and work in Arab territories. The Palmach participated in several dangerous missions. Its members were among twenty-three men who vanished at sea on their way to a commando action near Tripoli in Vichy-occupied Lebanon, and when the British forces invaded Vichy Syria and Lebanon, Palmach scouts led the vanguard units. (One of these scouts, Moshe Dayan, lost his eye in the battle.) Palmach men were also among the Palestinian parachutists dropped behind enemy lines in Europe. When it seemed that the Germans would invade Palestine, the Haganah drew up the so-called Carmel Plan, which called for fortifying and concentrating most of the Jewish community on Mount Carmel. The Germans would be fought to the end much as the defenders of Masada had fought the Romans in A.D. 70.

When Rommel was defeated by the British and the danger of Nazi attack abated, the British decided to halt their cooperation with the

Palmach. Nevertheless, the Haganah resolved to maintain the Palmach framework. In 1943 one of the leaders of the kibbutz movement suggested that Palmach units be attached to kibbutzim where they would devote half their time to training and the remainder to farming, which would cover eighty percent of the Palmach's expenses. It was thus that the Palmach took on the character of a workers' army rooted in the land and imbued with egalitarian ideals. Moreover, it was enriched by the graduates of youth movements who were drawn to the kibbutzim.

In 1944, the Palmach numbered 1,000 men and 300 women, organized in battalions, and another 400 reservists on call. It was to play a key role in the struggle against the British postwar, and its men escorted the illegal immigrant ships that ran the British blockade. When Yigal Allon succeeded Sadeh as Commander in May 1945 Palmachniks were sent to the displaced persons camps in Europe and Cyprus to train young people in the use of weapons. The Palmach also organized Jewish communities in the Arab countries for self-defense and emigration.

The unique quality of the Palmach lay in its *esprit de corps*. It was an elite volunteer unit with the highest level of training in the Haganah and was especially noted for its ideology. Commanders emphasized educational and informational activities that inculcated socialist ideals, for the education of the soldier was considered the basis for discipline. Their slogan was taken from one of the lines of the Palmach anthem: *Rishonim Tamid Anahnu!* (We are always first!)

In the postwar period, the Haganah steadily developed in strength and scope. Its command received its orders from the Executive of the Jewish Agency, which was the pre-state authority over the Yishuv, and within the agency it was Ben-Gurion who controlled defense matters. His assistants were the chiefs of the Haganah, Yisrael Galili and Yaakov Dori. In the spring of 1947, the Haganah boasted 46,000 men, and its activities extended beyond the borders of Palestine to Europe, where it arranged for smuggling tens of thousands of Jewish refugees to Palestine in defiance of the British ban. Finally, hoping to wash their hands of the increasingly explosive situation, the British decided to relinquish their mandate over Palestine.

On November 29, 1947, the United Nations voted to partition Palestine into a Jewish and an Arab state. The Arabs immediately rallied their forces in an attempt to crush the Jews and to prevent the State of Israel from coming into being. Thus a new war began in

Palestine and the underground Jewish forces—the Haganah, its commando force the Palmach, and ETZEL—went into battle. Before that war was over, these fighting groups would be merged into one army—*Tzva Haganah Leyisrael,* the Israel Defense Forces.

Notes

1. Collected letters of Orde Wingate. Haganah Archives, Tel Aviv.
2. *Ibid.*
3. Yigal Allon, *Shield of David* (London: Weidenfeld and Nicholson, 1972), p. 104.
4. Speech at Kibbutz Ein Harod, 1939. Haganah Archives, Tel Aviv.
5. *Ibid.*

The War of Independence

ZAHAL, the Israel Defense Forces, came into being in the midst of Israel's hardest and cruelest war, the War of Independence. On the eve of that conflict, in November 1947, Israel's very existence was in peril; an Arab victory could have destroyed the dream of Zionism together with the politically independent Jewish state.

Israel did win her War of Independence, but the result was armistice, not peace. The loss of Jewish life in the war was heavy. Out of a population of some 600,000, more than 6,000 men were killed—one out of every 100 people—and many more wounded. Nor was the specter of future hostilities dispelled. To this day, with the sole exception of the frontier with Egypt recognized in the recent peace treaty between the two countries, Israel has no permanent, recognized borders as far as her Arab neighbors are concerned.

On November 29, 1947 the UN General Assembly voted to end the British Mandate over Palestine by May 1, 1948 and to partition Palestine into a Jewish state, an Arab state, and an International Zone comprised of Jerusalem and its environs, extending as far as Bethlehem. Perhaps only one whose people had been denied freedom for thousands of years and then had struggled to regain it could appreciate the joy that enveloped the Jewish nation on November 29, 1947. But the celebrations were short-lived, for Arab threats to thwart the UN resolution had not been empty, and the opponents of the resolution sought to alter it by force of arms. Scattered incidents resembling the guerrilla and terrorist tactics of the anti-Jewish actions of 1929 and 1936-39 quickly assumed the dimensions of full-scale hostilities.

The War of Independence began as a confrontation between two populations: the Jewish Yishuv and the Arab community, which at that time numbered about 1.2 million. But Amin el-Husseini, the Mufti of Jerusalem and religious leader of the Moslems in Arab Palestine, sought to involve the armies of his allies. Before the war was over, Jewish forces had battled with the regular armies of five Arab states that had invaded Palestine to foil the creation of an independent Jewish nation. The Jewish force began as an underground organization but emerged from the battle as an organized national army of twelve brigades. Facing well-equipped enemy forces, the Jewish fighters began with scanty equipment but in the course of the war received aircraft, ships, tanks, guns, and ammunition.

The Arabs of Palestine and the neighboring countries set out to prove that the UN resolution was unenforceable. On November 30 a Jewish bus was attacked en route to Jerusalem and five Jews were killed. This was the starting gun for a war which was to last intermittently for a year and seven months, reaching its formal conclusion when an armistice agreement was signed with Syria on July 17, 1949 after similar agreements had been signed with Egypt on February 24, 1949, with Lebanon on March 23, 1949, and with Jordan on April 4, 1949. The Iraqi Army withdrew from Palestine without any formal cessation of warfare.

When hostilities broke out the mobilized Jewish force consisted of the 2,100 members of the Palmach, while another 1,000 reservists could be called upon. The Supernumerary Police numbered 1,800 men on regular full-time duty, but the Haganah could also quickly muster 9,500 men in the eighteen to twenty-five age group. Two other Jewish military organizations, the ETZEL and the LEHI, numbered 4,000.

At that time military cooperation existed between the ETZEL and LEHI and the Haganah, though these forces would not be merged into the unified IDF until after May 1948. As the war escalated, the Haganah began to recruit from the higher age groups, and an estimated 32,000 men were recruited in stages throughout the war. Another 9,500 youth from ages fifteen to eighteen were organized in GADNA youth battalions.

At the beginning of the war the Jewish community possessed what few weapons had been collected one by one over the years. The arsenal inventories listed 10,000 rifles, 3,500 submachine guns, 160 medium machine guns, 885 light machine guns, 670 light mortars, and 84 three-inch mortars. There was no heavy armament, but the Haganah had nine light aircraft and forty pilots, including some who had served as fighters for the RAF and U.S. Army's air force in World War II.

The Arabs possessed more weapons and more fighters, but their organization was weak, especially as the Palestinian Arab political leadership had been splintered since the failure in the uprisings of 1936–39. An exception was the extremist Mufti who controlled two Palestinian Arab military organizations, the Najada and the Futuwa. Altogether some 6,000 local Arabs had acquired military training in the British Army and almost every male Arab villager was experienced with weapons. Moreover, about 3,000 Arabs were enlisted in the British Palestinian Police but were at the immediate disposal of the Arab military. Finally, a number of units of the British-trained Jordanian Arab Legion were in the country and assisted the local Arabs, even capturing some Jewish settlements for them. Both sides accepted volunteers from abroad, but the Arabs were initially more successful in this respect: some 6,000 volunteers, the majority Syrians, were organized in fighting units and sent to Palestine as the Arab Liberation Army. Volunteers also poured in from Egypt, drawn from the Moslem Brotherhood and from among Yugoslavian Moslems, ex-Nazis, and deserters from the British Army. The Palestine Liberation Army force was led by an Arab officer, Fawzi Kaoukji, who had commanded terrorist bands during the Arab Revolt and had spent World War II in Nazi Germany. Another military leader who had spent time in Germany was Hassan Salameh, whose units fought in Central Palestine. But the most talented Arab military leader in Palestine was unquestionably Abdul Kader Husseini, who commanded units in the Jerusalem area.

The Jews had the advantage of superior organization, a resolve to fight to the bitter end, and a united political and military leadership. The main Arab advantage, in addition to better armament, was geographic strength: much of the area allotted the Jewish state by the UN partition plan was either in fact in Arab hands or was isolated, such as the bulk of the Negev Desert and part of Eastern Galilee. Jewish areas such as the Etzion bloc near Jerusalem and Western Galilee were surrounded by Arab districts. Jerusalem, with its Jewish majority, was surrounded by Arab communities; Tel Aviv and Haifa were adjacent to large Arab towns and settlements. The Arabs also controlled the major transportation arteries, and even more important the Arab community enjoyed land frontiers with neighboring Arab countries while the sole border through which the Yishuv could bring vital supplies was the sea.

The ports were in British hands until their departure from Palestine, and in May 1948 the British forces, displaying open hostility to the Jewish side, endeavored to hand strategic points over to the Arabs. This antagonism had its source in the years of the Yishuv's struggle against the British regime, when hundreds of British police and soldiers were killed by the ETZEL and LEHI. The Egyptian and Iraqi armies and the Arab Legion were equipped with British weapons, and the latter was commanded by English officers. Even after the evacuation of the British Army, which numbered some 80,000 men, British hostility to the young Jewish state continued. During the final stage of the War of Independence, London threatened Israel that she would implement her mutual-defense pact with Egypt.

December 1947–March 1948:
The First Stage

In the first four months of the war the initiative was mainly in Arab hands. Fighting broke out in mixed Arab-Jewish towns, such as Jerusalem, Haifa, Tiberias, and Safed, and between neighboring towns like Tel Aviv and Jaffa. Sniping and sabotage were the order of the day, with the Arabs often sending camouflaged vehicles packed with explosives into Jewish districts. Thus, for example, they exloded a car on Ben Yehuda Street, a main thoroughfare in Jerusalem, killing fifty people. A short while later, with the help of a driver from the American Consulate, they exploded a consulate car in the courtyard of the Jewish agency building in Jerusalem, taking twelve lives.

As fighting went on in the towns, a battle began for the country's roads. The Arabs' objective was to isolate and destroy the individual Jewish settlements and to impose blockades on the towns. Hoping to hold off the Arabs while building up its forces for the later battles, the Jewish command took a defensive stance.

Soon the question arose whether it would be wise to shorten supply lines and evacuate isolated settlements—an issue that became even more acute when Kaoukji's Arab Liberation Army, Abdul Kader Husseini's units, and the Moslem Brotherhood began to mount attacks on isolated Jewish settlements. A number of Jewish military experts contended that it would be best to evacuate those settlements in danger of falling. But the decisive consideration was political, rather than military, and it was decided to risk the settlements on the assumption that the size and borders of the Jewish state would ultimately be determined by the area that the Jews succeeded in holding. There was also no possibility of strategic withdrawal without adversely affecting the Yishuv's morale. There were about 300 Jewish settlements throughout the country. At first commanders refused to permit even the evacuation of women and children, for the assumption was that where there were children and wives to be defended, the effort would be more spirited. As pressure grew children and some of the women were evacuated from the Etzion bloc, but in the Negev settlements children remained until the Egyptian Army's invasion.

The Jewish military effort at this stage was directed toward maintaining communications with isolated settlements by means of armored truck and bus convoys. The armor was prepared by placing wood between two layers of steel, thereby earning the name "sandwiches" for the armored vehicles. These convoys carried supplies and ammunition to Jerusalem and other settlements, but the Arabs improved their methods of warfare and heightened the blockade of Jerusalem daily. Most of the offensive actions in this early stage of the war were carried out by Arabs. Things went badly for the Jews. The convoys were hard hit, especially on the road to Jerusalem. In Jerusalem itself, one of the regular convoys to Mount Scopus and the Hadassah Hospital fell victim to an assault in which scores of doctors and research personnel were killed.

On March 27, 1948 a large convoy was trapped on its way back to Jerusalem from the Etzion bloc. The following day, forty-two men were killed in the Galilee while manning a convoy to isolated Kibbutz Yehiam. A force of thirty-five, mostly students and Palmach men, went on foot to reinforce the Etzion bloc, but they encountered Arab villagers en route and were wiped out. On March 31, 1948 the road to Jerusalem was cut and a convoy was forced to turn back after sustaining heavy casualties. Abdul Kader Husseini's forces were not particularly large, but he could summon thousands of villagers every time a Jewish convoy approached. They would shoot and hurl rocks at the vehicles, slowing them down and thereby increasing their vulnerability.

In March 1948 the daily Jewish losses reached their peak: an average of ten men per day. The total death toll at this stage was 1,200 Jews, of whom half were civilians.

Equally ominous was the fact that the success of the Arab offensive, coupled with Jewish military failures, influenced diplomatic developments. U.S. support for the partition plan waned to the point where on March 19 Hershel Johnson, the U.S. representative in the United Nations, suggested reviving the international trusteeship plan for Palestine. In effect this was a proposal to repeal the UN resolution to establish two states in Palestine. Yet it turned out that Truman had not been consulted before this proposal was raised. Surprised by his own officials the President ordered them to drop the trusteeship proposal, especially when the Pentagon calculated that its implementation would require the commitment of 80,000–100,000 soldiers, while in Palestine the Jews were finally managing to turn the tide in battle.

Failures in the field, coupled with the British transfer of such strategic points as the army camps at Sarafand, Tel Litwinsky, and Lydda Airport to the Arabs, forced the Jews to acknowledge the need for a counteroffensive. It was clear that the Haganah could not be strong everywhere at once, and the only hope was to concentrate forces at a strategic point. The site chosen for the first major counteroffensive was Jerusalem, a city under siege. The fact that Jerusalem was a religious symbol to Jews was an important factor in the decision. "The Arabs were right," Ben-Gurion said. "The capitulation, conquest or destruction of Jewish Jerusalem would strike a heavy, perhaps mortal, blow to the *yishuv* and would break Jewish willingness and ability to withstand Arab aggression."[1]

April 1948: Stage Two—The Counteroffensive

On April 3, 1948, Jewish forces began Operation Nahshon. Named for a biblical hero, this military action marked the beginning of the second stage of the War of Independence. Nahshon was the first operation in which Jewish forces actually moved on the offensive to seize territory. Until then units had ventured out only to return to their starting points, or had broken through on roads that would again be closed. According to the new operational plans a breakthrough would be made on the road to Jerusalem and control of the areas on both sides of the main road would be secured prior to the dispatch of a large convoy to the besieged city.

Haganah was used for this operation, which relied on surprise and boldness. The boldness lay in a willingness to expose other fronts, which would be depleted in manpower and weapons in order to focus strength at one point. It was the first time a Jewish force had operated in large formations. At the beginning of the War of Independence, the largest operative unit was the company; in Operation Nahshon three battalions or about nine companies participated in a single action. Because of the large number of men rank badges were distributed for the first time in order to differentiate between officers and enlisted men. To equip this force it was necessary to transfer arms from fighting units on other fronts and to strip some settlements of almost all their defenses.

On the eve of the operation March 31 a transport plane flown by a hired American pilot landed with the first delivery of arms purchased from Czechoslovakia: 200 German rifles and 40 machine guns. These were immediately transferred to the Nahshon command. A second and even larger shipment from Czechoslovakia arrived the following day by sea on the SS *Nora*. Over 4,000 rifles and 200 machine guns were hidden beneath a load of onions.

Operation Nahshon succeeded in securing the road to Jerusalem, but only temporarily. For the Haganah's new strategy was promptly countered by the Arabs, who likewise activated large units. Kaoukji's forces attacked Kibbutz Mishmar Ha'Emek in the Jezreel Valley, using artillery for the first time, while a battalion of Druze (non-Moslem Arabs concentrated mostly in the Galilee) attacked another kibbutz. Nonetheless Kaoukji's forces found themselves in danger of encirclement and retreated, though the Haganah had insufficient men to exploit its success.

The battle with the Druze at Kibbutz Ramat Yohanan was decisive for the future of the Western Galilee, for it decided not only the fate of the Kibbutz but also the control of the only road that connected the Galilee with the rest of the country. After their repeated assaults were repulsed, the Druze finally abandoned their attack. In fact, the Druze mounted no further operations against the Jews during this war, and many of their settlements in the Galilee announced their willingness to assist the Jewish forces. They later became staunch allies of the Jews and have served in the IDF and in the Border Patrol units.

In April a battle which was to become a milestone in the Israeli-Arab dispute took place on the outskirts of Jerusalem. This was the battle for Dir Yassin, a small village that controlled the road to Jerusalem. The attack was mounted on April 9 by the ETZEL and LEHI, with the knowledge and approval of the Haganah commanders in Jerusalem—although afterward when the outcome of the action became known, the Haganah repudiated it. Of 400 inhabitants of the village, 250 men, women, and children were killed. Though the ETZEL commanders did not condone the killing of civilians, they later contended that the conquest of Dir Yassin was of strategic significance since it was an armed village and the first Arab village to be conquered by a Jewish force.[2] The battle caused masses of Arabs to flee in fear of further atrocities, making the battle for distant Haifa all the easier for Jewish forces. As the story of the massacre spread among the Arabs it gathered gruesome detail and became a serious blow to the morale of the civilian Arab population. The wealthier classes had already been moving to neighboring countries, and now the middle class and proletariat panicked and fled despite Jewish appeals that they stay. They hoped to return within weeks supported by the Arab armies.

In May, the Jews won additional victories, one of the hardest won in the north of the country when the siege of Safed was lifted. In this ancient town 1,200 Jews faced 12,000 Arabs. The Mufti was convinced that victory was at hand for him and had even planned to establish a Palestinian government in this town. But the faulty organization of the Arabs was their undoing. The town's Arab inhabitants, hearing of Dir Yassin, had begun to flee, and the Jews readily assisted in the exodus from surrounding villages by spreading rumors and threats.

The conquest of Safed was carried out as part of a broader operation named Yiftach, in which Jewish forces took control of part of the Eastern Galilee. During the fighting, when Lebanese forces and local Arabs descended on Moshav Ramat Naphtali (which was also called Yemin Orde after Orde Wingate), Wingate's widow came to visit Palestine. At her insistence the Jewish command put her aboard a reconnaissance plane that flew over the settlement named for her husband. She dropped a parcel to the fighters containing a Bible and a letter that read: "To the defenders of Yemin Orde: Since the spirit of Wingate is with you, even if he cannot command you in person, I am sending you the Bible that he carried with him on all his war travels, and from which he drew the inspiration of his victories. Let this be a mark of the pact between you and him, in victory or defeat, from now to eternity!" The Jews broke the Arab siege of Yemin Orde and the settlement was saved.

Before long the local Arab leadership began to crumble and the Arab military leaders could not overcome the disintegration or stem the exodus, especially after superior military leaders were killed in battle—Hassan Salameh and the talented commander Abdul Kader Husseini. But the Jews continued to pay heavily in losses. In this second stage of the war another 1,253 Jews, among them 500 civilians, were killed, and following Operation Nahshon the road to Jerusalem was again closed to Jewish convoys. Grimmer yet, in mid-May four settlements of the Etzion bloc near Jerusalem fell. Earlier proposals made to the Haganah command to evacuate the bloc settlements had been rejected, but the shock caused by the fall of the block resulted in a decision to evacuate a number of settlements around Jerusalem (Atarot, Neve Yaakov, and Hartuv, and the potash works at the north of the Dead Sea).

The Arab irregular forces that descended on the Etzion bloc settlements were joined by a battalion of the Arab Legion, and the final charge was mounted on the morning of May 13. Legion armored cars penetrated the village of Kfar Etzion, followed by thousands of armed men from the local Arab villages. One hundred and fifty inhabitants of Kfar Etzion were massacred. In the last stage of fighting, only eighty men and women remained. After surrendering, they were brought to a field and cut down by machine-gun fire. A few tried to reach their weapons, but then all were killed save four. Two of these succeeded in reaching a nearby settlement; one hid and was saved by an elderly Arab; while the other, a girl, was caught by two irregulars who attempted to rape and kill her, but an Arab Legion officer shot them and took her prisoner. When the fate of the inhabitants of Kfar Etzion became known the following day, the three other settlements of the bloc surrendered. Two hundred and fifty defenders of the Etzion bloc had fallen in battle.

The name of the Etzion bloc has been recorded in awe in Israel's annals of courage. It is often claimed that by their bravery the settlers saved Jewish Jerusalem, although the truth is that the Etzion bloc was conquered by irregular forces and a small Legion unit before the Arab regular armies invaded Palestine. In this respect the role played by the Etzion bloc differed from that played by settlements like Yad Mordechai and Negba, which were on the invasion route of the Egyptian Army to the south and effectively delayed the Egyptian advance on Tel Aviv. More than once the question arose whether it would not have been better to evacuate the bloc at a certain stage and transfer the defenders to Jerusalem, where they were sorely needed.

The fall of the Etzion bloc marked the end of the second phase of the War of Independence, during which the Haganah had an opportunity to establish territorial continuity within and between Jewish areas, as well as to extend Jewish control over areas previously held by Arab forces. Most of the Arab attacks during this period were repulsed and Jewish forces conquered vital areas, including the Upper and Lower Galilee, which included several Arab towns and mixed Arab-Jewish towns like Safed and Tiberias. Jaffa was taken by ETZEL and Haganah forces, and Haifa and sections of western Jerusalem were captured along with several strategically significant villages. Nahshon was typical of the operations undertaken to clear the Jerusalem corridor.

The Haganah suffered heavy casualties during this period and Jewish convoys were hit hard. But as a result of their successes and experience during the second stage, the Jewish fighters were prepared to meet the third phase of the war, which lasted from May 15, the day after Israel's statehood was declared, until June 10.

On May 14, 1948 in a museum in Tel Aviv housed in a squat, white stone building, David Ben-Gurion proclaimed the birth of the State of Israel, the first Jewish republic in 2,000 years. Soon afterward he moved to unify the Jewish fighting forces and create the IDF. The Haganah was the basis of the new state's official army. The ETZEL and LEHI were ordered to disband and gradually integrated into reorganized battalions. The Palmach command staff was integrated into the IDF likewise, but three Palmach brigades were kept intact. All the troops took an oath of allegiance to the State, an official uniform was introduced, and ranks were created for officers and NCOs. The Chief of Staff of the Haganah, Yaakov Dori, became the new Chief of Staff of the IDF with the rank of major general.

Toward the end of the war, the entire field army consisted of twelve regular brigades and one armored brigade, including the Palmach brigades. The Israeli forces were still numerically inferior to those of the Arabs, but were now better equipped. The army had Czechoslovak and French arms and the air force had acquired a number of Czech-built Messerschmitts and British-built Spitfires—all bought in Europe.

An attempt by the ETZEL in June 1948 to land the *Altalena,* a ship loaded with sorely needed rifles, ammunition, armored vehicles, bombs, and other arms, was at first agreed to by the new government and then opposed, presumably because the government feared an armed revolt by the dissident ETZEL. The IDF sank the ship and the arms, while several men were killed on shore. Although the incident might have been seen as cause for civil war, Menachem Begin, who lost one of his closest friends in the shelling of the *Altalena,* vowed that his men would not use arms against fellow Jews. Civil war was avoided but the *Altalena* Affair haunted Israeli politics for many years to come and was the cause of a bitter feud between Begin and Ben-Gurion.

May 15–June 10, 1948:
Stage Three

The third phase of the war brought the simultaneous offensive of the neighboring Arab armies on all fronts. The initiative had returned to the Arabs, and the encounter with regular armies, supported by aircraft, armor, and massed artillery, was a shock for the Jewish units. At the end of this stage the Arab armies had indeed been blocked, but at the cost of a staggering 1,176 Jews, of whom 300 were civilians. Israel was in fact saved by the first truce of the Independence War, which was declared by the United Nations on June 11 after four weeks of bitter fighting.

The defeat of the local Arab irregulars in the early stages of the war convinced the Arab states that they would have to commit their armies, tipping the scales in favor of invasion. In April 1948 King Abdullah of Jordan, King Hussein's grandfather, announced that he intended to take control of the UN-proposed Arab part of Palestine. A month earlier the British had given their stamp of approval to Abdullah's plan in the belief that it would be better to support the Bedouin ruler of Transjordan than choose the Palestinian alternative, which would have meant recognition of the Mufti—a collaborator with the Nazis who was considered a war criminal.

Abdullah's decision gave rise to considerable anxiety among Egyptian and other Arab leaders. The Egyptians feared that the inter-Arab balance would be upset and that King Abdullah would gain strength. There was also talk that Abdullah intended to reach an understanding with the Jews of Palestine. Before the invasion, Abdullah did indeed receive a Jewish delegation headed by Golda Meir. In fact it was these fears that induced the Egyptians to invade Palestine, even though the Egyptian Chief of Staff warned his government that the army was not prepared for war.

The Arab armies lacked an overall operational plan. They did not use their weapons efficiently and because of conflicting interests abstained from coming to each other's assistance in time of need. It was agreed that Abdullah would head the coordinating staff of the Arab armies, but from the beginning he formulated a limited strategy against the Jews. It was widely believed that a secret agreement would be reached between Ben-Gurion and Abdullah whereby both would employ a limited strategy. Hence the Jordanian Arab Legion did not invade the areas allocated to the proposed Jewish state. The large-scale clashes between the IDF and the legion were in the Jerusalem sector, which was explained by the fact that Jerusalem, according to the partition plan, was to be a part of an international zone.

British experts, among them Field Marshal Montgomery, esti-mated that the Yishuv would be destroyed within two weeks, for in their estimation the Jewish force could not withstand the heavy weapons. Acting on this evaluation, the British increased diplomatic and economic pressure on the nascent State of Israel by expelling Is-rael from the pound-sterling currency bloc and then abrogating all existing arrangements for the supply of vital commodities.

The armies of five Arab states invaded Israel: Syria, Transjordan, Lebanon, Iraq, and Egypt. Token units of other forces, such as the Sudanese Army, were added to the Egyptian Expeditionary Force. On May 15 Tel Aviv was bombed for the first time by Egyptian air-craft (the city was to be bombed another fifteen times before the first truce). Ben-Gurion, who had already become the leader of a fighting Israel, related how one morning returning from a bombed area he saw the faces of people peering out at him from the windows of their homes and he knew that this nation could stand in war. "I saw anx-iety in their eyes but no sign of panic, and this convinced me that the nation would be able to sustain the many sacrifices it could ex-pect."[3]

Even before the battle began, Ben-Gurion understood that this would not be a war of armies alone. The victor would be the side that could mobilize all its resources. "We will not win by military might alone," he told IDF commanders. "Even if we could field a larger army, we could not stand. The most important thing is moral and intellectual strength."[4]

When the first Chief of Staff Yaakov Dori fell ill, the main bur-den of directing the war fell on the shoulders of a talented young officer who was head of the Operations Division. His name was Yig-ael (Sukenik) Yadin, a student of archaeology who had been sum-moned in October 1947, at the age of thirty, to head the Operations Branch of the Haganah.

Yadin assumed command mainly during the third stage of the war when the Arabs had a clear advantage both in terms of weapons and equipment, and manpower. With the invasion May 15 the Jewish community mobilized an additional 30,535 men, including the defenders of settlements. From the beginning of the war a supreme effort had been made to acquire additional weapons, but the 21,000 rifles that had been secured was not sufficient to equip all the soldiers. The heavy casualty rate among officers resulted in a disturbing decline in the quality of the junior command; however, their ranks were slowly replenished, and luckily the new officers adapted themselves quickly to regular warfare tactics. Young men who had been squad commanders in a partisan force at the beginning of the war were subsequently transformed into company and battalion commanders in a regular army with heavy support equipment.

A considerable part of the fighting force came from abroad while the fighting was in progress. Thousands of new immigrants brought from refugee camps in Cyprus and Germany joined the ranks of the army straight off the ships. The second, more professional force that came from abroad consisted of the men of MAHAL (*Mitnadvey Hutz Learetz*—Foreign Volunteers in the War of Independence), overseas volunteers who came from all over the world. Most were Jews, but many were also of other religions. Among them were veterans of World War II who had been called to the aid of the Jews. Some were legendary figures, such as George Bass Barling, an American pilot who had downed thirty-two German aircraft. (He was killed in Rome, while taking off in a fighter aircraft to fly to Israel to fight.) Another such American was Ted Gibson, the son of a Protestant minister who had received his father's blessing to volunteer for the Israeli Army. Ted was a squadron commander in the Israeli Air Force.

The men of MAHAL made a considerable professional and technical contribution to the young army. Apart from pilots, there were gunners, tank crews, naval officers, doctors, most of whom spoke English. In those days, orders were given in a babel of tongues, the most prevalent being Yiddish, English, and Russian. One of the volunteer pilots whose plane was shot down landed near an IDF outpost. He spoke only English and, fearing that he would be shot by IDF soldiers, he blurted out the two "Jewish" words he had heard in his parents' house: gefilte fish!

There can be no doubt that what blocked the advance of the invading Arab armies was the string of Israeli settlements, primarily kibbutzim, that stood in their path. The Arab commanders erroneously believed they would be confronted solely by armed bands.

They knew little of the Jewish fighting force and almost nothing of the morale and determination of Israel's citizens. Consequently, they lost countless soldiers in small clashes, but more importantly, they lost time. For the Jewish army, which needed every minute to organize, that time was golden.

The smallest Arab army to invade Palestinian territory was the Lebanese. This sector of the northern front was also the only place where IDF units had initiated operations in advance of the invading force. A Palmach-IDF unit penetrated into Lebanon by night and demolished the bridge over the Litani River, thereby seriously disrupting Lebanese troop movements. The Lebanese Army contented itself with taking one kibbutz and some areas close to the Lebanese-Palestinian border. In this way the IDF contained the Lebanese force and foiled the Syrian plan to act jointly with the Lebanese in cutting off the Upper Galilee.

The clashes with the invading Syrian Army were more severe. A Syrian column, accompanied by armor, concentrated on the area south of the Sea of Galilee with the intention of breaking through toward Tiberias and Nazareth. First it took the Arab township of Semach, inflicting heavy losses on IDF units. A day before its renewed offensive a delegation from the settlements of the region reached the Israeli General Staff and begged for reinforcements and heavy weapons. A number of Ben-Gurion's comrades from the Second Aliyah were included in this delegation, and it was a particularly grim conversation for Ben-Gurion, replete with pleas and even tears. But Ben-Gurion was compelled to reject the demand on the grounds that the reinforcements were needed on the Jerusalem and Egyptian fronts. All the delegation gained were two 65mm mountain artillery pieces of nineteenth-century vintage, named Napoleonchiks which had reached the country two days earlier.

To block the Syrian armor, Yigael Yadin told the men of Kibbutz Degania, which would be the first to face the Syrian breakthrough, "There is no choice but to let the Syrians approach the fences, and then to fight face to face with their armor!"[5] And that was exactly what happened. The tanks broke through the fences of Degania and were set afire by Molotov cocktails thrown at close range by the defenders. The Napoleonchiks opened fire from the hills above and the Syrian attack was blocked. The invaders retreated to Semach.

This battle persuaded the Jewish settlements on the front lines that a regular army with heavy equipment could be stopped. Degania and the whole of Jordan Valley were safe. Two other settlements, Masada and Sha'ar Hagolan, had been abandoned by night without prior approval from the High Command, for its members feared that an additional advance by the Syrian Army would isolate them completely.

The Syrians made no further attempts to flex their muscles on this front. Instead, they transferred their efforts northward and in the new area of operation succeeded in taking control, after bitter fighting, of the settlement of Mishmar Hayarden. But they halved their advance at that point and made no further moves until the end of the war.

The Iraqi Army entered Palestine further to the south. One prong occupied the Naharayim Power Station but was unable to advance further, even though Napoleonchiks, summoned to bombard the Iraqi column, were not very accurate. Another column forged ahead into the Arab regions of Judea and Samaria on the west bank of the Jordan River and threatened the center of the country. Minor battles flared up in this sector and one of the Jewish settlements changed hands. The IDF tried to draw the Iraqi Army's attention northward and opened an attack of brigade strength on the Arab town of Jenin. The opening proceeded well, but because it lacked coordination the IDF sustained one of its most severe defeats and retreated from Jenin and the surrounding hills. Still, the advance of the Iraqi Army had been blocked. The achievements of the Arab armies were limited to occupying positions on the periphery.

Meanwhile, the Negev Brigade of the Palmach and the Givati Brigade were attempting to halt the advance of the Egyptian Army through the south of the country. The latter numbered five battalions with 2,750 men; at the time there were twenty-seven Jewish settlements in the Negev area. The Egyptian Army, which was the largest of the invading Arab armies, advanced in a two-pronged attack with the larger column moving up the coast toward Tel Aviv and the second turning eastward to Beersheba and from there through Hebron to the south of Jerusalem. The major problem facing the IDF was to delay the column advancing toward Tel Aviv in order to gain time to organize defense lines.

This task was assigned to the Israeli settlements along the line of Egyptian advance. Though the inhabitants numbered only a few score men, some of these settlements were formidable obstacles to the Egyptians' advance. At first the Egyptian Command decided to concentrate on the settlements, thereby granting the Israelis considerable time. Fierce attacks were directed against Yad Mordechai, a kibbutz named in honor of Mordechai Anilewitz, one of the leaders of the Warsaw ghetto uprising. On May 24 the settlement was evacuated after most of its buildings had been destroyed and the majority of its defenders were killed. A second settlement, Kibbutz Nitzanim, fell to the Egyptians after substantially delaying them (the women and children of Nitzanim had been evacuated earlier). In their northward advance the Egyptians finally reached Ashdod but stopped at a bridge twenty miles south of Tel Aviv, where they were attacked by four Israeli fighter aircraft. This was the first time that fighter planes, brought from Czechoslovakia and assembled in Palestine by Czech experts, had gone into action, and the Egyptians were shocked by the presence of aircraft in Israeli hands. The Negev remained cut off, but the Egyptian Army advanced no further. The bridge where it was stopped by Israeli aircraft has been known ever since by the name *Ad Halom!* (thus far).

The most serious blows sustained by Israel's army were on the Jerusalem front in the fighting with the Arab Legion. When the legion joined the irregular forces that encircled the Jewish quarter of Jerusalem's Old City, the defenders were no longer able to prolong their resistance; on May 28 the quarter fell into Arab hands. Its twenty-five hundred inhabitants were sorted out and all the men taken prisoner. The IDF's success in taking control over some of the Arab districts of Jerusalem outside the walls was not enough to compensate in even the smallest degree for the loss of the quarter with the Western Wall and its ancient synagogues. It was a demoralizing blow.

The IDF sustained another stinging defeat in the battles for the Jerusalem Road. There the battles centered on the Latrun Police Fortress that commanded the road to Jerusalem before its entry into the Sha'ar Hagai ascent. The IDF attacked the police station five times, including once supported by a number of tanks, but each assault on the fortress was driven back. Some 200 men sacrificed their lives in these battles, the most costly attack being that of a brigade that had been organized only a few days earlier and consisted of many new immigrants who had just come off the boats. Though Yigael Yadin opposed this attack, Ben-Gurion would not rescind his orders. All his energy was devoted to easing the pressure on Jerusalem. Many of the new immigrants were killed by Jordanian artillery fire without even having seen the country for which they died.

Ben-Gurion devoted most of his attention to Jerusalem, and it was to this front that he sent Colonel Mickey Marcus, an American-Jewish graduate of West Point who had come to Israel as a volunteer. Marcus was given command of the Jerusalem front over the objections of a number of Israeli officers. He was killed one night when he left his tent to urinate and was challenged by a sentry in Hebrew. Marcus was asked for the password and when he replied in English the sentry shot him.

By the time of the first truce, the Israeli forces had opened a roundabout mountain route, called the Burma Road, through which they transported the first food to reach starving Jerusalem in weeks. Hundreds of men over call-up age were brought to the Burma Road to carry sacks of flour and crates of food on their backs.

At about the same time Israel's small air force had its opportunity to flex its muscles. Just before the truce an Israeli transport plane dropped bombs over Amman, the capital of Jordan. This was the first Arab capital to be bombed and, it caused considerable shock among the Arabs, who didn't know the Jews had any planes. Later Damascus was bombed as well. The bombings of Tel Aviv continued until two Egyptian planes were downed in aerial combat, a success achieved thanks to the fighter aircraft that Czechoslovakia had sold to Israel.

Israel's arms deals with the Communist bloc are an interesting aspect of her War of Independence. A few years before his death, the first Prime Minister and Defense Minister of Israel David Ben-Gurion told me in an interview: "They saved the State. There is no doubt of this. Without these weapons, it's doubtful whether we could have won. The arms deal with the Czechs was the greatest assistance we received."[6]

Ben-Gurion related that the contacts with Czechoslovakia began during the days of the democratic regime in that country and continued after the Communists took over. This arrangement was not only business for the arms industry; it was backed by the Communist Party and the government and, according to all signs, had received Stalin's approval. The Secretary of the Israeli Communist Party, Shlomo Mikunis, reported being told by Communist officials in Bulgaria in 1949 that Stalin was the moving force behind Eastern-bloc assistance for Israel.

It seems that the Communist countries were interested in supporting any means to help remove the British from Palestine. At that time Ben-Gurion had declared that Israel would maintain a policy of neutrality, but the Russians certainly thought they could acquire influence in the region through aid to the new state. The assistance encompassed a number of Communist-bloc countries: Bulgaria agreed to release Jewish youngsters for immigration to Israel and even offered to equip them with light arms; Rumania also agreed that 400 Jewish youths could go to Israel as volunteers; Poland announced that she would be willing to accept Palestinian Jews into her staff officers' school; and a few volunteers arrived from the Soviet Union.

But the greatest help came from Czechoslovakia, whose leaders were even prepared to establish a brigade of Czech-Jewish volunteers (who were subsequently split up among all the units in Israel). The Czech trained pilots and tank crews from among the Jews who asked to immigrate to Israel. Yet the arms transaction, in which Israel paid the full price, was the major affair. Prague demanded payments in dollars and its prices were high. Nevertheless, for Israel the deal was most worthwhile. At one point, when it became known to the Czechs that the IDF needed heavy mortars for the battle of Jerusalem, they bought twelve such pieces in Switzerland and delivered them to Israeli agents. Tens of thousands of rifles and thousands of machine guns were also transferred to the country.

The foundations for the Israeli Air Force can also be attributed to Czechoslovakia. In all, eighty-nine fighter planes were acquired there. The first were German Messerschmitts and they were followed by British Spitfires. The Czechs also began to train Israeli pilots within the Czech Air Force. Moreover, an Israeli base, named Etzion, was established near the Czech town of Zatec, and most of the weapons acquired in America and in Europe were brought there and then flown on to Israel. Three Flying Fortresses acquired in the United States also landed at Etzion and flew to Israel via Cairo, where they dropped one and a half tons of bombs near one of King Farouk's palaces. Ninety-five missions were flown from Etzion to Israel until August 1948, when Prague gave in to American pressure to close the base and put an end to the aerial bridge.

The CIA was also worried over the fact that planes taking off in the United States were "vanishing" behind the Iron Curtain. After two Czech flying officers who had defected to West Germany reported an aerial link that began in the U.S. and extended from Czechoslovakia to Israel, Washington submitted a formal complaint to the Prague government and even noted the names of American citizens who were involved in the airlift. The United States threatened to bring the matter before the United Nations. America also put pressure on the Bulgarian government not to permit Jewish youth to go to Israel to join the IDF.

A stalemate developed in late spring, as Arab armies lost the offensive momentum and the Israelis were not yet ready for large-scale offensives. Both sides welcomed a breather and they agreed to a one-month cease-fire that began on June 11.

During this period the IDF made its plans for the future. Israeli forces were to take the initiative after the cease-fire with first priority going to dissolving the threat to Tel Aviv and its immediate surroundings by capturing the towns of Lydda and Ramle. Next they planned to move into the hilly country east of the coastal plain to lift the siege of Jerusalem; then to outflank the Transjordanian-held Old City from the north. Another task was to secure the Haifa region by taking Nazareth and the remaining parts of the Lower Galilee. At the same time the Egyptians in the south, the Iraqis in the east, and the Syrians in the north had to be held back by the settlements until offensive action could be taken.

It was clear to the Israeli General Staff that once the fighting resumed, they would enter the decisive stage of the war. Four weeks of truce allowed for rearmament and reorganization, and the IDF now stood on its feet. There was no doubt that the Arabs had made a military error by agreeing to the truce. In addition to the weapons that arrived from Czechoslovakia, Israel had acquired material from other countries, including fifty Krupp 75mm guns and six ships for the Israeli Navy.

The army intensified its training and divided its forces among four fronts. Severe conflict erupted between the General Staff and Ben-Gurion over the appointments of commanders for these fronts. Ben-Gurion wanted to appoint Shlomo Shamir and Mordechai Makleff, graduates of the British Army, to these positions in place of officers whom he apparently considered to be leftists and thus politically less reliable. Yigael Yadin submitted his resignation.[7] Ben-Gurion in turn announced his own resignation, and it was only thereafter that a temporary solution was found by the appointment of Yigal Allon, Commander of the Palmach, as commander of Operation Dani in the Tel Aviv area, which was slated to begin when the truce ended on July 9, 1948, for the prestige associated with the appointment placated the officers. It was also decided to move on the weakest enemy of all: Kaoukji's Arab Liberation Army in Galilee.

July 9–July 18, 1948: Stage Four

Fighting resumed on July 9 and raged for ten days through July 18, at which point the United Nations again imposed a truce that lasted until October 10, 1948. The IDF remained on the defensive on the Egyptian front, but the Egyptian Army was repeatedly repelled by the residents of Kibbutz Negba, who effectively prevented its northward advance. Another settlement, Kfar Darom in the Gaza Strip, was evacuated on July 7 under Egyptian pressure. This was the last Israeli settlement to fall during the War of Independence.

During the ten days of battle, Israeli naval vessels shelled the town of Tyre in Lebanon and land forces began operations against Kaoukji on the northern front. By penetrating from the rear they succeeded in gaining control over the Arab town of Nazareth and in conquering a considerable part of Lower Galilee.

Yet the biggest and most important operation of the ten-day battle was Operation Dani, which was designed to drive the Arab Legion from the area of Tel Aviv and relieve the pressure on Jerusalem. The Arab towns of Lydda and Ramle fell into IDF hands. Yigal Allon commanded a force of almost four brigades, including some armor (half-tracks and eight-tracks) and artillery. Yitzhak Sadeh, the founder of the Palmach and a past commander of Allon's, led the armored force. Moshe Dayan led a raiding battalion of commandos. This was the IDF's largest offensive operation and it led to the taking of Lydda Airport. Some 50,000 Arab inhabitants of Lydda, Ramle, and neighboring towns fled the region, this time without the Israelis preventing them or suggesting that they remain.

The second truce came into effect on July 19 when the Israeli offensive was at the height of its momentum. During the last ten days of fighting Israel learned that the Arab military coalition in effect had crumbled; when one of the Arab armies was hit the others failed to come to its aid.

October 10, 1948:
The Final Stage Begins

When fighting resumed on October 10, Israel held the initiative on all fronts in what was no longer a war of few against many. The Arab forces had lost the numerical advantage and at best the opposing forces were equal in number. The Jewish community had mustered all its resources and at the peak of the battle fielded an army of 120,000 men. Weapons flowed into the country in considerable quantities, and in the final stage of the war the IDF had 60,000 rifles, 220 artillery pieces, and 7,000 vehicles of various types.

The Israelis had the advantage of superior organization on their side. Throughout the war and during the cease-fire period, the IDF had undergone an evolutionary change. It began to take on the marks of a regular army, with ranks and a well-developed command. The Arab armies by contrast were large but they were peasant armies, the vast majority of fighting men being illiterate and the gap between soldier and officer immense. Organization was faulty, ammunition stores ill-prepared, and medical facilities inadequate.

The IDF carried out four major operations, three in the south and one in the north. In the north Kaoukji's Arab Liberation Army was driven out of the country in Operation Hiram, named for a biblical king of Tyre in the days of Solomon. The rout lasted only sixty hours with four brigades operating in Upper Galilee under the command of Moshe Carmel. The objective was to cut off Kaoukji's army without clashing with him directly, and the move succeeded with relatively few losses, although Kaoukji and most of his army managed to escape to Lebanon. The IDF chased his units as far as the frontier and took twelve Lebanese border villages. Vanguard units even reached the banks of the Litani River but withdrew from Lebanese territory when the armistice agreement was signed with Lebanon.

The IDF's major effort, however, was directed southward to the Negev and was motivated by diplomatic and political considerations. The UN mediator, Swedish Count Bernadotte, had proposed a new plan for the partition of Palestine in which he suggested removing the Negev from Israeli hands. Israeli leaders suspected that the British were behind the plan, which would permit them to establish military bases in the Negev. At that time the area was under siege by the Egyptian Army, which refused to allow convoys to reach the blockaded Israeli settlements. The Israeli offensive was based on the short-term goal of breaking the siege and blockade on the settlements, and the long-term goal of securing the Negev against later attempts at a partition of the area.

On October 15 the battles of Operation Yoav began according to a plan that was one of the finest in the War of Independence. For the first time during this war the offensive began with an aerial bombardment by the Israeli Air Force on Egyptian planes stationed at the El Arish Airfield. Three brigades opened the offensive and were joined toward the end by a fourth and a battalion of armor. Planning was based on the assumption that the other Arab armies would not interfere or even open fire.

Before the breakthrough began various diversionary actions were carried out, with forces from the besieged settlements attacking Egyptian supply lines from the rear. The only frontal assault took place around an Arab-held police fortress located on the main road to the Negev. IDF forces attacked the fortress unsuccessfully a number of times before they took it and broke through to the Negev.

The Egyptian Army began a general retreat while the IDF was taking the Negev capital of Beersheba, but 5,000 Egyptian soldiers remained behind in an area called the Faluja Pocket. One of them was a young officer named Abdul Nasser who would later become the President of Egypt. The Egyptians sustained another defeat in the course of the operation when the *Emir Farouk,* flagship of the Egyptian Navy, was sunk by Israeli frogmen.

The commander of Operation Yoav was Yigal Allon, then thirty years old and the army's most talented field commander. One of the breed of farmer-soldiers, Allon had been born in Kfar Tabor in Galilee, the birthplace of the Hashomer organization. He later studied in an agricultural school and joined Kibbutz Ginossar. He began his military career in the Palmach and was a student of the doctrines of Orde Wingate and Yitzhak Sadeh. Allon also followed Sadeh as Palmach commander and his strategic theories were instrumental in shaping IDF military doctrines.

On December 22, while the siege of the Faluja Pocket continued, the last operation of the war, Horev, began. Based primarily on mobility rather than frontal attack, this offensive resulted in the total rout of the Egyptian Army. Five brigades including one armor participated in the operation. In the beginning a small force penetrated the enemy rear and secretly moved along one of the mountains that controlled the main road. When it reached the peak it announced its success by the dispatch of a carrier pigeon, the signal to begin the attack. While the bulk of the forces were pushing forward one division moved along an old Roman road that had not been used for hundreds of years. This unit appeared suddenly in the rear, in the Nitzana region, and totally surprised the Egyptians. It was a brilliant application of Liddell-Hart's theory of the indirect offensive.

The main Egyptian positions on the road were taken by the assault. The follow-up was in hand-to-hand battles between the remaining Egyptian forces and a unit of MAHAL volunteers who were veterans of the French underground in World War II. The road thus cleared the IDF broke through to the Sinai Peninsula. On December

30 the army reached Abu Ageila and raiding forces penetrated deep into Sinai.

The Egyptian command was badly shaken, and the fate of the Egyptian Expeditionary Force in Palestine was nearly sealed when diplomatic circumstances extricated Cairo from total defeat. Invoking her 1936 Defense Pact with Egypt, Great Britain delivered an ultimatum demanding immediate withdrawal of Israeli forces from Egyptian territory. It was delivered through the U.S. Ambassador in Israel together with a warning from President Truman that it would be wise to heed the English demand. Yigal Allon, the commander in the field, cabled the General Staff: "There is no military reason for retreat!"[8] He then left the front and flew to Tel Aviv, but his efforts to convince Ben-Gurion that withdrawal should be delayed until the Egyptians were destroyed were in vain. His orders were to withdraw within twenty-four hours. A few days later another ultimatum demanded the removal of IDF forces from Gaza. These forces had driven a wedge into the Gaza Strip, by way of Rafiah, which effectively prevented the safe retreat of Egyptian forces from Palestine. Diplomatic intervention clearly saved Egypt from total defeat. A day before the Gaza ultimatum a message radioed to Cairo by the commander of the Egyptian Expeditionary Force had been intercepted by Israel. Its text: "The chances of solving the Palestine problem by military means are nil. Try diplomatic means!"[9]

Allon sent a strong message to the General Staff: "I am shocked by the withdrawal order! This is the second time that we are throwing away a certain chance of inflicting a final defeat on the Egyptian enemy!"[10] Again Ben-Gurion was resolute. He believed that by agreeing to withdraw IDF forces he would achieve Cairo's agreement to negotiate for an armistice. He ordered the Chief of Staff to inform the commander on the scene that he was not entitled to interfere in diplomatic matters and was forbidden to criticize the management of the war. On January 6, 1949 Egypt did indeed announce her willingness to negotiate. Yigal Allon refused to participate as a representative in the Israeli delegation; he later contended that Israel had made a diplomatic mistake in accepting an armistice without guarantees instead of demanding a peace treaty.

The last battle on the southern front was not with the Egyptians but with the British. British fighter planes flew over Israeli territory and opened fire on IDF forces. Five RAF planes were shot down in aerial combat with Israeli planes and by ground fire. Among the Israeli pilots who took part in this battle were some who had served in the RAF during World War II. The joy of victory was tempered by sorrow over the fate of the pilots who were downed. The Israeli squadron sent a telegram to the British squadron that was stationed in Cyprus: "Comrades, forgive us. But you were on the wrong side of the fence."[11]

With the Egyptian Army defeated, attention turned to securing the southern Negev as far as the Red Sea, the gateway to Africa, the Indian Ocean, and the Persian Gulf. This operation was also based primarily on rapid movement and proceeded almost without a shot being fired. The Jordanians retreated to Aqaba across the gulf when they saw IDF forces approaching. Upon reaching the place where the town of Eilat stands today, the commander of the Israeli force radioed: "We have reached the end of the map!"[12]

King Abdullah tacitly recognized Israeli rule over this important area, and in return Israel acceded to the Arab Legion's occupation of all areas of western Palestine that were originally allocated by the UN for the Arab state. Ben-Gurion would later regret this agreement. In a conversation with UN Secretary-General Hammarskjöld he admitted that had he known how relationships with the Arab states would develop he would not have conceded those sectors to Jordan. Nineteen years were to pass before the Six-Day War, when the IDF again conquered this part of Palestine.

The IDF's last operations showed considerable progress in the level of strategic planning by the Israeli General Staff. The Israeli forces proved that they excelled in defense. They were not as noteworthy for their offensive tactics yet they were impressive in maneuvers of large-scale forces and in the creation of operative situations which stymied the enemy. The IDF came out of the War of Independence confident of itself. The feeling was that peace was at hand. Only a few saw otherwise. Yigal Allon, for example, summed up the war to his officers: "We won the war, but lost the peace!"[13]

Following the signing of armistice agreements in February, March, and April of 1949, Israeli forces evacuated Lebanese territory south of the Litani; the Syrians evacuated their bridgehead in Upper Galilee; the surrounded Egyptian brigade was allowed to leave the Faluja Pocket; and Egypt retained the Gaza Strip, which together with Jordan's takeover of the West Bank and the Old City of Jerusalem prevented the establishment of an Arab state in Palestine as prescribed by the UN partition plan. Israel emerged with more territory than the original plan had allocated to her—although much less than was within her military ability to win.

Notes

1. Israel Defense Forces, *Toldot Milhemet Hakommiyut* [History of the War of Independence] (Tel Aviv: Maarachot Publishers, 1964), p. 49.

2. For ETZEL's version of the episode, see Menachem Begin, *The Revolt* (Los Angeles: Nash, 1972), pp. 162–65.

3. David Ben-Gurion, *Behilahm Am* [A People's Struggle] (Tel Aviv: Mapai Publications, 1951), p. 34.

4. *Ibid.,* p. 11.

5. Israel Defense Forces, *op. cit.,* p. 169.

6. Interview with author, originally published in *Ha'aretz,* September 1969.

7. For Allon's account of this period, see *The Making of Israel's Army* (New York: Bantam, 1971), pp. 34-51.

8. Yeruham Cohen, *Leor Hayom Oobemachashach* [By the Light of Dawn] (Tel Aviv: Amicam Publishers, 1969), pp. 239, 250.

9. Allon, *Keshet Lohamim* [Shield of David] (Jerusalem: Wedenfeld and Nicolson, 1972), p. 218.

10. Cohen, *op. cit.,* p. 250.

11. *Diary of the First Combat Aviation Squadron,* internal publication, Israel Defense Forces.

12. Cohen, *op. cit.,* p. 266.

13. Allon, *Making of Israel's Army,* pp. 48–49.

The First Years

T HE ISRAEL DEFENSE FORCES emerged from the War
of Independence as a victorious army but nevertheless faced a
myriad of new problems. It had been formed in the heat of
battle—a hodgepodge of fighting men quickly organized to respond
to the pressing defense needs of the Yishuv—but after the war it was
the national defense force of a new state. While there was much to
be accomplished in those early days, soon it became clear that Israel's
defense was a major priority, that readiness for war would always be
essential, and that the task of the IDF had just begun.

The IDF was a young army lacking in traditions and occasionally
it seemed to be little more than a fighting rabble founded by idealists
but totally lacking in form. The immediate focus of operations gave
way to peace-time problems; above all it was necessary to decide on
the structure and character of Israel's army. But the first order of
business was demobilization and return of thousands of soldiers to
civilian life.

At the end of the War of Independence, the IDF numbered 120,000
soldiers—an immense figure in view of the fact that the entire Jewish
population of Israel was no more than 600,000. The debate over the
organization and structure of the IDF, as well as the role it would
play in the new Israeli society, was punctuated by two important events
that left a lasting mark on both the defense establishment and the
country as a whole. One was the Altalena Affair, the other the dis-
banding of Palmach: both shared the distinction of being the product of Ben-Gurion's desire to rule out any possibility that private armies
would exist within the young state. His fears in this regard were focused on both the right and the left, but the standing of the leftist
parties concerned him more because they had played a pivotal role in

the Haganah and the Palmach, and many of the IDF's senior officers during the War of Independence belonged to them.

At the beginning of 1948, when two leftist parties merged to form Mapam (which regarded itself as a viable alternative to the ruling Mapai Party), Ben-Gurion's apprehensions were stoked ever further. Signs of friction arose while the fighting was still at its height and before the official formation of the IDF. After the establishment of the People's Administration, effectively Israel's first provisional government, Ben-Gurion decided to dissolve the post of Chief of the Haganah National Command. It just happened to be held by Yisrael Galili, a member of Mapam and one of the most outstanding figures in the Haganah. When his post was dissolved, a few members of the General Staff, headed by Yigael Yadin, joined in expressing their objection to Galili's dismissal and threatened to resign. Ben-Gurion was forced to accept a compromise, but it was only a stopgap and within a few months he had succeeded in deposing Galili for good.

In June 1948, during the first truce, the Altalena Affair took center stage and almost caused a civil war. The command of the ETZEL informed the People's Administration that it had arranged for a ship (named the *Altalena*) loaded with arms to sail to Israel from a French port. It was agreed between the two sides that the arms would be turned over to the government of Israel and its army, although the ETZEL demanded that a portion of the weaponry be set aide for its units in Jerusalem. As the boat approached the Israeli shore the government announced that the ETZEL had violated the agreement, and soon fighting broke out between ETZEL and IDF units. Ben-Gurion assigned units of the Palmach and Moshe Dayan's commando battalion to handle the fighting, which included shelling the boat offshore. In the end the *Altalena* went down in flames, all the arms were lost, and both sides sustained losses in the fighting. Yet Ben-Gurion's fear that the dissident organizations would refuse to disband proved unfounded. The ETZEL and LEHI agreed to merge with the IDF and were swallowed up by the new army. Even so officers who had come out of these two movements found their advancement in the IDF blocked during the early 1950s.

Although Ben-Gurion had used the Palmach to quash the ETZEL and the LEHI, his doubts were not assuaged about the loyalty of its officers, most of whom were members of Mapam. Not long after the Altalena Affair the commander of the Alexandroni Brigade, Dan Even, was approached on Ben-Gurion's behalf and asked to have one of his battalions ready to act in the event that the Palmach attempted to carry out a putsch. And toward the end of the war, Ben-Gurion decided to disband the Palmach command, explaining this move on purely military and organizational grounds but also intimating that the command was an important tool for a certain political party. Some of his associates tried to persuade Ben-Gurion that it was in the country's interest to maintain units loyal to the Histadrut (and the Left in general) if cases like the Altalena Affair were to recur, but the Prime Minister dismissed such counsel out of hand.

Even before dissolving the Palmach command, Ben-Gurion had tried to dispose of a number of Palmach officers who happened to have been among the most talented in the War of Independence. In one case, after the Prime Minister refused to appoint Yigal Allon, the Commander of the Palmach, and Shimon Avidan as front commanders, the then Chief of Operations Yigael Yadin tendered his resignation. In response Ben-Gurion announced that he too was resigning and renounced all responsibility for the conduct of the war. This incident occurred in the midst of the war so that within days a compromise was hammered out without the resignations becoming public. Yigal Allon was in fact appointed commander of the southern front and led his troops to victory over the Egyptian Army. But as in the case of dismissing Galili Ben-Gurion ultimately found a way to maneuver Allon out of the IDF. Right after the war, while Allon was on a tour of French Algeria, the Prime Minister appointed Moshe Dayan to replace him as head of the southern front, and upon returning Allon resigned from the army.

Soon the Palmach as a whole became the object of Ben-Gurion's zeal. Its three brigades, the finest in the IDF, were among the first to be disbanded at the end of the war on the grounds that no privileged units should be allowed to exist within the framework of the army. Hundreds of officers left the IDF in Allon's wake, rejecting the call to join the newly formed regular army—and it must be said that the leaders of Mapam encouraged their decision not to remain in uniform. Nevertheless, some of the Palmach's commanders did stay in the army, despite the fact that at first they were denied deserved promotions—sometimes for years. In addition to Allon six of the IDF's twelve brigade commanders resigned from the army following the War of Independence. Their decision not to join the regular army affected both the level of the IDF and the morale of its command.

Some military leaders, such as Mordechai Makleff, who became the IDF's third Chief of Staff in 1952, were convinced that there was a positive side to the exodus of senior Palmach officers:

The bulk of those who resigned were the ones who had political aspirations. The lower echelon of Palmach officers, who were able to contribute to forming the young army, for the most part remained. Had the senior commanders remained in the IDF, we would have been compelled to waste another two years in disputes over organization. Thus, matters were decided far more quickly, and we didn't waste valuable time on pointless discussions.[1]

Ben-Gurion's fears of a political challenge from former Palmach and Haganah commanders increased his reliance on those officers who had acquired their experience in the British Army during World War II. In making his early appointments to senior positions, he chose a large percentage from among the graduates of the British forces. He felt they were the only ones with formal experience in administration, ordnance, and the use of support weaponry. This policy was hotly debated and increased the already serious factionalism within the IDF.

In December 1949, after much consideration, Ben-Gurion finally yielded and decided to transfer the command of the IDF into the hands of the younger generation of officers. Yaakov Dori was replaced as Chief of Staff by thirty-two-year-old Yigael Yadin. Despite his youth, he had served as Chief of Operations in the wartime General Staff and had filled in as acting Chief of Staff when Dori was ill. He brought into the command echelons other young officers who participated in vital decisions. Notable among them was Mordechai Makleff, who was appointed Yadin's deputy. Another future Chief of Staff, Chaim Laskov, was among the members of Yadin's brain trust. Yadin himself emerged as a leader of true stature, and it was during his tenure that the IDF's foundations were laid.

The first problem faced by the General Staff was determining the size of the regular army. It was clear from the outset that Israel's economy could not support a large standing army. The manpower needs in other sectors of national life were too great and the population of the country too small. Nonetheless, Israel's defense requirements were also important. The threat of future Arab incursions had not been eliminated by the War of Independence and many officers believed that a large army would have to take precedence over the lesser needs of the economy. But Ben-Gurion rejected that view. Another suggestion was that the army be based on selected volunteers, an approach Yadin described as follows: "Whether to create an army from the 600,000 selected Jews who resided in the country before the War of Independence and treat the others as trash or to conceive of the IDF's problems as part and parcel of the problems of a state that is absorbing immigration, with all the attendant difficulties and risks."[2]

The debate ended in the establishment of a small standing army and a large reserve army that would include new immigrants. The standing army comprised draftees—men and women alike—plus the members of the regular army, and at first it numbered no more than 37,000 people.

Yadin went to Switzerland to study that country's organization of reserve units and was followed by generals Makleff and Aharon Remez in 1950. The IDF generally adopted the Swiss system, though it had to alter a number of aspects to suit Israel's needs. For example, Swiss reservists take their weapons home, a detail that could not be duplicated in Israel because her stores were not sufficiently rich to risk the loss of such weapons. It was feared that the immigrant soldiers would not act responsibly regarding their weapons. Furthermore, Israel's borders were far from safe, and bands of marauding Arabs were attacking border settlements and stealing everything they could get their hands on. The IDF command was aware that reservists' weapons could easily fall into Arab hands in that manner. Special arsenals were set up for the reserves, while the emergency-warehouse system made it possible to keep the weapons both secure and readily available when needed.

The IDF's original organization followed the model of the British Army. After a sharp debate, and despite opposition from the air force, a common General Staff was established for all branches, but territorial commands were set up in relation to the surrounding Arab states: the Southern Command was stationed near the Egyptian border, the Northern Command was opposite the armies of Syria and Lebanon, and the Central Command faced the Jordanian Legion. The commands were attached to the General Staff, and the territorial brigades, the largest operative formations, were directly subordinate to the commands.

The General Staff is the supreme command of the IDF, including the air force and the navy, and is an integrated and centralized body. The air force and the navy both have their own commands and enjoy the status of arms, but in wartime their commanders assume the status of the Chief of Staff's professional advisors. This accent on centralization and the integrity of command have facilitated the conduct of fighting since the War of Independence, but it has also created problems in terms of building and training the army in times of relative quiet. Training is handled by the territorial commands that direct the forces in wartime.

At first the General Staff was built as a triangular structure with three branches: Operations, Quartermaster, Manpower. But in 1953 a special branch was established for Military Intelligence, and after the Yom Kippur War a fifth branch, Planning, was added. Another structural change, introduced after the War in Lebanon, was the establishment of a Ground Forces Command responsible for training these forces during times of quiet but not for commanding them in war. The General Staff is headed by the Chief of Staff, who is also the Commander-in-Chief of the Armed Forces and is responsible to the Cabinet through the aegis of the Minister of Defense. The minister is also in charge of the Defense Ministry proper and its various extensions, such as the arms industry.

Once the system of reserves was established, the basic doctrines of the IDF still had to be forged. Because the early leaders of the IDF were almost entirely infantrymen, infantry strategy was paramount. It was only later that armored forces became crucial.

One of the questions confronting the commanders of the IDF was the type of war for which they should prepare. The popularly held assumption in the early 1950s was that if a war broke out, it would be a full-scale confrontation, whether it was along one or all of the country's frontiers. In 1951 the IDF held its first major maneuvers to evaluate the entire military system. During the exercise (called All-Purpose) over 200,000 men were mobilized within forty-eight hours. The plan for the first exercise was predicated on the assumption that Israel would be attacked by all the Arab armies. In coming to the country's defense the IDF would deal first with the most menacing of these forces, and only after neutralizing that threat would it then take on the other Arab armies—which is precisely what happened sixteen years later during the Six-Day War.

In the early 1950s a special effort was also made to replenish the IDF's eclectic arsenal. The Israeli Army had emerged from the War of Independence with a collection of arms of World War II vintage, at best. Weapons procurement had been a patchwork affair, if only because most countries had refused to sell arms to Israel—at least openly. Emissaries from the IDF and the Israeli Ministry of Defense scoured the globe to acquire used armaments that had been consigned to the scrap heap. Among these purchases were worn Sherman tanks that the United States Army had left in the Philippines, field guns from Canada, Italian antiaircraft guns, and Mexican frigates. The method of the day was to purchase the hardware wherever it could be obtained and only then worry about its compatibility with the prevailing mode of combat. As a result the equipment purchased was often unsuitable to the army's needs. The IDF was, after all, the poor army of a poor country that was weighed down by such awesome problems as the absorption of masses of refugees displaced by World War II and the need to provide its population with food that it could not itself produce.

Under these circumstances the struggle over the new army's budget was understandably a bitter one. With the national treasury empty for the better part of the year, it was difficult to justify the allocation of large sums to an army that had just won a war (Israel's defense budget at the start of the 1950s was about 150 million Israeli pounds, with the Israeli pound being equal in worth to the pound sterling); and debates about the defense budget went on within the confines of the army as well. Mordechai Makleff related that as Chief of Staff he was summoned to appear before the Cabinet after having requested an additional million pounds for the purchase of arms. Some of the ministers remarked that he could receive the sum but it would be at the cost of opening a hospital and a number of schools. Makleff objected that it was unfair to ask him to determine the state's order of priorities, but by the end of the discussion he felt obliged to withdraw his request.

One of the IDF's critical problems in its early days was officer training. The army had lost the cream of its officers in the War of Independence, and a survey after that war revealed that only a small percentage of IDF officers (about 400) had had professional training of any sort, with fewer still having completed an officer's course in either the British Army or the Haganah. Thousands of officers, in both the regular army and the reserves, had received their commissions without undergoing special training. Thus an immense training operation was launched in the early fifties. General Laskov was placed in charge of the operation, whose objective was to train 27,000 officers within eighteen months. Thirty military schools were established and for the first time in the history of the Israeli fighting force uniform instruction was instituted (previously each commander had trained his men his own way, with the methods he considered best). Under the newly designed program there was a single training base for the absorption of new recruits and a single officers' course. After basic training candidates moved on to specialized training in the various branches.

In these early years the IDF did not have its own training literature and most of its officers, who had disrupted their secondary education to participate in the struggle against the British and the War of Independence, did not know any foreign languages. "One of the first things that I did," Laskov related, "was to teach many officers English so that they could read foreign military literature."[3] Efforts were also made to send officers for advanced training in foreign armies. This was only mildly successful because most foreign military officials were initially reluctant to accept Israeli soldiers. A course for battalion commanders and a staff and command school were developed within the IDF.

The years immediately following the War of Independence were a period of decline for the Israeli Army primarily because the great immigration of Jews from underdeveloped North African and Mideastern countries filled the ranks of the IDF with manpower of the lowest standard. The army absorbed thousands of illiterate recruits who had to be taught basic grooming, reading and writing, in addition to soldiering. They lacked motivtion and regarded service in the army as a punishment. They filled the combat units and thereby reduced the IDF's operational level, while sabras and the educated filled the higher ranks and served in the offices of the General Staff and the various commands. Mordechai Makleff recalls that he was often approached by officers concerned about the low level of the average Israeli soldier. His reply was that the average enemy soldier, the disadvantaged Arab, was likely to be even more backward.[4]

Still, the problems experienced in absorbing the new immigrants into the IDF, especially those from the Mideastern communities, particularly worried Ben-Gurion. He was driven by a desire to see commanders emerge from the Oriental population for he believed that this would ensure their integration into the army and Israeli society at large. At Ben-Gurion's instigation, therefore, the IDF attempted an ultimately disappointing social experiment. Makleff described the program as follows:

We decided to try to prove that it was possible to produce good commanders from among new Oriental immigrants with the help of an accelerated process. We selected 150 candidates from different countries and tried to indoctrinate them with the help of the best teachers and officers and the assistance of sociologists and psychologists. The course lasted for ten months and was the first and last of its kind. We achieved nothing. Altogether we succeeded in producing fifteen sergeants but not one officer. The disappointment was terrible but we learned that it was impossible to take shortcuts and that progress would have to be slow and would take many years.[5]

The decline in the level of the IDF was most evident in the small-scale retaliatory actions against *fedayeen* (Arabic for those prepared to sacrifice themselves) that the IDF staged from time to time. Many missions failed because of the low operational abilities of the Israeli soldiers. The IDF was finally shocked out of its lethargy by a disgraceful performance in battle against the Syrians.

In May 1951, Syrian regular and irregular forces crossed the Jordan River where it flows into the Sea of Galilee and occupied a hill in Israeli territory. A small IDF force summoned to that point was quickly repulsed. A larger force followed, but it proved difficult to stage an assault at the rocky area of battle. It was also a hot Saturday, and the IDF custom at the time was to feed soldiers a heavy Jewish Sabbath pudding—*cholent*—cooked the preceding day because of the prohibition against cooking on the Sabbath. That day the cholent was bad, and many of the soldiers went into battle with upset stomachs and diarrhea. During the assault the soldiers held back in fear of Syrian fire. The assault was repulsed and twenty-seven Israeli soldiers were killed. The Syrians were finally pushed back over the border when additional forces were brought up with the support of heavy artillery.

The IDF viewed the battle as a sign that combat units filled with new immigrants were not ready for battle. The General Staff convened for a post mortem, and Yigael Yadin, Chief of Staff at the time, later explained the reasons for failure: "In accordance with government directives, the IDF was not then oriented to immediate war. An army that has no combat challenge, that marks time, is faulty. This did not derive from lack of combat willingness in the General Staff or the senior echelons."[6]

Another military action reflecting the nadir to which the IDF had sunk during that period took place in the Jordanian village of Falma. On January 28, 1953 one of the battalions of the Givati Infantry Brigade, one of the most outstanding units in the War of Independence, attacked the village. As the battalion approached the village fence one of its men was wounded, and for over an hour twelve riflemen of the Jordanian National Guard held the entire battalion at bay, preventing it from penetrating the village. In the end the battalion abandoned the assault and withdrew. The action demonstrated a flagrant failure of will and performance that set off alarms about the substandard operational ability of many IDF units.

One of the immediate reforms was to assign sabras to combat units. A special effort was made to enhance the quality of junior officers in combat units, and a combat school was set up to train junior commanders under battle conditions. But the IDF realized that a broader program was needed to improve the standards of its soldiers. Training in combat was not enough. Morale, literacy, and a sense of mission had to be part of the approach. Women soldiers were assigned to eliminate illiteracy in immigrant settlements and assist in the assimilation of the immigrants. The army began to grow potatoes and tomatoes on its farms to ease the shortage of food. Yigael Yadin recalled:

New immigrant soldiers would visit their parents in transit camps and find them in leaking tents and degrading deprivation. I saw in this an extreme danger from the viewpoint of national security. I suggested to Ben-Gurion that the IDF adopt the transit camps. We tended to educational, housing, and food supply problems. These activities may have hampered the effort to build the army and its fighting spirit, but they assisted the State of Israel no less than combat actions.[7]

The conflict over priorities, in light of Israel's enfeebled economy, finally resulted in a bitter dispute between Ben-Gurion, who was both Prime Minister and Minister of Defense, and his Chief of Staff. The immediate outcome was Yadin's resignation, but the ultimate result was a streamlining of the IDF. In the early 1950s, before Egypt began to send fedayeen against Israel, Ben-Gurion estimated that the country would be safe from war for the next five or six years. He decided accordingly that defense should not be considered Israel's leading priority but that the emphasis should be shifted to social and economic development. He ordered a drastic cut in the defense budget and proposed that the IDF withdraw from functions not directly connected with combat.

Chief of Staff Yadin was unhappy about the plan to reduce the defense budget but was prepared to comply if the government insisted. The focus of conflict was determining on whose authority the cuts would be made. Yadin contended that as Chief of Staff it was up to him to decide exactly where cuts would be made; Ben-Gurion, for his part, ordered the arbitrary dismissal of 8,000 regular army men and another 10,000 civilians employed by the IDF. Yadin refused to authorize the dismissals and submitted his resignation.

At the time of Yadin's resignation, Deputy Chief of Staff Mordechai Makleff was in London studying economics in preparation for his demobilization from the army. He was called home to replace Yadin. Makleff supported Ben-Gurion's position in the dispute: "I realized that if we were released from maintaining military hospitals, laundries, etc., we'd have more funds for purely combat missions."[8]

Makleff reduced the IDF budget by one-sixth and dismissed thousands of regular army men and civilian workers:

My plan was to trim the administrative fat without damaging the fighting force. I rejected a proposal to thin out units and instead we eliminated commands and units that weren't essential. We examined the file of every officer and decided on dismissals. I knew that in the heat generated by our drive to establish a regular army quickly we had absorbed a high proportion of incompetents. I knew that the money we would save would be channelled to important social objectives. Ben-Gurion thought that a weak civilian population would cause the army to be weak, and I agreed with him.[9]

Appointed Chief of Staff at a young age, Makleff continued the youthful tradition begun by Yadin. Ben-Gurion welcomed Makleff to his new position with the words: "Your life is a tragic model for the younger generation."[10]

Mordechai Makleff had been thrust into the conflict that engulfed Palestine at the age of nine. He lived with his parents and three brothers and sisters in the village of Motza near Jerusalem, which was attacked by Arabs from neighboring villages in the 1929 riots. Makleff escaped through a window and hid in the branches of a tree from where he heard the screams of his family; when the attack ended, he found them dead.

Adopted by relatives at an early age, Makleff joined Orde Wingate's special night squads. During World War II he served in the British Army where he rose to the rank of major.

Makleff's acceptance of the appointment as Chief of Staff proved to be of greater historical significance than anyone could have suspected at the time. For having won the budget dispute and secure in the knowledge that the Chief of Staff held views consonant with his own, Ben-Gurion began to hint that he was considering retirement. No longer young, he periodically fell victim to bouts of depression, spoke increasingly about death, and mused about the immortality of the soul. He wanted to cap the end of a long political career with one last flourish. He believed that if he went to one of the desert kibbutzim, Israeli youth would follow his example. In 1953 Ben-Gurion did indeed resign as Prime Minister and Minister of Defense and appointed Pinhas Lavon to succeed him in the latter position, a move he was later to regret. Makleff had finished the year he had agreed to serve as Chief of Staff, and before Ben-Gurion departed for the Negev kibbutz of Sde Boker he appointed Moshe Dayan the fourth man to hold that position.

Notes

1. Previously unpublished interview with author, 1973.
2. Interview with author, originally published in *Davar Hashavua,* March 17, 1972.
3. Previously unpublished interview with author, 1973.
4. *Ibid.*
5. *Ibid.*
6. Interview in *Davar Hashavua, ibid.*
7. *Ibid.*
8. Previously unpublished interview with author, 1973.
9. *Ibid.*
10. Letter from David Ben-Gurion to Mordechai Makleff, 1952.

An Army of Farmers

THE DREAM that Jews would one day be farmers in the Land of Israel was closely tied to the Jewish defense of Palestine. In pre-statehood days, this was indeed a revolutionary notion, since the Jewish people had for centuries possessed neither military capability nor a physical tie with their homeland. The creation of NAHAL, an acronym for *Noar Halutzi Lohem*—Pioneering, Farming Youth Corps—as an integral part of the IDF reflected this early visionary thinking. The importance of the warrior-farmer to the future of Israel was aptly expressed by Yigal Allon, Commander of the Palmach: "The true frontier of the State of Israel moves and forms according to the movement and location of Jewish workers of the land. Without Jewish settlement, defense of the country is not possible, even if we double the force of the army." [1]

David Ben-Gurion dreamed of making the IDF a farmer's army. He envisioned the IDF as a working army that would combine superior combat ability with an agricultural education to create a brotherhood of fighting pioneers. The emphasis was to be on settling and developing the resources of the Negev Desert, another of Ben-Gurion's cherished dreams. This vision of an army of farmers was influenced by earlier Zionist thinkers who stressed that the redemption of the Jews was to be found in labor in their historic homeland. The original idea that each soldier devote a year of his military service to agriculture was eventually subsumed by the more urgent demand for specialization and technical training. But NAHAL, as a standing unit of the IDF, remains the embodiment of Ben-Gurion's dream.

Ben-Gurion's original plan found expression in the Defense Service Act of Israel (1949), which specifically imposed the obligation of agricultural service on every recruit. This law is still on the books in

Israel, although it is no longer enforced. Article F of the law states: "The first twelve months of regular service of a recruit will be devoted, after preliminary military training, primarily to agricultural preparation as shall be determined in the regulations, except for a recruit sent to serve in the air force or navy."

As the massive waves of immigration to Israel got underway, especially after 1948, Ben-Gurion saw that the number of new settlers exceeded that of the veterans and native Israelis. Many of the new immigrants came from Arab countries, from stagnating ghettos, and even from primitive cave dwellings in parts of Yemen and North Africa. As the sons of the new immigrants entered the ranks of the IDF, problems were bound to arise. One of the commanders of the IDF at the time, Brigadier General Yitzhak Pundak, recalls: "There were boys who didn't know what shoes were. Others had never seen soap before. The first thing we did was put them in a shower."[2]

Ben-Gurion hoped that the encounter between immigrant youth and sabras at IDF agricultural settlements would accelerate the process of immigrant absorption. In August 1948, when submitting the law for defense service to the Knesset, he noted:

There are fifty-five nations of origin represented in the army and you have no concept of how great are the distances and how considerable the differences between these national groups. The great majority of our nation is not yet Jewish, but human dust, bereft of a single language, without tradition, without roots, without a bond to national life, without the customs of an independent society. We must mend the rifts of the Diaspora and form a united nation. An efficient army will not emerge in this country, which is a land of immigration, if the youth, and especially the immigrants, do not first accept the agricultural education that will accord them roots in the life of the homeland, will accustom them to physical labor, will give them a language, cultural mores, and a routine of discipline before they enter the regular army. A year of agricultural preparation is designed in the first instance to build the nation, to crystallize this dust of man collected together from all ends of the earth into one national entity.

An even more pressing rationale for making the IDF into an army of farmers could be found in Israel's economic situation at the end of the 1940s and the beginning of the 1950s. Some three-quarters of the country's area was wilderness. The agricultural populations of the young state was only twelve percent of the nation's total. Israel urgently needed additional farmers to feed its burgeoning population. Food shortages during the years of austerity in the 1950s led the General Staff to develop agricultural farms on which to grow potatoes for the needs of the army and the public at large. Two such farms were founded with a company of soldiers assigned to each. These soldiers were to work the fields within a military regimen, but under the supervision of veteran farmers from kibbutzim. Once the food supply improved, however, the IDF's agricultural farms were disbanded.

1948: NAHAL Is Born

The idea of integrating military service and agricultural settlement appealed to youth movements and to the members of the settlement groups they sponsored. With the encouragement of the kibbutzim, a delegation of youth movement leaders approached Ben-Gurion in 1948 to request that rather than be separated and sent to various army units they be inducted as groups and assigned to agricultural settlements for the duration of their national service. Ben-Gurion liked the idea and ordered the General Staff to organize the fighting, pioneering youth. It was thus that NAHAL was born.

The first recruits entered the army in seven homogeneous groups. Most of them came from the same schools and had spent a few years together in their youth movements. The recruits were accompanied by their youth-movement instructors, who shared the task of supervision with the regular IDF command. The members of the NAHAL entered the army with a common purpose: to serve on an agricultural settlement and adapt to that way of life for at least a few years. This high motivation accounts for the fact that NAHAL members are for the most part superior soldiers with high morale.

The resemblance NAHAL bore to the Palmach so aroused the suspicions of Ben-Gurion's political opponents that following the dissolution of the Palmach in November 1948, the Prime Minister was accused of merely attempting to mold a new Palmach that would remain loyal to him alone. But his rivals misinterpreted Ben-Gurion's actions. His rationale for dissolving the Palmach was not, as they believed, an objection to its aims but rather his objection to the existence of separate armies within the state. He was all too aware of the tendency in Jewish society to splinter into factions over relatively unimportant issues, and he knew that the young state's only chance to stand up to the Arabs lay in a unified and concentrated armed force. The Palmach's spirit of pioneering and self-sacrifice was worth preserving, however, and Ben-Gurion sought to keep it alive in the NAHAL.

Inevitably there was internal dissension over the formation of the NAHAL. Many members who came from the left-wing youth movement resisted the new framework. They had aspired to an armed force like the Palmach and justified their resistance and resentment toward the NAHAL on ideological grounds. Desertion and breaches of discipline encouraged by the Mapam Party and its kibbutz movement plagued the NAHAL in its early days.

The continuation of the Palmach tradition was further emphasized in the design of the badge for the new unit. The Palmach badge had featured two ears of wheat with a sword lying diagonally across them. The badge of the NAHAL featured a sword and sickle with a common handle overlaying two ears of wheat. In a sense, this design perpetuated a tradition that had begun with Hashomer, whose badge depicted a plough and a rifle with the slogan: "The way of strength is labor." All three badges employed the same motifs: a blend of arms with agricultural tools or ears of wheat to symbolize labor on the land, the implication being that the arms were tools to protect the achievements of building and labor.

The first NAHAL recruitment in 1948 was known as the "Children's Draft." The IDF was a poor army then living from hand to mouth and vital equipment was earmarked for combat units. In their first military parade, the new NAHAL soldiers looked bedraggled, wearing sandals and slippers, and sporting many individual touches in their dress. At first the NAHAL units had to train with sticks instead of rifles. At the same time, the feeling among the many of its soldiers that the NAHAL was a continuation of the Palmach tradition created specific disciplinary problems because they wanted to preserve the democratic feisty spirit of the Palmach commandos. Some objected to having to work outside the settlements in addition to military training. Their desire to create a special life-style of civilian-like camaraderie inside a military camp gave rise to much friction. "We had to prove that we were an army and *not* partisans,"[3] Yitzhak Pundak, the Commander of the NAHAL, recalled.

The Palmach had encouraged self-discipline and individualism, rather than formal, imposed regulations. Members of the NAHAL who wanted to preserve that tradition sparked a debate over the issue of saluting, which arose when rank badges were first distributed to commanders. Despite the general desire to preserve a popular spirit in the IDF, there was no alternative to the use of rank badges as a means of identifying officers. At first officers had worn red crosses on their shoulders; then permanent ranks were instituted. And that was when the question of saluting arose. Until then the custom had been to stand at attention in front of an officer. "Doesn't saluting damage the Israeli spirit?" many soldiers asked. "What's wrong with just standing at attention? Why do we have to imitate foreign armies? We show respect for officers without the external marks of rank!" the opponents of saluting insisted. In the NAHAL the controversy was even sharper. Soldiers cited the Palmach, where officers had not been saluted, and claiming NAHAL's spiritual legacy, insisted that the formality be dispensed with.

It was also widely believed that a NAHAL private should have the right to oppose an officer and dispute his orders. This approach was also reflected in other objections to disciplinary formalities raised by the soldiers of NAHAL. They insisted, for instance, that polishing boots should be left to the individual's discretion and not be subject to orders from the commander. Such matters, they believed, had little to do with operational discipline. Similarly, where dress was concerned, the NAHAL members chose to wear their shirts outside their pants, in imitation of a custom that began in Palmach. Because each NAHAL unit was jointly supervised by an IDF officer and the NAHAL settlement coordinator, a question arose about who had final authority on such matters as work arrangements, details related to kibbutz life, and the issuance of passes. The unit coordinator was chosen by the NAHAL unit itself, and many members felt that he should have priority over the IDF officer in charge. But the NAHAL commanders stood their ground and protected their prerogatives. They did not want to forgo such tokens of discipline as saluting and a decent military appearance, although they were prepared to grant many powers to the NAHAL soldiers' committees, including the power to recommend a soldier's release from a unit if he should so desire.

A persistent propaganda campaign was not enough to ensure the enforcement of discipline. There was a frequent need for arrests and courts martial. One of the severest breaches of discipline in the NAHAL was a case of political mutiny that occurred in 1952. IDF regulations forbade the display of photographs of political personalities in soldiers' rooms, other than pictures of the President of Israel, the Prime Minister, Minister of Defense, or the Chief of Staff. At the beginning of the 1950s, when the Soviet Union was holding the show trials over the alleged Doctors' Plot (which involved mostly Jewish doctors), one of the pro-Soviet left-wing parties in Israel was split over whether to protest the matter to the Kremlin. One group split off from Mapam and merged with the Israeli Communist Party, which justified the purge. At a NAHAL settlement comprised of Hashomer Hatzair (Mapam) members, pictures of Stalin were found hanging in a number of soldiers' rooms. When ordered to remove them the soldiers refused.

The Commander of the NAHAL Colonel Moshe Netzer, came to discuss the matter with members of the NAHAL unit. The soldiers emphatically justified their refusal to remove Stalin's photo from their rooms in the name of freedom of expression. They insisted that in a democratic army *and* an independent unit a soldier should be permitted complete freedom of action and expression outside of training hours. Faith in Stalin and the Soviet Union did not, they contended, clash with the spirit of the IDF; and again reference was made to the spirit of Palmach as the paragon of independence within the armed forces.

Nor was this an isolated incident. The enormity of Stalinist atrocities and the extent of Soviet anti-Semitism had not yet come out, and Mapam was conducting a pro-Soviet propaganda campaign that leveled sharp criticism at the Israeli government. Disseminating political propaganda within the IDF was counter to orders of the high command, and concern grew about the spread of such insubordination as had occurred at that particular NAHAL settlement. Therefore, to prevent the spread of what the army regarded as mutiny, the NAHAL commanders and the General Staff decided to disband the offending unit and reassign its members to other units outside the framework of the NAHAL.

The NAHAL recruits who had joined up as members of youth movements were oriented to the combination of agricultural work and military training, but those soldiers assigned to NAHAL from other units did not always welcome the requirement to engage in farming. Some of the new immigrants regarded physical labor as degrading and did not understand the need for farmwork during their military service. In certain cases there was no alternative but to court-martial those who refused to go to work. One instance of organized resistance occurred in 1950 at Kibbutz Nir Am in the Negev when a platoon of ninety-two soldiers refused to work in the kibbutz. NAHAL commanders sent to quell the mutiny were told that the dissidents were not afraid of going to military prison. They carried placards proclaiming: "We don't want a settlement, we want the Army," implying that they wanted to be regarded as soldiers, not armed farmers. The affair ended when six of the ringleaders were sent to prison and the remainder returned to work.

During the few years that the program of agricultural training for all soldiers lasted, it was the NAHAL that organized the training. In November 1949 fifty camps wre built in various kibbutzim to absorb the first draft of agricultural soldiers. At the same time hundreds of youngsters who had grown up on kibbutzim and moshavim (semi-collective agricultural settlements) attended a course for squad commanders to prepare them to serve as a noncommissioned cadre for the thousands of soldiers who would come to the farms. The Defense Ministry prepared a special contract that the kibbutzim were asked to sign when they took in army units for work. Under its terms the kibbutz undertook to employ each unit for at least nine months and no more than twenty-five percent of each unit would be employed in the kitchen, laundry, and other service work. The army's intention was that the soldiers not be required to perform menial labor and that they would receive proper agricultural training. The kibbutzim agreed that the soldiers would undergo military training for five days a month and attend lectures one day a month. The new immigrants among them were entitled to half a day a week to learn Hebrew.

The great dream of converting the IDF into a working army that devoted half its time to agricultural training ran aground quickly. By 1950 it was clear that if Israel wanted to have a progressive army equipped with modern weapons, full-time professional training would be necessary for all its branches. Army commanders urged Ben-Gurion to revise the Defense Service Law, and in 1950 the first amendment was introduced, freeing soldiers needed for professional service from agricultural training. Soldiers who entered the army over the age of twenty were also to be exempt from work on the land. These were followed by two more amendments: at first, the Defense Minister was authorized to defer the period of service intended for agricultural training or devote it to ordinary military service; then the program of universal agricultural training was shelved altogether.

It met its end because Ben-Gurion's vision of a large farmers' army could not compete with the pressures for a professional armed force. The great demand for soldiers capable of performing tasks that re-

quired full-time training took precedence over the dream. The years
of terrorist infiltration and border skirmishes were upon Israel. Larger
numbers of soldiers were needed in well-trained combat units. After
the 1956 Sinai War the crop of young people eligible for call-up de-
creased, since the birth rate had declined in the difficult years of World
War II. During this time the army had, of necessity, entered a period
of greater specialization in weapons systems that demanded longer
training periods. So the universal agricultural-training scheme was
doomed.

From the outset the NAHAL took on auxiliary duties in addition
to agricultural work. Toward the end of the War of Independence its
men serviced planes engaged in bombing Arab positions. In April 1949
all the members of the NAHAL were dispatched to pave a road from
Sodom to Ein Gedi, the furthest point the army had reached along
the Dead Sea. Then the NAHAL turned southward to build fortifi-
cations around the first houses of Eilat, Israel's new Red Sea port.

But by far the NAHAL's greatest accomplishment was the establishment of a network of fortified settlements in strategic border areas.
During the War of Independence the High Command of the IDF
was convinced that the best defense for the young state lay in the
agricultural settlements, since these settlements, and especially the kibbutzim, formed obstacles to the invading armies. Whenever an Arab
force came up against agricultural settlements it had to fight much
harder and risk heavy losses. Consequently, after the War of Independence the IDF tried to continue filling in gaps on the borders with
these settlements. The problem was that manpower was lacking for
the rapid constuction of civilian settlements. So it was decided to create settlements manned with soldiers. The idea originated not in Israel but in imperial Rome, whose retired legionnaires built settlements
along the empire's borders. Members of the Palmach had also founded
a number of such settlements before the establishment of the state,
but the NAHAL was to endow this operation with an impetus that
changed the map of Israel.

Known in Hebrew as *heachzuyot,* or "holding settlements," these
points are maintained jointly by the army and civil agencies. The men
engage in guard and patrol duties as well as farm and work in light
industry. The women gravitate to the traditionally domestic chores.
Many holding settlements have eventually become permanent civilian
settlements.

NAHAL soldiers sent to holding settlements are required to remain there for at least a year and enjoy all the privileges of regular soldiers—wages, leave, and the like. At the end of the year they may remain in the holding settlement, and if they choose to form a permanent agricultural settlement, all the livestock and equipment remains at their disposal.

On July 23, 1951 the first holding settlement was established facing the Gaza Strip, which was teeming with Palestinian refugees and Egyptian soldiers. A young commander named Danny Matt, assisted by junior commanders, who had been raised on kibbutzim and moshavim, and a company of NAHAL soldiers climbed a small hill and named the settlement Nahal Oz. A month later Gonen, the second NAHAL holding settlement, was founded on the Syrian border. Like Nahal Oz it also was to become a successful kibbutz in the ensuing years. In October 1951 the NAHAL went south and founded Yotvata, the third holding settlement, in the Arava Plain by the Jordan border. In the next two decades the NAHAL founded or rehabilitated thirty agricultural settlements, and dozens of the holding settlements became permanent kibbutzim.

After the Six-Day War the holding settlements took on a clearly political character since they indicated that Israel might retain large portions of the territories captured from the Arab states. They sprang up on the Golan Heights, a strategic point from which the Syrians had bombarded Israeli settlements filling the Jordan Valley, and dotting the landscape of northern Sinai and the Gaza Strip. Many of these have since become permanent settlements. However, the fact that the holding settlement is in essence an army camp with an agricultural role gives the army and the government the right to order its dissolution. After the Israeli conquest of the Sinai Peninsula in 1956, Nahal Ophir was set up in Sharm el-Sheikh. But it was promptly dismantled when the government decided to retreat from Sinai. Similarly, NAHAL holding settlements were evacuated along with a cluster of civilian settlements when Israeli pulled out of Sinai after the signing of a peace treaty with Egypt.

In 1977, after the Likud bloc came to power in Israel, Israel's settlement policy in the territories occupied during the Six-Day War underwent a fundamental change. The new approach called for establishing settlements in areas densely populated by the area's Arab inhabitants, where formerly the emphasis had always been on areas close to the border and usually devoid of residents. The NAHAL was exploited to implement this new settlement policy, and that inevitably led to a dispute between the Defense Ministry and the kibbutz movement, which opposed the new policy and argued that the NAHAL must not be involved in an issue on which the nation was sharply divided.

Despite the NAHAL's achievements, the opposition of many professional soldiers persisted and even grew more severe as the IDF felt the manpower pinch in the early 1950s. When Moshe Dayan became Chief of Staff he expressed grave doubts about the wisdom of diverting considerable manpower to kibbutzim at a time when the army needed superior fighters. Dayan proposed that NAHAL members receive advanced military training at the expense of their agricultural duties. He suggested that they be trained as paratroops and be included in a special battalion of the IDF airborne forces. The men of the NAHAL paratroop battalion, who wear the NAHAL badge on their sleeves and the paratroops' red beret, have taken part in many military operations and compiled an exemplary record.

Still, some opposition still remains on the part of military men who feel that in periods when the IDF is starved for superior manpower, the cream of the recruits are often directed to the NAHAL. And it is true that many of the privates in the NAHAL could have become fine officers had they gone to other units. The IDF thereby loses many officers not only during the period of compulsory service but also during the years they would serve in the active reserve.

The NAHAL continues to fight for its existence but also adapts to a changing reality and to pressures from within the army. After the Six-Day War, when the IDF needed more tank crews to man the greatly increased number of armored units, the NAHAL agreed to divert some of its men to armored training. What's more the routine of service in the NAHAL has been changed considerably. Of the thirty-six months of compulsory service, only twelve or so are now devoted to agricultural training and settlement on a kibbutz. The remaining time is given to regular military training and operational employment. Those who are not in prime physical condition volunteer for second-line combat units, such as long-range gunners, and combat engineers.

Notes

1. Yigal Allon, *Masach shel Hol* [Sand Screen] (Tel Aviv: Hakibbutz Hameuchad, 1959), p. 233.

2. Previously unpublished interview with author, 1973.

3. *Ibid.*

5

Terror and Retaliation

T HROUGHOUT 1949, the first year following the end of the War of Independence, the Israelis still harbored the hope that the armistice agreements would be merely a temporary arrangement to be followed by standard peace treaties. Despite Arab frustration over defeat on the battlefield, at first there were some encouraging signs of reconciliation in the unofficial relations between the two sides. Egypt and Israel maintained a joint camp in the demilitarized zone at Nitzana and manned joint patrols (with the participation of UN observers) along the cease-fire line. Egyptian and Lebanese delegates to the armistice talks had even accepted the invitation of their Israeli counterparts to visit kibbutzim in Israel.

A different but equally promising sign was Egypt's desire to disengage from the Gaza Strip. Cairo regarded this salient as an economic and political burden on the Egyptian body politic and was alarmed by the voracity of the Palestinian refugees. In 1950 the Egyptians considered handing over responsibility for the strip to the Palestinian government of Gaza, and they sent a military man out to establish a local militia meant to replace the Egyptian Army. In their desire to induce the withdrawal of British troops from their country, the Egyptians even suggested that the British transfer their forces from camps along the Suez Canal to the Gaza Strip. However, they effectively scotched the idea by making it conditional upon the stationing of British troops on the Israeli side of the border as well!

The relations that developed between Israel and Transjordan to the east can best be described as correct. They remained so due to the realistic approach of King Abdullah who realized that if he wanted to strengthen and extend his kingdom he must first obtain the agreement of the nascent Jewish state. From time to time Abdullah held secret meetings with Israeli representatives in his palace; at one of these the Bedouin potentate told Moshe Dayan, then Commander of the Jerusalem District, that he personally was amenable to a peace treaty but was under heavy pressure from the British ambassador not to enter into any such commitment. Abdullah surmised that the ambassador's opposition to an accord stemmed from the fear that a peace treaty between Israel and Transjordan would further undermine Britain's position in Egypt.

He may well have been right, for Britain continued to stir the Israeli-Egyptian caldron. As the Egyptians increased their pressure on London regarding a troop withdrawal, the British began to drop ominous hints that Israel was planning an attack on its southern neighbor. In July 1950, for example, during a visit to Egypt by the Chief of the Imperial General Staff they planted the notion that if the international situation deteriorated as a result of the Korean conflict Israel might well attack Egypt. Whitehall was hoping to mute the Egyptian demands for troop withdrawals, and these warnings did indeed arouse concern in Cairo. In fact the Egyptians stepped up their patrols on the Israeli border, laid mines to protect their coasts, and stationed two units on the islands of Tiran and Sanafir in the Straits of Tiran—none of which bode well for the future.

At first the violations and incidents along Israel's border with Egypt had more to do with economic motives than military. Many of the Palestinians who had abandoned their homes during the war took up what they assumed would be temporary residence in refugee camps near Israel's borders. When they discovered that they would not be allowed to return to their homes, some of them began to steal across the border to salvage belongings in their deserted dwellings or harvest fruit in what used to be their orchards—or, merely to plunder whatever they could from Israeli settlements. The dire economic situation in the refugee camps, which deteriorated even further when the Arab states abandoned the refugees to their fate, was the chief factor behind this infiltration movement. Even the minor border incidents that occurred during this period were related to disputes over agricultural land along the armistice lines. Nevertheless, the porous border was a matter of great concern to Israel because it created a sense of insecurity in whole sectors of the country.

In 1951 the general situation took a turn for the worse when the ban on shipping to and from Israel through the Suez Canal became a matter of principle for Egypt. In September of that year the UN

Security Council called upon the Egyptians to allow for the passage of Israeli vessels, but to no avail. Soon threats of war filled the Arab press, as editorials urged the Arab governments to purge the stain of the 1948 defeat, and the penetrations into Israel not only multiplied that year but were joined by acts of murder.

Israel also contributed its share to the climate of tension by its relentless efforts to gain control of the demilitarized zones, especially along the Syrian border. Not to be outdone, the Syrians likewise moved to take their share of territory, and it was in the course of one of these incidents centering on the demilitarized zone that a full-scale battle broke out in 1951 at Tel Mutilla (where the Jordan River flows into the Sea of Galilee). Israel also took strong measures against its Arab citizens suspected of collaborating with the enemy. Many Bedouin dwelling along the northern border were driven over the frontier into Syria, while in the Negev the Azazma tribe was expelled to Sinai after some of its men had been found responsible for attacks on traffic, and the residents of the town of Migdal were expelled en masse to the Gaza Strip.

As part of the spiral of violence the nature of the incursions into Israel also changed, for many of the infiltrators were now working in gangs. What's more the incursions were no longer a phenomenon limited to desperate refugees; in a number of cases wealthy Arabs from Jordan organized the gangs as a business venture. Either way the bands would penetrate Israel nightly and make off with anything of value: herds, motors, irrigation pipes, building materials, and fruits and vegetables. During the citrus season Arab vehicles crossed the border in the heart of the country and returned to Jordan ladened with oranges. Whenever possible these thefts were accompanied by the brutal murder of Jewish settlers. The infiltrators also engaged in acts of outright sabotage, such as burning fields, destroying water installations, uprooting trees, and tearing up railroad tracks. In the south of the country the Bedouin were known to lay mines just so that they could make off with parts of the mauled automobiles.

In the middle of 1951 Israeli Intelligence received reports that Amin el-Husseini, formerly the Mufti of Jerusalem and the leader of the Arab Revolt in the 1930s, was organizing bands of saboteurs. Incidents of murder unaccompanied by any attempt at theft or plunder had in fact begun to occur in the vicinity of the border. The Egyptian Army and Transjordan's Arab Legion were officially opposed to the Mufti's independent endeavor, but their Intelligence Services nevertheless exploited the infiltration movement for their own purposes by agreeing to turn a blind eye with selected infiltrators if they brought back information of military value along with their plunder.

Not a week passed without incidents and casualties, and before long it seemed as if whole regions of the country were wide open to these assaults. The consequent atmosphere of vulnerability had a particularly detrimental effect on the settlements populated by new immigrants, though the bands did not spare veteran settlements or cities either. One infiltrator from Jordan was caught in Tel Aviv after having successfully carried out five thefts. In Jerusalem infiltrators were known to steal tires right off cars. Soon they had taken to murdering Israeli security guards for their weapons and not even the IDF was immune on this score; infiltrators brazenly stole into army camps to make off with arms. In one case they penetrated the camp housing Central Command's headquarters, and in 1952 three tons of food were stolen from an army camp in Eilat. The impotence of the Israei border patrols reached new heights during this period. They failed to stop even the gangs that specialized in stealing telephone wire, which was subsequently sold for its copper content. These gangs regularly "shaved" whole regions of their phone wires. For example, in July 1951, 55 kilometers of such wire were stolen in the center of the country alone. The thefts also spread to the south and their audacity peaked in March 1952 when infiltrators pulled up and made off with thirty-five telephone poles.

Most infiltrations occurred along Israel's longest border—with Jordan—and the majority of the Israeli casualties also were at the hands of saboteurs coming from the east. Of the 137 Israeli casualties incurred in 1951, 111 were along the Jordanian frontier. The following year saw the statistic rise to 114 (out of a total of 147 nationally). After the assassination of King Abdullah the penetrations from Jordan mounted from month to month and relations between the two countries deteriorated sharply. By 1952 matters reached the point where the Israeli General Staff inclined toward the view that an all-out war was preferable to allowing the raids to continue. For the first time since the War of Independence there was talk of sending the IDF to conquer the West Bank. The operation's contingency plan was predicated on the establishment of an autonomous Arab administration for the area, with Aqaba and Eilat on the Red Sea becoming a joint port. In effect the West Bank would function somewhat like a condominium, with the conduct of defense and foreign affairs retained by Israel.

Such plans were never acted upon, however, and the IDF remained plagued by the security problem posed by the sabotage raids from neighboring states. Dealing with the infiltrations was Israel's first military challenge since the War of Independence, and its initial efforts resulted in a string of failures. The General Staff was convinced that the war against the infiltrators could not be limited to defensive actions, and many Israeli officers believed that to have any effect it would have to be conducted as a war against the Gazan refugee camps and Jordanian villages in which the Mufti was recruiting his fedayeen. Following this thinking, the General Staff arrived at a policy of reprisal actions against the villages harboring infiltrators. The counterstrikes were conceived as a way of creating popular pressure on the infiltrators to halt their activities. The IDF initiated systematic reprisal actions in 1951. The military literature concentrates mainly on the raids carried out in 1955 and 1956, but the fact is that as far back as 1950 the Israeli Army had already engaged in four reprisal actions, and in the following year (in which eighteen actions were carried out) the policy became axiomatic. In the early years, however, Israel did not own up to these actions. On the contrary the IDF consistently denied claims by the Jordanians, Egyptians, and the UN that its units had operated over the border.

For the most part these early reprisal raids were modest operations directed against civilians or units of the Jordanian National Guard. Even so many of them were marked by a poor level of execution. Units would fail to locate or reach their objectives, or they aborted missions *and* left valuable equipment behind in enemy territory. Ambushes came to grief because the soldiers lacked combat ability. The methods employed in these reprisal actions were varied from laying mines in enemy territory (in response to similar acts on Israeli soil) to retaliatory thefts of irrigation pipes, telephone wires, even herds of goats and sheep. Deserted villages inside Israel proved to be a lodestone for infiltrators were razed, and tracts that had been planted by Jordanian villagers on the Israeli side of the frontier were harvested by the IDF. But none of these measures prevented the infiltration movement from gathering momentum.

Before long the Israeli General Staff had come to the conclusion that the counterraids were not an adequate answer to the problem. Of the eighty-five reprisal actions undertaken through the end of 1953, only thirty-eight were considered successful; forty-one were judged by high-ranking officers to be unqualified failures, and the remaining six were deemed only partially successful. There was a period during which the IDF was careful to send out only small units on the ironic assumption that the failure of a few men would cause less psychological damage in the ranks. In their search for a viable solution, the IDF's leading commanders decided to turn to ex-army people, most of whom had served in the Palmach and leading commando units and were living in kibbutzim, and ask them to take on the reprisal missions for the army. A few operations officers went so far as to organize units of this sort, often without the knowledge of the General Staff. One of these officers was David Elazar (who was to become Chief of Staff in 1972). Dado, as Elazar was widely known, recruited veterans of the Palmach's Harel Brigade and members of moshavim on the coastal plain. Having obtained permission from Moshe Dayan (then Chief of Operations Branch in the General Staff), he proceeded to dispatch them over the border on his own initiative.

Still, calling these old war horses back into service was not a solid solution either. The accumulation of failures and search for a better way finally led to a turnabout in the summer of 1953, when the Commander of the Jerusalem District Mishael Shaham decided to go after a saboteur known as Samweli who had cast his terror over the settlements in the area. Samweli lived in the West Bank village of Nebi Samwel, just over the border, and he added new Israeli victims to his hit list every week. Shaham would have sent a military unit into Samweli's village had he not been deterred by the fear that the punitive operation would only end in failure, as so many had before. Then he recalled a student at the Hebrew University who could surely accomplish the mission handily, if only he could be persuaded to take it on. The man he had in mind was a twenty-five-year-old major in the reserves who had been released from the regular army a year earlier after having served as an intelligence officer in the north. His name was Ariel Sharon and he had a reputation for daring.

Sharon had been raised in a small town on the coastal plain, had fought in the War of Independence, and was wounded in the battle for Latrun. It was only due to the efforts of a new immigrant who had come to the battlefield straight from the boat, and had the presence of mind to carry Sharon to safety on his back, that the young man was saved from the fate of the dozens of other wounded Israelis who met their deaths on the battlefield. After a few years' service in the regular army, Sharon decided to leave the IDF and register on the Faculty for Middle Eastern Studies in Jersualem.

Mishael Shaham had little trouble persuading Sharon to take on the mission. His one condition was that he be allowed to take along some friends—none of whom was then serving in the army—and he proceeded to assemble them from kibbutzim and moshavim around the country. The makeshift unit did not manage to catch Samweli that night, but their action nonetheless inaugurated a new era in the history of the Israeli Army. For soon Sharon and Shaham were proposing the establishment of a single commando unit specializing in reprisals against saboteurs. The idea was duly raised before the General Staff, but not everyone was enthusiastic about it. One reason for reserve was a fear that the creation of a special unit would further damage the morale of the rest of the army. Nevertheless Chief of Staff Makleff decided in favor of it because he calculated that if the bungling of the regular units were allowed to continue a feeling of weakness and failure might engulf the army. Initially the other units might take offense at the fact that all the reprisal operations were being assigned to one unit alone—and an elite unit at that. On the other hand, its chances of succeeding were good and a thirst for victory would eventually spread throughout the entire army.

The new unit's name was simply "101." It existed as an independent for only half a year, but that was enough time for it to light the necessary spark. At its peak Unit 101 numbered no more than forty fighters, each of whom was a character in his own right. Ariel Sharon handpicked his men, and rank was not a very important distinction among them; more than once a sergeant was known to command an officer, and some—like Sharon himself—had been commissioned as officers without completing officers' school. For the most part the members of Unit 101 came from kibbutzim and moshavim and were men of the soil. Their unit resembled a group of partisans more than a regular army unit: the camp placed at their disposal was a paragon of disorder; most of the men dressed haphazardly, and were armed as suited them best; in fact, quite a few were eccentrics. But none of this prevented them from excelling in combat and fieldcraft.

Perhaps the most celebrated member of 101 was Meir Har-Zion, whom Moshe Dayan promoted to the rank of captain though he never took an officers' course. The keen senses of this young kibbutznik became legendary, and in the course of time Dayan would see fit to praise him as the greatest Jewish soldier since Bar-Kokhba.

Dayan had reason to recall his first meeting with Har-Zion, during the early days of Unit 101, following a battle with Bedouin near the Sinai border. Dayan went down to visit the new unit, and standing in the field he suddenly noticed a large eagle perched on the corpse of a camel that had been killed in the fighting. Dayan instinctively grabbed a rifle and aimed it at the bird, but suddenly a heavy hand came down on the barrel, shoving it aside. It belonged to the twenty-one-year-old sergeant who commanded 101's reconnaissance section, and his name was Meir Har-Zion. "What are you doing?" the sergeant barked at the general. "That's an eagle! I won't let you harm it."

Dayan, momentarily stunned, studied the young man carefully and abandoned the idea of shooting the eagle. In time the two men grew close despite the differences in age and rank, and when Har-Zion was critically wounded in a reprisal raid Dayan sat by his bedside for hours until he regained consciousness.

As Unit 101 began operating over the border, initially in patrols that reached dozens of kilometers into enemy territory and later in actions against selected targets, its operations became bolder and inflicted more pain on the enemy. Sharon set the rule (which was subsequently adopted by the paratroops and the IDF as a whole) that his men were not to return unless they had successfully completed their mission. Still, 101's operations remained relatively modest until the reprisal action that became a watchword in the history of the Israeli-Arab conflict: Kibya. It took place in October 1953 after Israel was shaken by the gruesome murder of a woman and her two children in a settlement for new immigrants near Lod by saboteurs from Jordan. The assailants had thrown hand grenades into the victims' house, and this time there was no doubt that Israel would respond vigorously.

The commander of Unit 101 and the deputy commander of the IDF's paratroop battalion were called into a meeting in the Operations Room of Central Command. The main objective of the reprisal operation was the village of Kibya, which was assigned to the paratroops, while 101 was charged with smaller actions in two villages nearby. Hearing the plan the paratroop commander reacted with diffidence: he suspected that his men were not polished enough to take on an operation of that order; clearly he feared another fiasco and was reluctant to accept command. This was the opportunity Sharon had been waiting for. He promptly volunteered to take command of the paratroops and the operation as a whole, and his offer was accepted. One of the leading players in the bloody war between Israel and the Arab states, a man of meager restraint, had entered onto the stage of history.

Sharon knew that the success of that particular operation would greatly affect—if not wholly determine—his future in the army. (The fact is that within three months of the Kibya action the twenty-five-year-old major had been appointed commander of the paratroops— an impressive leap forward.) Thus prior to leaving their base, he told the ninety paratroopers and twenty-five members of Unit 101: "We're not coming back until we've completed the mission! We must break the chain of failures!" This was a tune very different from what the men of the IDF were accustomed to hearing. Sharon further prepped his men by reading an account of the murder that had sparked the operation. He ordered his soldiers to carry with them not less than 700 kg of explosives.

Kibya fell after a short battle, and the Israelis destroyed forty-six of its 250 houses. They assumed that most of its inhabitants had fled at the outbreak of fighting; instead, sixty-nine men, women, and children met their deaths while hiding in their demolished homes.

When the truth became known a wave of horror spread through Israel. The military command was sure that the Jordanians had incurred no more than ten deaths as a result of the action, and the government was equally caught off balance by the magnitude of the action. Judging by the results, UN observers ventured that no less than 600 soldiers had taken part in the attack. Rather than set the record straight the Israeli government remained true to its policy of not admitting to operations undertaken in enemy territory and denied any association with the Kibya action. But since it could not get around issuing some statement on the affair, the eventual communiqué was evasive and inevitably mendacious. "The government of Israel," Ben-Gurion stated on October 9, "vigorously denies the preposterous claim that 600 men of the IDF took part in an action against Kibya. We have done a rigorous check and have found without doubt that not a single military unit, not even the smallest, was absent from its camp on the night of the attack on Kibya." Afterward a story was floated that the attack on Kibya had been the work of Israeli settlers whose families had been victimized by infiltrators.

The Kibya action also left its mark on the IDF, primarily by spawning the decision that acts of reprisal were to focus on military targets and as much as possible avoid harm to civilians. The new Minister of Defense Pinhas Lavon (who had been appointed to the post after Ben-Gurion withdrew from public affairs for a year and a half) was more scrupulous than ever before about establishing the limits of every action. At the same time Sharon's position changed when

Unit 101 merged into the paratroops, and he was appointed the new paratroop commander.

Just before beginning his leave (during which he was replaced as Prime Minister by Moshe Sharett and as Minister of Defense by Pinhas Lavon), Ben-Gurion appointed Moshe Dayan to succeed Mordechai Makleff as the fourth Chief of Staff of the Israel Defense Forces. Before long, however, communications faltered and a dangerous rift opened among the three men new to these three key posts. Sharett had repeatedly asked Lavon for copies of the operational orders of the reprisal raids. Before long the Prime Minister was accusing Lavon of failing to report to him—and the Cabinet—on operations that had been undertaken across the border, complaining that many had in fact taken place contrary to the Cabinet's wishes. Relations also soured between the Minister of Defense and the Chief of Staff, especially after Lavon summoned officers to his ministry and questioned them on why their reprisals had exceeded the bounds of their original plans. When the relations between Lavon and Dayan deteriorated in 1954 to the point of open rupture, envoys from the ruling Mapai Party made off for the Negev in the hope of drawing Ben-Gurion back into the government. Even Dayan did his share by informing Ben-Gurion of the intolerable situation that had evolved in the Defense Ministry.

It was against this background of flawed relations that the so-called Lavon Affair began to run its long course. Its roots traced back to the rather childish notion, broached within the confines of Military Intelligence, that acts of sabotage against British and American targets in Egypt would prompt the British to postpone the withdrawal of forces. As a bid to undermine Egypt's relations with the two Western powers, the idea attested more than anything else to Israel's fear of being left to face the Arab states alone. Be that as it may, orders were given to put the plan into action, and as it turned out the execution was flagrantly amateurish. The members of the network in Egypt—all of them Jews—were readily apprehended, tried, and two subsequently were executed. On top of that accusations were aired that one of the members of the network—an Israeli—had betrayed his comrades to the Egyptians.

It was not until the Egyptians had rounded up the network and issued a communiqué that the affair became known to Prime Minister Sharett and his Cabinet. Sharett demanded a full report from the Defense Minister, while the latter claimed that he was as surprised as everyone else. Lavon conceded that he had known about the planning of the operation but had not authorized its execution, whereas Chief of Military Intelligence Benyamin Jibli countered that he had received the minister's approval to proceed with the operation—and even produced documents to prove his claim. Thereafter, however, a number of Intelligence people testified before an inquiry commission that they had been ordered to forge documents that would place responsibility for the debacle on Lavon. The whole unsavory episode only heightened the clamor for Ben-Gurion to return to government, and on January 21, 1955 he took over the defense portfolio in Moshe Sharett's government. A few months later Ben-Gurion replaced the Chief of Military Intelligence, and on November 2 he again became Prime Minister.

Ben-Gurion's return to the Defense Ministry was regarded as a victory for the "activists" on defense issues—and with good reason. For the fact is that about a month afterward on February 28, 1955 the IDF delivered a sharp blow to the Egyptian Army in the Gaza Strip. This operation, known in the General Staff as Black Arrow, was a milestone in the history of Israeli-Egyptian relations. Its plan called for a company of paratroopers under Sharon's command to attack a camp of the Egyptian garrison in Gaza. Sharon wanted to broaden the objectives of the action and received permission to blow up the Gaza's railroad facilities and the city's waterworks. Thirty-six Egyptian soldiers were killed in this action and twenty-eight were wounded; the Israelis suffered eight dead, twelve wounded.

The vehemence of this move against the Egyptian Army puzzled many observers, for January had been a relatively quiet month along the border. Admittedly five days before the Israeli action a squad from Egyptian Intelligence had penetrated seventy kilometers into Israeli territory and murdered an Israeli laborer, but that was not what had sparked the Israeli decision to respond so forcefully. Instead the operation appeared to signal a thoroughgoing change in Israel's reprisal policy toward Egypt, prompted by Egypt's reinforcement of its blockade on Israeli shipping through the Straits of Tiran as well as by the harsh sentences passed by a military tribunal in January 1955 on the members of the Jewish network involved in the sabotage operations behind the Lavon Affair. Another radical change was Israel's new-found willingness to own up to its deeds. Until the Gaza operation the Israeli government had consistently denied all association with the reprisal actions; now these operations were to become the country's official policy.

The communiqué issued by the IDF spokesman after the Gaza operation did include some fabricated details. (Israel contended, for example, that an IDF unit had been attacked on Israeli territory and that it was during the pursuit of the Egyptian assailants that a battle had developed in the Gaza Strip.) Nevertheless the statement was an admission of responsibility, and from then on Israel would always confirm that the IDF was responsible for the reprisal actions.

Rocked by the shock waves of the attack, the Egyptians sent reinforcements into Sinai and the Gaza Strip. Nasser would later contend that the Gaza action had prodded him into his first arms deal with the Communist bloc. And although Cairo did not believe that it would be capable of taking on Israel in a full-scale war in the foreseeable future, Egypt felt obliged as the leading country in the Arab world to respond to the Israeli move.

It is highly doubtful that the Gaza action is what really prompted Nasser to enter into an association with the Soviet Union by means of an arms transaction. On the other hand there is little doubt that it was among the prime factors behind the Egyptian decision to send fedayeen units out to wreak mayhem on Israel. The most portentous aspect of the matter was that, for the first time since the War of Independence, a sovereign Arab state stood behind acts of infiltration and sabotage against Israel. Thus the Gaza action set in motion a process of deterioration that led inexorably to the 1956 war in Sinai.

Israel's resolve to act vigorously against the Egyptians was not reached in a day. The search for a well-calibrated retaliation policy had been going on since 1950, when the first infiltrations began. The question was how to respond, when, against whom, and to what degree? These issues had been underlying Israel's doctrine of deterrence since the country's establishment. Jerusalem's retaliation policy from the outset was that the only way to deter the Arabs was to act according to the following three dictums:

1. Arabs understand and appreciate only the language of force.
2. If attacked, Israel must not remain passive; restraint will be interpreted as either fear or weakness, and invite additional violence.
3. A quid pro quo is not enough; Israel must exact twice the price—or more—for every attack.

Only in this way would the Arabs be moved to reconsider the advisability of every assault they planned against Israel.

On the eve of the Sinai Campaign, Moshe Dayan defined the retaliation doctrine as follows:

Although Israel cannot protect every tractor driver plowing close to the border or prevent the laying of mines on the roads of immigrant settlements, we are able to exact a heavy price for our blood. The aim of this policy is to prove to the Arabs that the Arab country responsible will not get off easily. Whenever the IDF operated in Arab territory, the forces of the countries involved have been incapable of contending with it. Their defeat was manifest to the citizenry, and the result was that instead of fedayeen actions enhancing the prestige of the regime, they have undermined faith in the government and its forces.

The first issue facing the Israeli General Staff was whom to punish, or through which channel to exert pressure on the Arab governments. Should the IDF retaliate solely against the perpetrators of the actions—the saboteurs themselves—or take up arms against army units or perhaps against the civilian population? Israel's strategy never reflected an unequivocal approach on this question. Instead the IDF experimented in its operations, the result being a swing from one extreme to the other. During the first stage, which drew to a close with the action in Kibya, small reprisal actions were mounted against civilian targets, creating the effect of terror against terror. The second stage, from 1954 until the Sinai Campaign, was characterized by actions directed primarily against military targets.

The axiom that twice the price should be exacted for every Arab attack inevitably produced an accumulation of unsettled scores and consequent large-scale actions by the IDF. The more difficult it was for Israel to cope with the fedayeen actions, the harsher its retaliatory strikes. In effect, the forcefulness of the IDF's reprisals spoke of Israel's weakness and her fear that a young state with such vulnerable borders would not be able to withstand a guerrilla war for very long. It also reflected the mounting frustration that, despite the vehemence of the reprisal actions, the fedayeen attacks did not stop. And this frustration was further stoked by public opinion internationally, which tended to ignore the multitude of small but costly actions by the fedayeen but react censoriously to the major Israeli reprisal operations that followed only after a long list of fedayeen provocations.

During the period when the reprisal raids were at their peak two men had a particularly profound influence on the IDF: Moshe Dayan, who established the policy of strong reprisals, and Ariel Sharon, who energetically implemented it. More than just executing orders, however, Sharon would exhort the General Staff to order a reprisal action each time Israelis met harm at the hands of fedayeen, and then he would immediately submit a variety of operational plans. He was bound to have an effect, if only because it was to his credit that for the first time since the War of Independence the General Staff had a first-rate force at its disposal on which it could rely to carry out any mission. On the battlefield Sharon usually tended to carry out his orders in the most thorough manner possible, and the tools he gave Dayan made it possible to pursue a policy of reprisal. Clearly this policy would never have been applied had it not been approved by Ben-Gurion; but Ben-Gurion was somewhat less than scrupulous about details because he was so often won over by the emphatic approach of his Chief of Staff.

The imprint made by Dayan and Sharon remained strong for many years, for they raised the IDF to a new level of ability in combat. It may be true that the standards demanded by these two had long been part of the IDF's tradition, but it is equally true that they pulled the army out of the decline into which it had fallen after the War of Independence. Their method was to work through an elite unit—initially with the small commando unit 101, then the paratroops—which the rest of the army eyed with envy. If at first they ran the risk of deflating the morale of all the other combat units, ultimately they infected the entire army with a yen for battle and a taste for victory. All aspired to the standards set by the paratroops.

While Sharon demanded that his men not return from an action unless they had carried it out, Dayan was even more stringent, warning that: "A commander who returns from a mission without having executed it and with less than fifty percent casualties will be dismissed!" The paratroops also renewed the combat approach cultivated in the Palmach that called for a commander to lead his men into battle and serve as an example to them. "Follow me. Attack!" was the standard IDF order, a sharp contrast to other armies' urging men into battle with the customary "Forward!" Another custom that took hold among the paratroops—and which became almost sacrosanct—was never to leave behind casualties, a practice that spread throughout the IDF and that sometimes reached questionable extremes during the period of the heaviest reprisal actions when paratroopers were prepared to sacrifice more and more men in order to retrieve one wounded comrade. In one instance, after a paratrooper had been taken prisoner by the Jordanians a number of actions were undertaken—at the cost of many lives—just to capture Jordanians who then could be traded for the Israeli.

The combat strategy favored by the paratroops was to stage a direct assault on their objective, attacking under any circumstances at any price. Sharon believed that only in close combat was it possible to defeat the Arab fighter and overcome the advantage in firepower he enjoyed. To enable his men to reach their objective with a minimum of casualties, reprisal actions were undertaken at night. His standing orders were to withhold fire until the actual assault began, not to shoot even if discovered and fired upon by the enemy. This was a tactic that confounded the Arabs, and the paratroops paid a high price as well. In September 1956 Dayan wrote in his diary: "I don't know whether there are any veteran commanders left in the paratroops who have not been wounded in one or another of their actions."

While cultivating the paratroops, however, Dayan took care to whip the rest of the army into shape as well, emphasizing building up the army's muscle. He also decided to rejuvenate the army by having officers retire at about age forty, to assure constant movement up the ranks, the introduction of fresh ideas, and a young and vibrant command. At the same time the officers leaving the army would retire at a young enough age to embark on a second career in civilian life.

The flaw in the line pursued by Dayan and Sharon was that the paratrooper's punishing blows did not bring peace to Israel's borders; just the opposite. Although Israeli paratroops exacted a heavy toll on the Egyptian Army, the Arab Legion, and even the Syrian Army, the infiltrations did not cease, they merely changed in nature. Instead of forays for plunder came raids bent on sabotage and murder.

During the early 1950s the Egyptians had sent their fedayeen against the British Army in Egypt; now these same units were transferred to the Gaza Strip to act against Israel. The 700 men in these units included criminals who had been released from prison after agreeing to join the ranks of the infiltrators, for a monthly salary plus bonuses for every border crossing and successful operation. Units were subordinate to the Intelligence Division of the Egyptian Army in Gaza. When Israeli reprisals grew more daring and damaging (in one paratroopers blew up the fedayeen Gaza Strip headquarters housed in the Khan Yunis police station), Egyptian military attachés began to organize fedayeen units in other Arab countries as well. It was not uncommon for fedayeen from the Gaza Strip crossing into Israel to complete their work and then retreat into Jordan, from where they were flown back to Egypt.

As Israel's frustration grew so did the force of the IDF's blows, and on April 5, 1956 Israel, straying from the principle established after the action in Kibya—to refrain as much as possible from attacking civilian targets—and in response to the Egyptian shelling of Israeli settlements, fired on the Market Square in Gaza and a number of refugee camps, killing sixty-six Arabs and wounding twelve others. The Egyptian response was to send dozens of fedayeen into Israeli territory that same night to wreak vengeance on Israeli civilians, including schoolchildren.

It was a vicious circle that neither country could break without taking some drastic step. Israel's sense of frustration and despair was probably best expressed by the eulogy that Dayan delivered at the funeral of Ro'i Rotberg, a twenty-two-year-old member of Kibbutz Nahal Oz, facing the Gaza Strip, who was killed in an ambush set in the kibbutz's fields.

Let us not condemn the murderers today. What do we know of their fierce hatred for us. For eight years they have been living in refugee camps in Gaza while right before their eyes we have been turning the land and the villages in which they and their forefathers lived into our own land. We should demand Ro'i's blood not from the Arabs in Gaza but from ourselves, for closing our eyes to our [cruel] fate and the role of our generation. . . . We are a generation of settlers, and without the combat helmet and the barrel of a gun, we will not be able to plant a tree or build a house. This is the fate of our generation, and the choice before us is to be ready and armed, strong and hard, or to have the sword snatched from our hands and be cut down![1]

The feeling of futility also sharpened by the steady rise in losses among the paratroopers from one action to the next. Because the IDF confined itself to military targets the operations began to take on the character of standard frontal attacks. The element of surprise eroded more and more with each passing day, for the Arabs expected an Israeli night attack to follow every murder by fedayeen, even predicting that such would take place opposite the given sector in which the fedayeen had operated. These operations peaked with the assault on the police station in the Jordanian town of Kalkilya, which followed the murder of two Jewish laborers in the heart of Israel's most populous area. Dozens of Jordanians were killed when the police station was blown up, but something went awry during the withdrawal and eighteen Israelis lost their lives as well.

Once again the General Staff was counseled to return to the format of the initial reprisal actions, albeit in a far more emphatic mode. If the Kalkilya police would not bring fedayeen activities to a halt, pressure to do so should come from the civilian population, which would happen only if the town were attacked and set ablaze. Dayan described the military solution he envisioned in more explicit terms:

> The consensus is that the current method must be revised. Actions that surprised the Egyptians and Jordanians at first, catching them unprepared, have now become routine. I have expressed the opinion that we cannot allow a situation of no peace and no war to continue and that we must force our Arab neighbors to choose between halting the terror against Israel and taking us on in a war. What is clear to us all is that we are at the end of the chapter of the nocturnal reprisal actions.

One alternative debated at the time was to capture a chunk of Arab territory and make its return conditional upon the cessation of terror. Egypt was the leading target in this plan, since it did not have a mutual defense treaty with any other nation (such as Jordan had with Great Britain).

This was not the first time that Dayan had expressed his desire for an all-out clash with Egypt—on the assumption that only in this way could Israel bring an end to the fedayeen attacks. The Chief of Staff first proposed mounting a major military operation against Egypt at the end of 1953, after the Straits of Tiran were closed to all shipping to and from Israel. In September 1955 Cairo announced that it was extending the blockade to flying over the straits—forcing El Al, Israel's national carrier, to suspend its flights to Africa—and on October 23 Ben-Gurion told Dayan to have the IDF ready to capture the straits. The army began drawing up plans and even sent a reconnaissance unit deep into Egyptian territory to establish routes for troop movement. Four days after the conversation between Ben-Gurion and Dayan, Nasser disclosed that he had signed a major arms deal with Czechoslovakia.

The threat that the balance of forces between Israel and Egypt would be totally destroyed now loomed very large. Dayan, firmly convinced that Israel should clash with Egypt as soon as possible, was quite surprised when Ben-Gurion informed him in December of that year that the majority of the Cabinet had voted down his proposal to open the straits by force. All he could do was send the Prime Minister a letter expressing his disappointment with the Cabinet's decision, noting that the failure to act essentially meant relinquishing Israel's freedom of shipping. He also warned that an action of this sort would entail a far greater risk in the future because of the infusion of arms that Egypt was to receive from the Communist bloc.

Dayan's preference for an all-out war and his statement dropping the curtain on the night raids were an indirect admission that the reprisal actions had failed to solve Israel's security problem—and may even have exacerbated it. They had demonstrated the IDF's might and raised the standard of combat in the Israeli Army, but they had not stopped fedayeen activity. In 1953 the number of Israeli casualties resulting from fedayeen incursions was 162, 20 at the Egyptian border; by 1954 the figures reached 180 and 50 respectively. A year later the number of Israeli casualties rose sharply to 258, 192 at the border. Altogether 1,237 Israelis were killed or wounded between the War of Independence and the Sinai Campaign. Considering the circumstances, it was only a matter of time before full-scale hostilities would break out, and Israel patiently waited for the best opportunity to present itself. It did in 1956.

Notes

1. Moshe Dayan, eulogy delivered at funeral of Ro'i Rotenberg, May 1, 1956.

6

The Sinai Campaign

ISRAEL'S SECOND WAR, the Sinai Campaign, began on October 29, 1956. Known in Israel as Operation Kadesh, the biblical name for the Sinai Peninsula, it lasted seven days and was waged on the Egyptian front only. Egypt was the target because of her sponsorship of increasingly frequent and effective fedayeen raids against Israel. She had further provoked Israel by closing the Straits of Tiran in 1951, and Israel saw her chance to reopen shipping to Eilat. Other Arab states bordering on Israel did not move their forces, despite their military treaties with Egypt.

The 1956 war cannot be understood without a review of the military relationship between Israel and France. Had it not been for this relationship, the war might not have begun when it did and would certainly have been of a different nature. The IDF's Sinai Campaign was developed to parallel the unsuccessful French and British Suez operation against Nasser's Egypt. The French chapter is also an important one in the history of Israel's military power; it began before the Sinai Campaign and continued until the eve of the Six-Day War, when President de Gaulle declared an arms embargo against Israel.

The first military contacts with France were made through the Haganah before Israel achieved statehood. With Haganah help representatives of Free France erected a secret radio station in Palestine without the knowledge of the British mandate authorities, and during the conquest of Vichy-held Syria and Lebanon, Palmach scouts led the Allied armies. The connections between the Zionist movement and the generation of the French Resistance were strengthened, and the French Gaullists, Socialists, and Communists gave their full assistance to the Haganah and ETZEL during the struggle to establish the Jewish state, helping the Jewish underground procure

Members of Hashomer, the Watchman, 1909. (*Israeli Army*)

A fence-and-tower settlement on the Lebanese border, 1936.

Orde Wingate's Night Squad, 1939. (*Haganah Archives*)

Yitzhak Sadeh (*center*) with Moshe Dayan (*left*) and Yigal Allon, as members of Palmach, 1938. (*Haganah Archives*)

Yigal Allon (*left*) and David Ben-Gurion (*right*) during the War of Independence.

New immigrant dying at battle for Latrun.

Food convoy moves toward the besieged city of Jerusalem during the War of Independence.

Chief of Staff Moshe Dayan (*right*) with
Minister of Defense Pinhas Lavon (*left*),
1954. (*Israeli Army*)

Training senior citizens in the use of arms during the siege of Jerusalem.

November 1956: Chief of Staff Moshe Dayan (*center*) at Sharm el-Sheikh with General Abraham Yoffe (*right*), commander of the capturing forces, and General Asaf Simhoni (*left*), who was killed two days later. (*Israeli Army*)

Herding sheep at a settlement in the Golan Heights.

Paratroop trainees.

The generals of the IDF posing with President Zalman Shazar after the Six-Day War. Directly to Shazar's right can be seen Lieutenant General Yitzhak Rabin, Chief of Staff at the time. On Shazar's left is Lieutenant General David Elazar, and behind him former air force Chief of Staff Ezer Weizman. (*Israeli Army*)

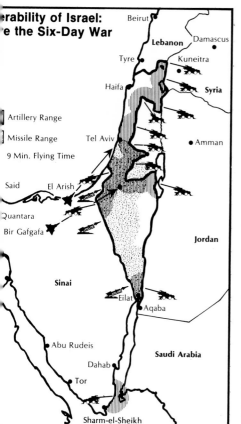

**erability of Israel:
e the Six-Day War**

Beirut

Lebanon

Damascus

Tyre

Kuneitra

Haifa

Syria

Artillery Range

Missile Range

9 Min. Flying Time

Tel Aviv

Amman

Said

El Arish

Quantara

Bir Gafgafa

Jordan

Sinai

Eilat

Aqaba

Abu Rudeis

Saudi Arabia

Dahab

Tor

Sharm-el-Sheikh

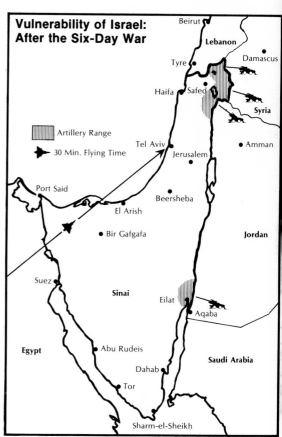

**Vulnerability of Israel:
After the Six-Day War**

Beirut

Lebanon

Tyre

Damascus

Haifa

Safed

Syria

Artillery Range

30 Min. Flying Time

Tel Aviv

Jerusalem

Amman

Port Said

Beersheba

El Arish

Bir Gafgafa

Jordan

Suez

Sinai

Eilat

Aqaba

Egypt

Abu Rudeis

Saudi Arabia

Dahab

Tor

Sharm-el-Sheikh

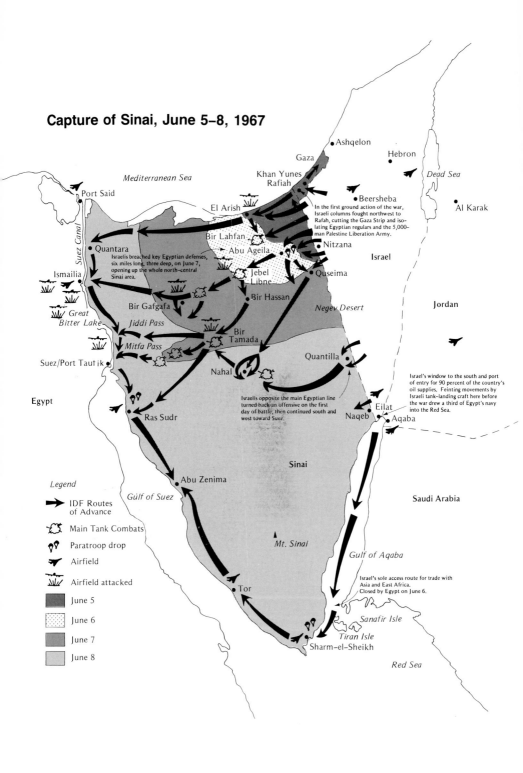

Capture of Sinai, June 5–8, 1967

Mediterranean Sea

Ashqelon

Gaza

Hebron

Dead Sea

Khan Yunes
Rafiah

Port Said

El Arish

Beersheba

Al Karak

In the first ground action of the war,
Israeli columns fought northwest to
Rafah, cutting the Gaza Strip and isolating Egyptian regulars and the 5,000-
man Palestine Liberation Army.

Quantara

Bir Lahfan

Abu Ageila

Nitzana

Israel

Ismailia

Israelis breached key Egyptian defenses,
six miles long, three deep, on June 7,
opening up the whole north-central
Sinai area.

Jebel
Libne

Quseima

Jordan

Bir Gafgafa

Bir Hassan

Negev Desert

Great
Bitter Lake

Jiddi Pass

Mitfa Pass

Bir
Tamada

Quantilla

Suez/Port Tautik

Nahal

Israel's window to the south and port
of entry for 90 percent of the country's
oil supplies. Feinting movements by
Israeli tank-landing craft here before
the war drew a third of Egypt's navy
into the Red Sea.

Egypt

Israelis opposite the main Egyptian line
turned back an offensive on the first
day of battle, then continued south and
west toward Suez.

Eilat

Ras Sudr

Naqeb

Aqaba

Sinai

Abu Zenima

Gulf of Suez

Saudi Arabia

Legend

→ IDF Routes
of Advance

Mt. Sinai

Main Tank Combats

Gulf of Aqaba

Paratroop drop

Airfield

Israel's sole access route for trade with
Asia and East Africa.
Closed by Egypt on June 6.

Airfield attacked

June 5

Tor

June 6

Sanafir Isle

June 7

Tiran Isle

June 8

Sharm-el-Sheikh

Red Sea

weapons and transfer Jewish refugees to Palestine.

At the end of the British mandate over Palestine, upon the establishment of the State of Israel, France wanted to play the Arab card but without discarding the Israeli hand. The Quai d'Orsay, the French Foreign Office, dictated the nature of relationships between France and Israel first by withholding recognition of Israel and later by placing restrictions on her policy toward the new state. The first signs of change in the French attitude attended the growing rift between France and the Arabs over control of the North Sahara countries: Tunisia, Algeria, and Morocco. With the Algerian War of Liberation at its height, it was believed that France would rely on Israel in her struggle against the wave of pan-Arabism. Dayan sensed the drift of French sentiment and spoke to the French Chief of Staff. "We face a common enemy, the Arabs," he said. "You are on the home front, while we are in firing lines. Don't you think that when the front lines are ablaze the arms should be transferred from the home front to the forward positions?"[1]

The first arms transaction, a shipment of Ouragan jet aircraft, was made at the end of 1954. Israel was asked to guarantee that she would not strike at Syria and Lebanon, which France regarded as being in her sphere of influence. The Quai d'Orsay was not in favor of the transaction, arguing that the supply of weapons to Israel should be coordinated with Great Britain and the United States, although these countries maintained a selective embargo against Israel.

The IDF had been compelled to live from hand to mouth and to rely on the generosity of small countries, often having to pay exorbitant prices to private arms dealers. When Israel realized that the French Foreign Office was hampering her efforts to find a way out of the maze of the embargo, she decided to bypass the Quai d'Orsay. The man in charge of this operation was Shimon Peres, the young and dynamic Director-General of the Israeli Defense Ministry. Peres was the man who wove the first web of contacts between the two defense ministries and between the respective armies.

Israeli emissaries found sympathetic ears in the French Defense Ministry, Army, and Ministry of the Interior. Events in Algeria had persuaded the French that Israel and France had a common interest, especially since France was convinced that Egyptian President Nasser was the main supplier of arms to the Algerian Liberation Movement. Major General Yehoshofat Harkabi, Head of Israeli Military Intelligence, became a regular visitor to the French Minister for Algerian

Affairs and the director of French espionage services. In retrospect, however, it is clear the Nasser's share in the Algerian rebellion was exaggerated by Paris and Israel.

The contacts and connections between the defense ministries of the two countries developed in tandem with the deterioration of the Algerian situation. In practice, these ministries maintained the foreign relations between the two countries. In April 1956 the French made one last effort to convince Nasser to halt arms shipments to Algiers. The Egyptian ruler promised that he would transfer no more weapons, but a week later the French fleet stopped an Egyptian ship off Algerian shores and found it loaded with arms. This marked the end of the French Foreign Office's attempts to scotch any rapprochement with Israel.

Two important events forced the issue and eventually led to war in the Mideast. The decisive date for Israel was October 27, 1955 when Nasser announced his first arms transaction with the Communist bloc. For France the decisive date was July 27, 1956 when the Egyptian ruler announced the nationalization of the Suez Canal, in reaction to United States and European refusals to finance the Aswan Dam. Egypt's first transaction with the Eastern bloc was made according to Soviet dictate with Czechoslovakia. It was believed in Israel that Moscow was making its first tentative steps in what would be an extensive penetration program. Since Russia was then convinced that the Middle East was a Western sphere of influence, she decided that the first transaction with Arabs should not be made directly but by way of the Czechs.

The Czech arms deal caused shock waves to rumble through Israel. It included 530 armored vehicles (of which 230 were tanks), 500 guns, 150 MIG-15 fighter planes, 50 Iluyshin-28 bombers, submarines and other naval craft, and many hundreds of transport vehicles. In one stroke the already precarious balance of power was upset. Until the Czech arms deal, Israel and Egypt had only 200 tanks each. The Egyptians had more than 80 jet aircraft, while Israel had about 50. Israel believed that the new Egyptian acquisitions were in preparation for war and that it was only a question of time before Egypt would mount an offensive. Thus Israel felt compelled to activate her war machine, and talk of preemptive war increased.

Inevitably, a debate arose as to the date by which the Egyptian Army would have absorbed the masses of Russian equipment. Chief of Staff Moshe Dayan was convinced that the Egyptian Army would be prepared for war in 1956. Major General Yehoshofat Harkabi's evaluation was that the Egyptians would not complete the assimilation of such quantities of arms before 1957. The outcome of the war proved Harkabi correct. Considerable quantities of Russian equipment had not yet reached the various units, and in many cases the new and modern equipment hampered the Egyptian soldiers.

This situation, which did not become known until after the war, revived the question as to whether the Egyptians had set themselves a date for an overall offensive against Israel. Years later Major General Harkabi commented on this: "The Egyptians did not intend to attack us at the time."[2] Major General Sharon, who commanded the paratroop brigade during the operation, was of the same opinion. "The Egyptians were not about to attack us. When we penetrated Sinai, we did not find an offensive deployment. This contention was sounded only after the war, in order to justify the operation."[3] The Head of General Staff Operations Division, Major General Meir Amit, added, "We knew of Egyptian planning and preparations and, had he the opportunity, Nasser would certainly have attacked us, but it would be exaggerated to contend that we knew Nasser was on the eve of a tangible operation against us."[4] Shimon Peres balances these opinions to some extent. "I am not convinced now, and I wasn't then, that Nasser had a final date for attack on Israel," he noted. "But we did have a great deal of evidence, and simple logic also indicated that he intended to strike out at us."[5]

France's willingness to supply Israel with considerable quantities of arms undoubtedly derived from her desire to see Egypt defeated. The French spoke of this in no uncertain terms, such as when the French Defense Minister, General Koenig, said, "Israel must be given more arms, so that her excellent soldiers can make use of them."[6] After Nasser's nationalization of the Suez Canal, the French specifically stated that they would like to see Israel act against Egypt with the aid of French arms. At the end of July 1956 the new Defense Minister Maurice Bourges-Maunoury asked Shimon Peres: "Aren't you thinking one day of acting on the southern borders? How long does your army need to cross Sinai and reach the Suez Canal?"[7] Peres understood from this question that the French government was itself thinking about a military operation against Egypt. His answer: "Our Suez is Eilat. We will never accept a blockade of the Straits against Israeli shipping."[8]

In September 1956 important decisions were made that resulted in a military alliance between Israel and France, and the first joint preparations for military action against Egypt. In July 1956 France had agreed to supply Israel with considerable quantities of weapons; the French stopped reporting to the joint committee of the three Western powers and did not ask its approval for the supply of arms to Israel. On July 7 Major General Amit visited Paris. It was known that France and Britain had begun planning a joint military operation, named Musketeer, designed to gain control over the Suez Canal. Amit was sounded out on the possibility of Israeli participation in Operation Musketeer. He argued that France and Britain had exaggerated Egypt's power and that the IDF could easily overcome the Egyptian Army in Sinai. France was not prepared to make a commitment regarding the Israeli share in the operation but did want to know whether Israel's airfields would be available to French planes.

As far as Israeli participation in the operation against Egypt was concerned, France was dependent on Great Britain. The grim memories of the mandate period and the War of Independence were not the only obstacles to understanding between England and Israel; Britain had mutual defense pacts with Jordan and with Egypt that Ben-Gurion viewed as a conflict of interests. Consequently, he feared that Britain was likely to betray Israel. Nor was London eager for open partnership with Israel, which might damage her status even in the Arab countries opposed to Nasser. France maneuvered on two separate levels between these conflicting interests.

Dayan and Peres were convinced that Israel had ample and good reason for acting against Egypt. They contended that joint action with France and Britain (or coordination with them) would safeguard Israel against intervention by the great powers, especially the Soviet Union. On the same day Amit visited Paris Dayan said in a General Staff session that "Israel must not find herself in a position where she will be compelled to forgo convenient diplomatic opportunities to strike at Egypt."[9] Three days later Dayan ordered the General Staff to prepare operative plans for the conquest of Sinai, the Straits of Tiran, and the Gaza Strip, emphasizing that Israel was not a party to the dispute over the Suez Canal but only with regard to Gaza and the straits.

At the end of September Ben-Gurion sent a ministerial-level delegation to Paris to coordinate a joint military action with the French government. The delegation included Foreign Minister Golda Meir, Transport Minister Moshe Carmel, Chief of Staff Moshe Dayan, and Shimon Peres. Mordechai Bar-On, the delegation secretary, wrote after the first day, "It became clear that France much preferred that Israel open an offensive in the Sinai Peninsula, alone and on her own initiative. Against this background, the French would be able to motivate the British into beginning their integrated operation. The IDF offensive is to be used as an excuse to cover military intervention in Egypt."[10] In the event that the Anglo-French operation did not take place, France was prepared to guarantee massive military support to Israel, and the French unofficially promised that in such an event Britain would not activate its defense pact with Egypt. At the same time the French transmitted a British warning that if Israel attacked Jordan she would be opposed.

The Israeli delegation returned from Paris with mixed feelings primarily because Britain's position aroused their distrust. Less than three weeks later, while Israel was carrying out a retaliatory action against Jordan, these suspicions were heightened when the British Chargé d'Affaires in Israel announced to Ben-Gurion that an Iraqi division was about to enter Jordan to defend that country against future IDF actions.

Military contacts with France grew stronger, however, to the point that the two armies established a kind of joint General Staff in preparation for their joint operation. The Commander of the French Air Force arrived in Israel at the beginning of October to survey the country's military needs. He was allowed to glance at the IDF operative plans and commented on his return to Paris on their simplicity. His impression was that the French and British commanders attached greater significance to the Egyptian Army than did the Israelis.

On October 16 Ben-Gurion received an invitation to a secret meeting with representatives of the French and British governments. The Prime Minister's misgivings about a joint excursion into war were increasing. He assumed that a day would come when Israel would have no alternative but to fight, but he did not want France and Britain to foist upon Israel the role of aggressor while they behaved as saviors of the region. Ben-Gurion worried about the morality of the three-way transaction and wanted a full, more open partnership. He was prepared to take great risks, but only if there were no other alternative; and he was not at all certain that a preventive war was the only choice. Dayan and Peres urged him to attend the meeting to seek answers to the two problems that bothered him most: aerial defense of Israel's civilian targets and a French promise that the British would not run out on them at the last minute.

The conference opened on October 22 at Sèvres on the outskirts of Paris. In that part of the meeting attended by the British, the atmosphere was fraught with tension. Fearing betrayal, Ben-Gurion refused to present Israel's operational plan in the presence of the British. He rejected a proposal that Israel's role be solely that of providing a pretext for the French and the British to intervene in the war. The lines of communication were on the verge of breaking down when Dayan made a proposal acceptable to Ben-Gurion as well as to the representatives of France and Britain. According to this proposal, Israel would not initiate an all-out war. The first move would be to drop a paratroop unit not far from the Canal Zone. Israel would not follow with an aerial attack or a general assault along the length of the Egyptian border. Thus it would appear to the Egyptians to be a large-scale retaliatory action. If the British and French kept their promise by going into action following this opening gambit, Israel would also continue her operation. If not the paratroops would be ordered to withdraw.

Ben-Gurion imposed other conditions as well. He demanded that Israel's allies begin bombing Egyptian airfields no later than thirty-six hours after the start of the Israeli operation, for he especially feared the bombers that Egypt had received from the Soviet Union. He also insisted that once control over Sinai had been achieved, Israel be permitted to maintain her hold over the island of Tiran in the Straits of Tiran.

At the end of the conference France agreed to dispatch sixty planes and pilots to defend Israeli airspace. They were to reach Israel a day before the beginning of the operation. France's agreement calmed Ben-Gurion, but in return the IDF was asked to change its first operational order: instead of limiting itself to the conquest of Northern Sinai, the Gaza Strip, and the Straits, the IDF was directed ". . . to create a threat on the Suez Canal by the taking of objectives in close proximity."[11] By making this concession, Israel effectively became an accomplice to the French and British conspiracy. It was now clear that the whole Israeli operation depended upon and was connected with the tripartite action; no longer did it stand on its own merits.

In his diary, published in 1965, Dayan admitted that, "If it were not for the Anglo-French operation, it is doubtful whether Israel would have launched her campaign; and if she had, its character, both military and political, would have been different."[12] Dayan continued by asserting that Israel would not have taken up arms even if the canal dispute between Egypt, Britain, and France had become a military conflict had not the Egyptian ruler adopted a hostile policy toward Israel. He likened Israel to a bicycle rider who chances upon a car while climbing a hill: the rider hangs onto the car, but lets go of it when their paths diverge.

The Israeli government was not consulted on the decision to go to war. There were ministers such as Golda Meir and Moshe Carmel who had prior knowledge because of their presence in France, but the full session of the Cabinet heard of the decision only when the machine was already in high gear. It was not until October 28, one day before the campaign was to begin, that Ben-Gurion brought the information and the proposal to the government. The commitments he had made during the conference in France had already been signed and sealed. Not one member of the government questioned this method of operation, and the proposal to go to war was approved.

Operation Musketeer, the strike by Israel's two partners, was a dismal failure because of a combination of political helplessness, military delay, and command hesitation. The Israeli operation, on the other hand, was a success. Inside of a hundred hours the IDF approached the Suez Canal and wrested away control over Sinai. The Egyptian Army, which received retreat orders at the peak of the Israeli action, lost some 3,000 men and more than 5,000 prisoners were taken. The IDF could have killed many more Egyptian soldiers but was ordered to limit itself to destroying the Egyptian Army's disposition.

The military plan for the Israeli operation was nothing short of brilliant. An indirect approach made what was in fact all-out war appear to be a mere retaliatory action. As a result the Egyptians were bewildered and for a full day failed to grasp what was actually happening. The accent was placed not on frontal attacks but on feints. The planners determined that there should be no assault at all on the Gaza Strip, which was closest to Israel, and that the conquest of that area should be attempted only toward the end of the operation, when the Egyptian Army in Sinai would be crumbling.

Dayan depended on the fact that while the Egyptian Army acted predictably, with its command posts located in the rear, IDF units could work more flexibly. He therefore ordered that every force going into action operate independently and seek to reach its final objective in its first thrust. Israel prepared a very detailed deception that was successfully activated before the operation, creating the illusion that Israel intended to attack Jordan. In General Staff meetings the number of those party to the secret was kept to a minimum until the last moment. Senior officers were asked to leave General Staff meetings when secret details were to be discussed. The Director-General of the Prime Minister's Office sensed something suspicious and asked Ben-Gurion what it was all about. Swearing him to absolute secrecy, Ben-Gurion told him that Israel planned a possible attack on Jordan! And on the eve of the operation, while French vessels carrying huge quantities of arms for Israel were offshore near the Kishon Harbor, the ships' captains were asked to tell their crews that they were anchored off the Algerian coast.

The order to mobilize reserve units likewise was issued only at the last moment. Armored units completed mobilization three days before the operation, while other units were ready on the two days before. When the scale of the mobilization was revealed, many countries were convinced that the objective was Jordan. The head of the UN observer team, General E. M. L. Burns, noted in his memoirs that up until October 28 he sensed nothing out of the ordinary and didn't receive any special reports from the American military attachés, who usually took care to keep him advised. Even when it appeared that Israel was mobilizing a considerable force, it did not occur to Burns that the IDF's objective was Egypt.[13]

On October 25, a few days before the action, Egypt, Syria, and Jordan announced that they had signed a tripartite military treaty and would establish a Joint Arab Command. Ben-Gurion was finally convinced that the operation was vital to Israel's safety.

On October 27 a planeload of Egyptian officers was lost over the Mediterranean returning from Syria, where the coordination talks had taken place. The Egyptians have always contended that Israel shot down the plane but Israel has never officially confirmed this. The result nonetheless was that on the eve of the war Egypt's command capabilities were severely diminished by the loss of these high-ranking military men.

At 4:20 P.M. on October 29 Israel's second war with Egypt began. Sixteen Dakota transport planes, one of which was piloted by a woman, dropped a battalion of Israeli paratroops forty-five miles from the Suez Canal. The battalion, numbering 395 men and commanded by Rafael (Raful) Eitan, grouped and took control of the entrance to the Mitla Pass. A short while earlier two Mustang fighter planes had completed another mission over Sinai. The propeller blades of these two piston aircraft cut telephone lines across the peninsula, thereby hampering Egyptian communications.

Israel used nine brigades on the Egyptian front, the remaining IDF force being positioned along the borders with Syria and Jordan in the event that these countries joined the war. (Despite the brand-new military agreement, Arab solidarity proved inoperative.) Of the nine Israeli brigades that operated on the Egyptian front, one was armored, two were mechanized. The remaining six were infantry, one a paratroop brigade. The Israeli force was faced by the Egyptian Third Division in northeastern Sinai, the Eighth Division and a few more brigades of Palestinians in the Gaza Strip, and more Egyptian units stationed to the rear with an armored force in the Canal Zone.

While the IDF carried out two surface penetrations on the edges of the front in conjunction with the paratroop drop, the rest of the paratroop force, headed by Ariel Sharon, penetrated Sinai. Its objective was to advance 125 miles and join up with the battalion dropped over the Mitla Pass under the command of Rafael Eitan, a farmer from one of the Jezreel Valley settlements. Further south near Eilat, the Ninth Infantry Brigade, commanded by another farmer soldier, Abraham Yoffe, began its grueling trek toward Sharm el-Sheikh. This force was to cross a nearly impassable tract and to advance as quietly as possible until it reached the straits, where the Egyptians were blocking Israeli shipping. At first it was thought that this march would last forty-eight hours, but it took the brigade a week to reach its objective.

The confusion in the Egyptian High Command was a major factor, for the Egyptians simply did not grasp the scope of the Israeli operation. They made do with activating their aircraft in the Sinai arena and dispatching reinforcements into the peninsula. Ben-Gurion, who was taken ill, rejected every proposal to activate the air force against Egyptian airfields, even after the war began.

According to plan the Seventh Brigade, the IDF's main armored unit, was to begin action on October 31 and break through the central axis of Sinai toward Ismailia. But two hitches surfaced on October 30. The head of the Southern Command, Asaf Simhoni, disobeyed an order and decided to activate the Seventh Armored Brigade a day early. Military need seemed more important to him and he did not concern himself with the political background. The second hitch was the French and British decision to delay the start of their bombing of Egyptian airfields by a day. The planes that were to take off from Cyprus were not prepared, and this was the first sign that the timetable of Operation Musketeer was out of sync. This communiqué, brought to Ben-Gurion's sickbed, caused him considerable anxiety. It was only Dayan's influence that prevented an order to immediately pull back the paratroops from the Mitla Pass and call off the whole operation.

On October 31 the battles spread out across the expanses of Sinai. An additional armored brigade burst forward in support of an infantry brigade near Rafiah, with the intention of penetrating along the northern Sinai axis toward Qantara. The breakthrough to Rafiah was carried out after French destroyers had bombarded some of the Egyptian positions from the sea. An intact Egyptian destroyer, the *Ibrahim el-Awal,* was seized close to Haifa Bay; it had begun to bombard Haifa coastal installations when French warships anchored nearby immediately opened fire. The destroyer fled with Israeli warships in hot pursuit. At dawn the Israeli Air Force joined the chase, and following a hit on the engine room, the ship stopped, and Israeli sailors took it.

The air force also saw action over Sinai, but aerial combat in this war was restricted to fourteen actions. The Egyptians lost eight planes, of which four were MIGs and four others were British-made Vampires. Israel lost nine planes, eight to ground fire and one reconnaissance plane to Egyptian aircraft.

On November 1 the action was more or less resolved. When it became clear to Nasser that he was also facing France and Britain, whose planes had begun to bomb Egyptian airfields, he ordered his forces in Sinai to withdraw. Within a few hours this pullback had turned into a rout. Air force planes began to swoop down on Egyptian convoys weaving through the desert and hit hundreds of Egyptian vehicles; many more were abandoned. A train left El Arish carrying Egyptian officers, while the soldiers retreated on foot toward the canal.

In the land battles, one of the bloodiest actions took place when the Israeli paratroops penetrated the Mitla Pass. (It was Dayan's contention that Sharon had disobeyed orders by entering the pass without permission.) The Egyptians fought properly from their fortified positions and more than forty paratroops were killed in taking the pass.

On November 2 IDF vanguard units approached the canal in the central and northern sectors while an infantry and an armored brigade began an attack on the Gaza Strip. Three days later Sharm el-Sheikh was also taken by the Ninth Brigade. This ended the military part of Operation Kadesh, which cost Israel 177 men. Two days after the fighting ended, Asaf Simhoni was killed when his plane crashed into Jordanian territory.

Operation Musketeer ran aground from the very start. The ships with landing units set off late; too much time was devoted to preparations; and each step was more complex than its predecessor. The misgivings of British Prime Minister Anthony Eden also caused delays in the timetable. By the time French paratroops finally took up position in the Canal Zone the whole operation was doomed to failure. The Israeli operation, meanwhile, drew to a close and with it, for all intents and purposes, the excuse for Anglo-French intervention. Israel announced that she was prepared for a cease-fire and withdrawal from the canal. The French were shocked by this declaration, and under pressure from them Israel announced that they would agree to a cease-fire only if the Egyptians would declare their willingness to renounce the state of war and enter into peace talks.

On November 5, the day on which Sharm el-Sheikh was conquered, the campaign of Soviet threats and pressures began. In letters dispatched to the prime ministers of Britain and France, Moscow threatened to take steps if their forces would not retreat from Egypt. The Soviet Union was encouraged by the fact that Washington was diverted by her own presidential election campaign and was angry with her allies over the operation in Egypt.

A letter from the Soviets sent to the Prime Minister of Israel contained a veiled threat to the existence of the state. The following day, France and Britain expressed their readiness for a cease-fire. That same day Golda Meir and Shimon Peres left for Paris to check with the French about her position in the event of Russian intervention against Israel. The French Foreign Minister promised that France would stand by Israel and would share military resources with her, but there was no ignoring the Soviet Union's numeric and military advantage.

Anxiety grew in Israel when reports were received of unidentified planes flying from the direction of Turkey to the Middle East. The United States increased the panic by spreading news, later proved incorrect, of Russian military concentrations in Syria. The Head of the Mossad Isser Halperin-Harel recommended withdrawal. The United States had by then opened a campaign of pressures on Israel: grants and the sale of surplus food were stopped, and negotiations for development loans suspended. There were also threats that contributions by American Jews would be subject to taxation.

On November 9 Ben-Gurion was compelled to announce that Israel was prepared to withdraw; his attempt to maintain Israeli jurisdiction over the Gaza Strip was in vain. On December 22 the British and French evacuated the Canal Zone. The Israeli withdrawal was more gradual, as the retreating Israelis destroyed the Egyptian military network of roads and airfields in Sinai.

In return for her withdrawal from Sinai, Israel was promised that the Gaza Strip would remain demilitarized. This promise was not kept for long, but when the Egyptian units returned to the Gaza Strip Israel did not renew the war. A UN Emergency Force was stationed along the border on the Egyptian side and carried out its function until the eve of the Six-Day War, when it withdrew at Nasser's demand.

President Eisenhower promised Israel free maritime traffic through the Straits of Tiran, but this pledge was not honored for very long. With the opening of the straits Israel took a giant stride toward the African continent. Her isolation was broken and she found herself on the international map as tankers laden with oil, mostly from Iran, began to reach Eilat. Freedom of navigation continued until 1967 when Nasser again closed the straits to Israeli shipping. But Israel had by then learned her political lesson: guarantees and demilitarization do not provide real security.

The only regrets after the war concerned the collusion between Israel, France, and Great Britain. When this conspiracy was uncovered many months after the war, the feeling among IDF commanders and the Israeli public was that Israel should have gone to war alone. From a military viewpoint, however, Operation Kadesh brought about a revolution in the structure of the IDF and gave foundation to new concepts of combat. On the eve of war there was a great fear that the reserve army would not be able to function on a sufficiently high level. These units included a considerable number of new immigrants who had come to Israel following statehood and many from Third World (especially Arab) countries as well. In the course of the war, however, it became clear that the reserve units did not fail; nor were they on a level much lower than that of the regular units.

The war revealed many faults in the operation of the IDF. The logistics system proved weak, and only an array of improvisations prevented serious hitches. The artillery arm did not keep up with the rapid rate of advance, and far more serious, the communications system did not operate properly. The Supreme Command of the IDF found it difficult to picture the battle as it was taking place, and most details were in fact received from the air force. Chief of Staff Dayan, who joined the fighting units, vanished and remained incommunicado for three days. But as for early and successful planning, it is doubtful whether it would have been possible to change and determine detailed moves in the midst of battle with such a communications system.

After Operation Kadesh it was decided to put greater energy into strengthening the air force, to ensure that in the future the IDF would not be compelled to rely on foreign air forces. The armored echelons also found their place on the map after the 1956 war. Before the war the question had arisen whether the 250 tanks at the IDF's disposal should be concentrated in armored units or be divided into smaller support units within the infantry. The armored corps men, headed by major generals Laskov and Zorea, and Colonel Benari, demanded the concentration of armor in large units. They felt it would strengthen the logistics system and broaden the communications networks. Dayan, who still viewed the infantry as the kingpin on the battlefield, demanded the dispersion of the armor as a support weapon for the infantry. The debate took place in the presence of Ben-Gurion and the decision was made in Dayan's favor. He then ordered the infantry to break through first with half-tracks and other vehicles, and the tanks to follow behind on transporters. Once the tanks carried out their allocated tasks, they were again to make way for mechanized infantry. In fact the war was carried out in a different fashion. Chaim Laskov and Uri Benari set the rate of advance with the help of the armor that they commanded.

Dayan admitted after the war that the commanders of the armored corps had been right. The IDF began its transition into a mechanized and armored army. From this standpoint the Sinai Campaign served as a kind of expensive exercise in preparation for the Six-Day War. Israel's victory in 1956 did not cloud the reformers' view. The Sinai Campaign gave Israel eight years of tranquility in which fedayeen activities were virtually unknown and which she utilized to develop, refine, and strengthen the IDF.

Notes

1. Michael Bar-Zohar, *Gesher al Yayam Hatichon* [Bridge over the Mediterranean] (Tel Aviv: Am Hasefer, 1964), p. 59.

2. Previously unpublished interview with author, 1972.

3. *Ibid.*

4. Interview with author originally published in *Ha'aretz*, October 1966.

5. *Ibid.*

6. Yosef Evron, *Beyom Sagrir* [On a Cold and Rainy Day] (Tel Aviv: Ot Paz, 1968), p. 18.

7. Shimon Peres, *Kela David* [David's Sling] (Tel Aviv: Am Hasefer, 1970), p. 49.

8. *Ibid.*

9. Moshe Dayan, *Yoman Ma'arachat Sinai* [Diary of the Sinai Campaign] (Tel Aviv: Am Hasefer, 1965), p. 25.

10. Mordechai Bar-On in *Maariv,* June 5, 1973.

11. Dayan, *op. cit.,* pp. 180, 182.

12. *Ibid.,* p. 3.

13. Burns, *op. cit.,* p. 117.

14. Schiff, *op. cit.*

7

The Making of the
Israeli Soldier

ALTHOUGH the Israel Defense Forces is by necessity similar to other armies in its recruitment, training, and operations, it differs markedly from most other fighting forces in its attitude toward discipline and its high sense of purpose and camaraderie. The army holds a uniquely central position in Israeli society and as such is the repository of the nation's hopes and fears, its commonality and its differences, its past and its future.

"IDF commanders have to deal with Jews," IDF Education Officer, Colonel Yeshayahu Tadmor, once wrote. "We have a keen awareness of events, a tendency toward skepticism and criticism. We are given to debate and dissertation. Our leadership is given no latitude unless it proves its capability. It can only succeed by constant persuasion, encouragement of thought and criticism and by safeguarding the soldier's dignity."[1] In a similar vein, Brigadier General Yitzhak Arad, former Chief Education Officer of the IDF, stated: "We are an army that asks many questions. We encourage the soldiers to ask questions too. From the weekly unit discussions, it is clear that IDF soldiers think. They ask about the government's diplomatic positions, the prospects of peace or war in the future—in short, our daily reality."[2]

Israel is fundamentally a small, intimate society. Everybody seems to know everybody else. This familiarity makes it difficult for the officers to create what would be an artificial distance between themselves and subordinates. The familial feeling is good for morale but it makes the imposition of discipline somewhat difficult. The IDF officer must win the esteem of his men; he cannot achieve it by title alone. Officers are selected from the ranks of enlisted men, and their comrades participate in the selection process—they are asked to name the members of their unit best suited to be officers.

Israelis grow up in a society closely identified with the army. In contrast to the traditional European Jewish societies, which set great store by intellectual achievement, Israel lavishes prestige on the man who rises in the ranks of the IDF. The Israeli's propensity for handling weapons and excelling at military tactics and actual combat are more than responses to the nation's precarious situation. These tendencies also represent a reaction to the image of the Jew in previous generations—the eternal student, the merchant, the money lender, the cosmopolitan intellectual to whom fighting was anathema. For modern Israel the historical example of the Diaspora Jew, afraid or unwilling to fight for his life, is a baffling and shameful one.

In her wars with the Arabs Israel has fashioned a fighting man of superior quality who is at once a source of pride and an example to Jews throughout the world. The pioneers who immigrated to Israel at the end of the last century came from generations of small businessmen and rabbis, as well as some scientists, writers, and musicians. These early settlers proved they could return to the soil and succeed as farmers; their sons and grandsons became the fighters. The continuing condition of Arab hostility necessitates that current and future generations of Israelis learn the skills of war also.

Most Israeli boys and girls at the age of fourteen are required to join a paramilitary organization called the GADNA (a Hebrew acronym for youth battalions). GADNA youngsters engage in military drills, receive rudimentary instruction in handling arms and map-reading, and tour Israel on camping excursions. At their sessions GADNA members wear khaki uniforms but do not hold rank. However, the movement has an emblem: the bow and arrow.

Some social critics have wondered aloud whether the existence of GADNA and the introduction of military training during adolescence is not a sign of militarism. The Israeli experience suggests that rather than militarism, it reflects the nation's predilection to direct the younger generation toward the military organization that has safeguarded the country's existence. GADNA commanders attest that in recent years the emphasis has shifted from the use of weapons to sports and physical training. Israeli educators often worry that the GADNA imposes the harsh reality of Israel's military situation at too early an age, since after all there will be no escaping this situation at a later age. Yet GADNA officers and many of the older generation of youth leaders, as well as parents, are convinced that recruitment of young Israelis into the GADNA eases their eventual entry into full-time military duty. Before called up for national service, the young Israeli has already spent time in an army camp, has met officers and NCOs, and has taken orders from them. He has slept in a scout tent, gone on daily hikes for distances up to twenty miles, knows what it is to be away from home, and has even learned to use a carbine.

Nevertheless, preparation of Israeli youth for army life is not the primary purpose of the GADNA. Rather it provides an awareness and appreciation of Israel's special security situation. GADNA members attend lectures designed to stimulate their consciousness of defense affairs. The younger generation is inquisitive and argumentative but generally does not tend to formulate a dissident view on Israel's security policies. It has been found that the GADNA experience confirms a sense of responsibility and inspires the youngsters to serve willingly and courageously.

The GADNA was founded in 1940 as a part of the Haganah. The sixteen-year-olds who were inducted into the Haganah took an oath of loyalty with a Bible and a revolver, as was customary in the Jewish underground, and were employed clandestinely distributing propaganda posters and gathering information on British activities and movements. By 1948, when the War of Independence began, the GADNA numbered thousands of youth and some of its units took part in the battles for Jerusalem and Haifa. When the IDF was formed, the GADNA became part of the military establishment; in 1954 it was structured as a nationwide command with six special training camps. The Ministry of Education is responsible for the GADNA units in the schools, with IDF officers serving as advisors to the Ministry. An emergency plan calls for the integration of the GADNA into the mobilized manpower system. During the Six-Day and Yom Kippur wars GADNA members served as orderlies in hospitals, replaced postal workers called up for duty, and helped out in essential civilian industries.

The GADNA school programs also embrace Moslem and Christian high school pupils and members of Israel's other minority communities such as the Druze and the Circassians. Training in arms begins in the last year of high school when GADNA members are sent to training camps for extended periods of time. The Arab boys and girls are not included in this later stage of GADNA training; however, the Druze boys who are eligible for military service join their Jewish friends at army training camp.

The GADNA also works with young delinquents serving sentences in reform schools—in response to a basic complaint by young offenders that without having done their military service they cannot find employment. The IDF has altered its policy of excluding youths with police records and has entrusted the GADNA with early rehabilitation counseling and military training. GADNA commanders feel that by giving delinquents an opportunity to serve in the army they are, in effect, restoring them to society. In some cases a number of young inmates, already beyond the call-up age of eighteen, have been released from prison to enlist in a special GADNA program. The IDF has achieved a high degree of success with integrating one-time, erstwhile delinquents into regular service. It has also broadened training to include vocational instruction so they can leave active duty with a trade.

Above all, national service is a passport to social acceptance. After completion of secondary school, Israeli youth are eligible for national service in the IDF, and the young man or woman who lacks discharge papers is treated with suspicion by prospective employers, these papers being the equivalent of a certificate of basic rectitude. The number of youngsters who try to evade military service is small because of the social stigma involved. In fact, those excused from military service for medical reasons often try to bring pressure to bear on authorities to allow them to serve, willing to release the army from responsibility for any risk to their health.

Compulsory service is three years for men, twenty months for women. There are some exceptions to this rule, however. A man over twenty-three who is married and the father of at least two children need serve only six months, and men over twenty-six serve three months of active duty, then are transferred to the reserves. The compulsory-service law does not apply to those over twenty-nine. If he desires, an older man can train for six weeks and then serve in the reserve force. This option is not available to women.

The willingness to serve in the IDF is almost axiomatic; few ask for and fewer still are granted exemptions. The conscientious objector is not generally recognized in the IDF. The number of such objectors hovers around ten a year. They are not excused from service, but each case is handled individually, and if their reasons are found to be sincere an effort is made to assign these soldiers to hospitals or border settlements where they can serve in noncombat roles.

Release for reasons of conscience is permitted for women only. Clause 30 of the Security Service Law permits a young woman to be exempted from military service "for reasons of conscience and religious conviction that prevent her from serving in the IDF." Requests for exemption based on this clause are usually on the grounds of religious conviction, very rarely pacifist beliefs. A woman's request for exemption is submitted to a public committee and must contain a sworn declaration and the signature of two guarantors—not close relations—who attest that the woman is devoutly religious. Approximately forty percent of the women reporting to recruiting officers are exempted from military service for one reason or another.

There is also a special arrangement for *yeshiva* students, based on coalition agreements that were signed in the 1950s between the Labor Party (which formed successive governments) and the religious parties, and that have remained in effect ever since. A yeshiva student who can prove that all his time is devoted to study can be temporarily excused from service. He must be enrolled in a recognized yeshiva, and upon completion of his studies must report for military service as the law requires. It is estimated that the total number of yeshiva students exempted from national service is about 6,000.

Malingerers, or "artistes" as they are called in Israel, are not a problem in the Israeli Army, while in many foreign armies they constitute a difficult problem for the doctors who strive to expose them. A former Chief Medical Officer of the IDF, Brigadier Dr. Reuven Eldar, says: "Contrary to other armies the number of malingerers in the Israeli Army is very small. They use such amateurish methods that it is easy to spot them. On the other hand, those who suffer from defects and do not declare them at the time of recruitment, so that they can join volunteer units, *are* a problem."[3]

Israel's limited manpower resources make the successful classification and preparation of the Israeli soldier all the more crucial. The aim is to achieve maximal utilization of this manpower. Some eighty-seven percent of the youngsters born in any one year who are eligible for induction actually reach the army. This is a relatively high figure in comparison with other Western countries that have compulsory military service. Of the thirteen percent of the males not inducted, about 3.5 percent are exempted due to severe illiteracy.

Although a cross section of Israeli society indicates that the average youngster is generally in satisfactory health, the physical condition of most of the draftees is not particularly good. This phenomenon, common to many Western societies, is a matter of concern to the military doctors in Israel. Another pertinent feature of Israel's young population is that a relatively high proportion of the draftees (estimated at close to twenty-five percent) wear glasses. The percentage of draftees who partake of drugs, on the other hand, is very low compared with other societies. Those who have been caught using drugs are not inducted into the IDF, and drug addicts are discharged from the army as soon as they are discovered. Dr. Eldar explains this policy as follows: "The military doctors are concerned by the fact that hashish and other drugs impair the user's ability to judge distances and time, as well as cause a light intoxication in the user while he's smoking. The result is that the soldier's alertness drops, and if he continues to smoke the drug he may develop a syndrome marked by lack of motivation and even apathy."

But inducting a vast proportion of the population is only half the battle; the next aim is to properly allocate each soldier to an active role that makes the best of his individual talents and qualities. Like other progressive armies, the IDF conducts numerous tests to aid in classification. The results of psychological tests are the most influential in making the actual assignments.

The first task of the classification system is to determine which recruits are suited to command positions and which are likely to cause problems. The classification process begins at age seventeen, when the young person is first summoned to register at the recruitment office about a year before his induction, and includes intensive personal interviews. Army psychologists believe that their work is easier than that of their colleagues in other armies since, on the whole, the Israeli youth is extremely frank about his personal ambitions and problems. The examiner seeks to determine the candidate's degree of motivation, devotion, independence, and sociability. The thrust of the selection process is directed toward placing superior manpower in field combat units, a principle that is almost sacrosanct in the IDF.

When Moshe Dayan was appointed Chief of Staff in 1953 the classification system was changed. Before that better-educated youngsters found their way to staff jobs, while the others went to field units where service was tougher. Now it is the fighting units that receive the cream of every new crop. A young person with a good medical profile has every chance of being sent to a combat unit. There are few exceptions to this rule: only children are not sent to fighting units unless they volunteer and receive the approval of both parents (the parents' signatures must be notarized by an attorney to prevent forgery), and young people from families that have lost one of their sons in war require parental agreement and approval by the military authorities.

Soldiers are divided into fourteen classifications, and only those included in one of the six high-quality groups can reach commissioned rank; soldiers from the four groups below these may reach noncommissioned rank. The other gradings are slated for lower enlisted ranks. Quality ranking in the IDF is determined by a number of factors: the results of the induction interview, IQ, education, knowledge of the Hebrew language, and health status. Upon completion of the primary classification stages, candidates are dispatched to volunteer units. Pilots and aircrew take pride of place in the division of the manpower cake, followed by submariners and frogmen, paratroops and volunteers to special reconnaissance units.

Each volunteer unit maintains its own tests for candidates (some of the methods in these tests, particularly in the air force, being secret). It is known that candidates for service in the Naval Commandos are taken on a ninety-five-mile march along the length of the coast. An army psychologist is attached to the march to examine candidates' reactions. Not all of those who display a good physical tolerance and reach the final line are necessarily accepted into the Naval Commandos and not all who fall by the wayside are necessarily disqualified. The true test is not endurance but the reactions of men to different situations. For example, eight food rations might be prepared for a group of ten men so that the reactions of the men can be observed and analyzed. These tests, and others, assist in spotting those who are less likely to cooperate with their fellow soldiers and assist them in time of need.

There is no shortage of volunteers for high-risk missions in the IDF. On the contrary, sometimes the number of volunteers is so high that two-thirds of them have to be rejected. This standard did not change after the war in Lebanon, even though it was the first of Israel's wars on which a national consensus was lacking. On the other hand, following the Lebanon War there was a noticeable drop in readiness to register for officers' school or to sign on in the regular army after compulsory service was over.

The volunteers come primarily from two opposite ends of Israeli society: the socioeconomic high achievers and the socioeconomically disadvantaged. Interestingly enough, IDF psychologists have come to the conclusion that a group made up solely of high achievers is not necessarily an outstanding unit, and they aim to organize units whose members come from a variety of backgrounds.

Psychological evaluations are heavily relied upon for other purposes as well. Teams of field psychologists are stationed in each unit, and with their help commanders can achieve maximum efficiency in organizing combat groups and teams. For example, a psychologist might suggest which individuals are best suited to serve as tank gunners and which as tank drivers. With an infantry unit the psychologists might indicate who is likely to be a good mortarman or machine gunner. Special emphasis is placed on the composition of tank, submarine, or mobile artillery teams. Evaluation has also influenced the composition of squads in infantry platoons. Based on a survey of professions, in this way the IDF can determine personality characteristics suitable for the operation of specific weapons.

One important test that has received special IDF attention is carried out within that unit itself: a sociometric test, a sort of straw poll among the soldiers about their comrades-in-arms. Every soldier in a field unit receives a questionnaire on which he is asked to note which of his comrades in the platoon, in his opinion, would likely make a good section leader. The poll is conducted again among the NCOs, with each soldier again asked to rate comrades in terms of being a good officer. The IDF's experience has been that this test provides an accurate indication of which candiates are destined to succeed as officers.

The social and educational gap dividing Israeli society that began with the massive waves of immigration in the early 1950s has still not been closed completely, and as a result pressure has been brought to bear on the army to take on deprived youngsters and teach them a profession. The truth is that with the reform of the Israeli educational system, the achievement level of the Oriental community has steadily improved. This change is reflected in the IDF also, which boasts more and more officers from the Oriental community. Their number is much greater than it was in the 1950s and 1960s, though still lagging behind the proportion of Oriental Jews in the overall Jewish population (more than 50 percent).

For the IDF the question has been how much to invest in the training of new soldiers from deprived backgrounds. An easy solution would be to place them in such nonspecialized jobs as kitchen or guard duty; the more demanding solution chosen by the army is to raise their performance levels and capabilities through education. It is a long-term process, but the IDF provides the opportunity for any soldier to complete his grade-school education, and the general rule is that an IDF soldier is not discharged until he has received a certificate of elementary education. On another plane, the IDF is perhaps the only army that must teach the language of the country to thousands of its soldiers. Upon induction each new recruit is examined for his proficiency, written and spoken, in Hebrew. Those found wanting are assigned to a course and must continue their studies until they receive a passing mark. Moreover they cannot be promoted without a suitable fluency in Hebrew. The IDF educational system in elementary and secondary education and language includes thousands of soldiers, and many thousands more learn technical professions during their military service.

Israel is the only country in which women must complete compulsory army service, making the IDF thereby unique. There are no units composed exclusively of women, however; the Women's Corps stands for the totality of women serving in the IDF and is referred to by the acronym CHEN (which in Hebrew means loveliness). Women serve in armies in many other countries, but they volunteer for service. In Israel the law requires every unmarried woman to report for military service at the age of eighteen, setting the length of service at two years—although this period can be shortened if conditions permit. To avoid conflict with Orthodox Jews who regard military service as incongruous with the traditional concept of womanhood, the IDF exempts women who declare themselves Orthodox. Exemptions are also granted to women whose educational level or IQ is extremely low. Upon completion of service, very few women are obliged to do reserve duty, but the army is entitled to call up women for reserve duty until the age of thirty-four if they have no children (men up to forty-nine).

The recruitment of women in the Yishuv stemmed from the pressure of circumstance rather than from an ideological impulse to achieve full equality between the sexes. The constant shortage of manpower forced the leaders of the community to fully utilize its human resources—be they male or female. This situation has remained unchanged since the establishment of the Haganah to the present. The population of Israel has grown but its precarious position as a small enclave surrounded by populous Arab states prevails.

The history of Jewish self-defense and the armed forces of the Yishuv is filled with women of valor. In 1920, when the settlement Tel Hai fell, two women—Devorah Drachler and Sarah Chizik—were among the ten defenders who perished in the defense of that northern outpost. A few years earlier, when the Jewish Legion was attached to General Allenby's expeditionary force, Rachel Yanait (later the wife of Yitzhak Ben-Zvi, the second President of Israel) demanded that women be included in those new battalions of the British Army. Sarah Aaronsohn, one of the settlers of Zichron Yaakov, was a leader of the Nili organization, a World War I espionage network that assisted the British forces against the Turks. In 1917 she was captured and tortured by the Turks, and she finally took her own life.

Thereafter, women played a key role after the establishment of the Haganah, and the number of women volunteers for military duty reached its peak during World War II. In 1942 the number of women members of the Haganah reached into the tens of thousands, while the percentage of women in the Palmach steadily increased until it was about a third of that commando force. Some 4,000 women were recruited into the auxiliary arms of the British Army, and most were sent to Egypt and Italy, where at the end of the war they assisted Jewish survivors of the Nazi extermination camps.

One of the chapters of consummate bravery during the world war was the participation of young Palestinian women in a group of Jewish parachutists trained by British Intelligence. The parachutists were dropped into Europe behind enemy lines for the purposes of espionage and sabotage, and to assist partisans in various countries. Two of the women, Hannah Senesh and Haviva Reich, were caught by the Germans and executed. Both had been members of kibbutzim, and Haviva Reich was in the Palmach. Hannah Senesh, who was twenty-three when she died, had come to Palestine from Hungary at the age of eighteen. She returned to her country with two other parachutists and was caught in action. Six years later, after the establishment of Israel, her remains were brought back for reinterment. Settlements in Israel have been named for these two women, remembered as war heroines of the first order.

Acts of heroism by women volunteers continued to mark the period of underground struggle and the War of Independence, the only war in which women actually engaged in combat. Twelve thousand women soldiers served in the IDF during the War of Independence, some being captured or killed while escorting convoys, others fighting to protect isolated settlements. Women were to be found at every level of command, and as late as the Sinai Campaign a woman pilot dropped paratroops over the Mitla Pass. They also served as radio operators and medical orderlies during the 1956 war, with many right on the firing line. (One woman who was with the armored regiment that assaulted Egyptian positions in its thrust across Sinai was mentioned in dispatches.) During the Six-Day War and the War of Attrition that followed it, although women were forbidden to engage in combat and generally were removed from the front lines, some inevitably found themselves in battle areas.

Today the emphasis in women's service is on auxiliary military tasks and noncombat duties. The basic training of a CHEN soldier lasts five weeks only and includes physical training, parade-ground drill, training in handling weapons, and a series of lectures. Afterward the trainees are sent for a week's agricultural work to one of the NAHAL border settlements. Those who wish to remain on the border settlements may so volunteer; the rest are sent to various vocational courses and then assigned to military units.

At one time paratroop training was forbidden for CHEN women because the army doctors believed the impact of landing could damage the reproductive organs. Some adventurous trainees acted against orders and jumped anyway, while many others expressed an interest in jumping. The doctors reconsidered their position, and parachute jumping is now permitted for women under certain controlled conditions.

Vocational options for IDF women are varied: clerk, driver, welfare worker, nurse, entertainer, sports organizer, radio operator, parachute handler, flight supervisor, psycho-technical examiner, and computer operator. Many women have penetrated a traditionally male province by being assigned as instructors of courses ranging from basic training to beginners' and advanced courses in Armor, Intelligence, and technical specializations for the air force. And as the IDF becomes more dependent upon sophisticated weapons systems, women become increasingly involved in technical vocations. They also carry out important tasks in Operations and Intelligence, and in the regular army women have reached senior rank in a number of key positions, with many others acquiring a useful profession while serving. "The IDF would not be able to maintain its present force without the girls," says former CHEN commander Colonel Devorah Tomer. "By taking over responsible positions, they release soldiers and officers for combat duties."[4] The army also profits from the fact that wherever women are found, they contribute to improved morale.

The women themselves grow and come into their own during their army service. And in addition to the serious business of defending the state, the army for many Israelis, both male and female, is a social experience as well. But with any coed setting for this age group, problems are bound to occur. A soldier who becomes pregnant, for example—even by her fiancé—is immediately released from the IDF. In fact a special clause in the army regulations provides for the discharge of a pregnant soldier within twenty-four hours of disclosure. The army does not invoke this clause arbitrarily, however; quite the contrary, military authorities are careful not to abandon a young woman in this situation for fear that her family may disown her. Her commander will often contact her parents, and if there are indications of a rift between parents and daughter, the appropriate authorities will seek a place for her outside the IDF.

Although procedures exist for assistance after the fact, the army has consistently rejected proposals that birth control pills be provided to women who request them. "We do *not* engage in preventive medicine of this kind," the commander of CHEN says. "We do, however, provide sex education. Army doctors deliver lectures to the women, and everyone is of course entitled to turn to a civilian doctor. A list of names is available in every unit and can be consulted without the knowledge of comrades or commanders."[5]

If the army is unwilling to arouse criticism from conservative sectors of the population by adopting a more supportive policy regarding birth control, it is prepared to protect the femininity of its soldiers in other areas. Many women justifiably complain that they put on weight because of the heavy, rich diet served in military camps. The IDF has responded by substituting fresh fruits and vegetables for a number of starchy items on the menu. It is impossible to do this everywhere, however, since in most units there is a much greater concentration of men than women, and the menu must be adapted to the needs of the men.

What is difficult to accomplish with diet is much easier to accomplish in the area of dress and cosmetics. For many years young women recruited into the IDF received coarse khaki uniforms with no consideration for cut and style. Occasionally items of clothing were contributed by donors from America or Europe. Today, however, the army no longer relies on the taste and generosity of donors. The women's uniforms have been fashionably designed, CHEN women are permitted to grow long hair if it is braided or pinned up, and army camps are opened to cosmetics consultants from various companies who give free advice on skin care.

A singular characteristic of the system of training and guidance in the Israeli Army is the frequency of exercises under live fire, whose purpose is to bring the soldier as close as possible to real combat situations and help the reserve soldier adapt to the sharp transition from civilian life. Another program peculiar to the IDF is instruction for noncommissioned officers; the squad leader's course is such a program. One of its primary objectives is to develop the initiative in the noncommissioned officer, stressing the cultivation of independent thought that will permit improvisation under battle conditions. Every noncommissioned officer is drilled in solving battle problems in unorthodox ways. Unlike similar schools in other armies, the IDF Staff College does not subscribe to prepared solutions to exercises and problems. General principles are taught and students are encouraged to search for their own solutions so that the Israeli commander will not find himself wedded to automatic solutions.

Although the Israeli Army depends primarily on mechanized and armored units, its commanders feel that it is the infantry officer who is most likely to exercise quick judgment and have to improvise in battle. Therefore all future Israeli officers are taught management of an infantry unit. Armor, artillery, and engineering officers then go on to specialized studies in other courses.

Perhaps one of the most striking traits of the Israeli Army is that does not play at soldiering. Little emphasis is placed on spit and polish, yet discipline is maintained because it is based on common sense and the very real need to defend the nation at a moment's notice. The younger generations of officers are professional military men who concentrate on enhancing the IDF's efficiency and combat readiness, but they are not militarists and they do not seek to set the army apart from the people. The absence of militarism is likewise reflected in the prevailing attitude toward discipline as a necessary tool for accomplishing the mission at hand. Hence there is little talk in Israel about the importance of blind obedience in shaping a soldier's character. On the contrary, every officer in the IDF can question extraordinary orders and demand to know their purpose. On more than one occasion soldiers who refused to obey orders they believed unlawful were exonerated. The excuse, "I was only following orders," can have no place in the army of the Jewish nation.

Today's high standards of conduct and performance essentially trace back to the days of the Haganah and the other underground organizations whose members were all volunteers. They cultivated a tradition of leadership and self-sacrifice that has lived on through two generations in the IDF. And since it is to the perpetuation of these qualities that the army can credit much of its inner strength, they will surely continue to take pride of place in the making of the Israeli soldier.

Notes

1. Israel Defense Forces, internal publication, 1970.
2. Briefing for military correspondents, 1971.
3. *Ibid.*
4. *Ibid.*

Doctrine

TO UNDERSTAND the IDF's doctrine of warfare and strategic approach, it is necessary to examine the five basic principles that guide Israel's thinking on national security: few against many, a war for survival, the strategy of attrition, geographic pressures, and the time factor.

Few Against Many—The fact that any armed conflict will pit the small population of Israel against an Arab camp many times its size has been a salient characteristic of the Arab-Israeli conflict since its inception. Israel's War of Independence broke out when the country's Jewish population was just over half a million, and by the time of the Six-Day War it had risen to somewhat more than 2.5 million. The State of Israel today, with a population hovering around 4 million, is immediately surrounded by some 61.5 million Arabs (about 45 million in Egypt), to which are added the populations of Libya, Iran, Iraq, and Algeria—countries that support terrorism and other hostile actions against Israel. The imbalance between the two sides becomes even more dramatic if we take into account the presence of a large Arab minority within Israel itself, as well as the Palestinian population of over a million residing in the territories controlled by Israel. It is clear that Israel's Jewish majority will diminish in time, and that the negative demographic trend may be accelerated substantially if Israel annexes the territories occupied since the Six-Day War.

Until the time of that war Israel covered a small area of some 12,500 square miles; after it, the territory under her control expanded to 50,000 square miles (including the Sinai Peninsula, since returned to Egypt). Even so the Arab states extend over millions of square miles that give them the distinct advantage of strategic depth. The gap between the two sides can also be seen in the natural resources at each's disposal. Whereas Israel's resources are meager, the Arab states are blessed with vast quantities of oil that yield billions of dollars in revenue and give them broad political leverage. Israel can rely only on the United States for political support, while Arab countries generally can count on the Soviet Union, China, and much of the Third World. One consequence is that over the years Israel has found herself in a perilous state of political isolation, which could affect her security in the event of a extended war. Hence relations with the U.S. have become the cornerstone of her security, and cultivation of this ally is a matter of the first priority.

A War of Survival—Unlike other nations, Israel faces an enemy whose aim is not merely to defeat her army or to conquer a specified area of land. The intention of the Arab governments has been (and continues to be) the liquidation of the Jewish state, making the Middle East conflict a war of survival for Israel. Many nations have lost wars yet continued to exist in one form or another, but Israel assumes that defeat in war would mean an end to the Jewish state— and she wages war accordingly. This concern with survival is also fueled by memories of the Nazi Holocaust, making the IDF and the Israeli people as a whole particularly sensitive about the loss of life. For example, the commanders of the IDF regard extensive losses on the battlefield as a threat to the nation's future, and this is an important consideration whenever the prospect of a prolonged war comes up in discussion.

The Strategy of Attrition—The Middle East dispute is marked by a flagrant asymmetry in the objectives of the two sides. Whereas the Arabs wish to destroy Israel, even if it so desired the IDF could not adopt a similar policy vis-à-vis the Arab world, and its strategic objectives must be realistic. The Israeli General Staff cannot think in terms of an absolute decision over the Arabs, only of defeat in specific battles or wars. The IDF, therefore, employs a strategy of attrition, trying to inflict heavy losses on the Arab armies in order to deter renewed aggression for as long as possible.

Geographic Pressures—Israel, a country with its back to the sea, was in a grave geostrategic situation prior to the Six-Day War. The ratio between the length of her borders and the depth of her territory was especially disadvantageous in terms of defense. Her only geographic advantage lay in short internal communications lines that permitted rapid movement of forces from one front to another, but even this was eclipsed by greater geographic drawbacks. The whole of Israel was no more than a patch in the Arab world surrounded on all sides by enemies and the easy object of sea blockades, whether in the Mediterranean or the Red Sea. Jerusalem, her capital, was cut in half by the frontier, and all her vital centers were within range of enemy artillery. Egypt had military bases close to Israel in the Sinai Desert and Gaza Strip; the Syrians in the Golan Heights enjoyed virtual control over a large part of her territory and a significant share of her water sources; and Jordan faced the country's narrow waistline and could cut the country in two by one armored strike at its center. Israel was a country with no depth. All its territory was a border zone, and it had almost no prospect of advance warning against approaching enemy aircraft.

This situation gave rise to a deep fear of a sudden Arab attack, which in turn produced an acute awareness that Israel would always have to make the first strike if she were to survive. Then the Six-Day War resulted in a drastic geographic change. Israel acquired considerable depth, and her ability to absorb offensive blows increased accordingly. For the first time in her history geographic conditions permitted Israeli strategists some peace of mind. Unfortunately it contributed to the complacent mood of the Israeli military establishment before the Yom Kippur War. For Israel's strategists failed to appreciate that based as it was on the territories captured in 1967, her newly acquired strategic depth heightened the Arabs' desire for war. While Israel had added a security belt to her borders, the Arabs had additional reasons for belligerency.

The Time Factor—Time is the decisive factor in all Israeli operative planning. Strategists and political leaders in Israel have always assumed that any outbreak of hostilities would immediately trigger intervention by the great powers of the United Nations to block or water down Israel's achievements, while there probably would not be any such intervention if the Arabs had the upper hand.[1] Hence Israel's strategy has always been designed to ensure that the Arabs would not achieve any territorial gains in war, with Israel attaining her objectives in the first stages of battle. The time factor takes on an additional importance because of Israel's limited resources, her sensitivity to losses, and the fact that her military power is based on reserve forces. Consequently, Israel will always strive to bring any war to its conclusion as quickly as possible. When it was drawn into the War of Attrition, for example, the IDF did everything possible to bring about a reversal in the military situation, even resorting to such drastic means as deep-penetration bombing in Egypt in 1970.

In the face of the Arabs' many distinct advantages, Israel has one outstanding strength: qualitative supremacy. The Arab countries at war with Israel are faced by a population that, although smaller than their own, is marked by a progressive social structure, a high level of physical health, and a generally superior level of education. The war for survival has impelled Israelis to aim for excellence, and while many sectors of civilian life in Israel are plagued by bureaucratic inefficiency and indifference, the army functions far more effectively.

Israel's doctrine of warfare evolved out of a search for answers to the problems stemming from the five basic principles outlined above. For example, an attempt has been made to compensate for the lack of strategic depth by establishing a regional defense structure based on border settlements, especially kibbutzim, and settlements on the second line, and organized for all-around defense, equipped with appropriate weapons, including antitank guns and mortars. According to the plan, they are to hold off an invader and wear down his strength while a general mobilization of reserve forces takes place. Regional defense saves money because it is based on existing settlements and not on army units holding a fortified line. Its operative importance lies in the fact that it releases crack units from the burdens of ongoing defense. Regional defense was crucial up until the Six-Day War, but its importance has diminished with the geographic changes brought about by that war.

Israeli strategists developed the doctrine of preemptive attack as an answer to the threat of defeat by surprise attack. In the conditions that prevailed until the Six-Day War, the opening blow was an essential element of Israeli planning. In 1958 Yigal Allon commented on the problem of initiative and the preemptive strike in his book *Sand Screen*:

Considering the country's situation, with its long and besieged borders, little depth and flat terrain . . . and the excessive proximity of Arab air bases and long-range artillery, Israel is unable to permit her enemies to take the initiative. Since the enemy could well set his first aim as the destruction of the Israeli Air Force on the ground, Israel is obliged to exercise her moral and political right to take the operative initiative into her own hands before enemy aircraft take off; otherwise she may be doomed at the outset of the battle. As long as the Arab rulers continue to maintain a technical state of war, the moral right of preemptive counterattack is the military guarantee of Israel's future.[2]

Another issue related to the mounting of a preemptive or deterrent strike is whether Israel should set down certain limits or taboos whose violation would be acknowledged as a *casus belli*. The approach to this issue has changed over the years. After the Sinai Campaign, for example, it was established unequivocally that if the Egyptians blockaded the Straits of Tiran again, Israel would respond by going to war. Such a blockade was no less valid a *casus belli* earlier in the 1950s, but at that time Israel was less disposed to respond to it; she was waiting for the right opportunity, which came along in 1956.

An issue that has occupied Israel for many years is the transfer of outside Arab military forces to bordering Arab countries in order to bolster the deployment near her border. Israel has been particularly sensitive to the stationing of Iraqi forces (or any other) in Jordan, and even with the West Bank under her control she is unable to accept such a move with equanimity. For in light of the buildup of the Arab armies and the growth of their armored forces, it would be highly perilous for Israel to allow for the concentration of outside forces in Jordan. The Israeli government nevertheless has refrained from articulating this position as official policy, and the fact is that Israel's stance on the entry of the Syrian Army into Lebanon has not been consistent. At times she has regarded the presence of the Syrian Army in Lebanon, and especially the stationing of antiaircraft missiles there, as grounds for military action; other times she has been prepared to yield on her own interdiction, provided that the Syrians were careful not to draw close to her northern border and refrained from introducing missiles into Lebanon.

Menachem Begin's government both established and publicly proclaimed yet another strategic imperative: the determination to destroy the nuclear stockpile of any Arab country at war with Israel if there are grounds to believe that the country is manufacturing nuclear weapons. This was the justification for destroying Iraq's nuclear reactor in the summer of 1981. At the same time Israel has played up her own scientific capabilities and nuclear achievements as a way of enhancing her deterrent power. Although she has never admitted to the possession of nuclear weapons, Israel has intimated more than once that she is certainly capable of producing them. What is more, while declaring that she will not be the first country to introduce nuclear weapons into the Middle East, Israel has refused to sign the antinuclear proliferation treaty. This seemingly contradictory stance has been described as the "bomb in the basement" policy, the result being that the Arab states suspect or are convinced that Israel has stockpiled nuclear weapons and would be prepared to use them if faced with defeat in a conventional war.

Another vital point of Israeli strategy is the need to transfer the war onto enemy territory. Because Israel lacks strategic depth and her back is to the sea, great importance is placed on rapidly shifting the fighting away from her populated areas and onto enemy territory, even if the enemy strikes first. This was again amply demonstrated in the Yom Kippur War when Israeli forces crossed the Suez Canal into Egypt and advanced into Syria to within a day's march from Damascus. IDF operational plans emphasize fast-moving, mobile attacks—the "blitzkrieg" strategy—especially as a mobile war makes the best use of the IDF's technological superiority. Following this doctrine, a precise order of preferences has been determined: the offensive arms receive top priority, first place going to the air force, followed by armor. High preference is also given to the paratroop brigades as a striking force. These units receive the best tools to guarantee rapid penetration and maneuverability in the difficult terrain of mountains and desert. And while the IDF has employed traditional combat methods, it has given them a distinctly Israeli character and set standards that are higher than the norm. An example of this is the Israeli Air Force's success in attacking Arab airfields and destroying hundreds of aircraft within just a few hours.

Of the three traditional battle patterns—defense, retreat, attack—the IDF has been outstanding only at the last, whereas the defensive method has been relegated to second place. The IDF made use of defensive tactics during the War of Independence, but since then the doctrine has remained on paper. The first time the IDF was compelled to think about defensive warfare was, in fact, during the War of Attrition. Instead, the name of the game has always been offensive action. The IDF had many advocates of this approach in its background, Yitzhak Sadeh and Orde Wingate being the most notable. Within the IDF itself, Moshe Dayan was noteworthy for his aggressive spirit, Ariel Sharon for the development of small-scale combat and highly mobile tactics, Israel Tal for tank warfare, and Ezer Weizman for the development of aerial combat. These commanders built a doctrine out of Orde Wingate's maxim "The best defense is attack."

The IDF excels in offensive planning, especially when the strategy of the indirect or improvisational approach is involved. But long-term planning has suffered from many faults because the General Staff has always been caught up with current problems. Much attention is directed toward how to overcome Arab superiority in firepower and combat weapons. Operative and tactical planning is based on the fastest possible route to face-to-face combat, in which the superiority of the individual fighter can be decisive. The IDF does not waste much time on preparing the classic opening moves. Commanders have learned not to make assault conditional on a specific number of hours of softening up by artillery or the destruction of ground-to-air missile systems. In the Six-Day War, for example, Israeli Air Force planes did not strike at the Egyptian missiles first but went directly to the airfields. The missiles were attacked only when they had begun to interfere with the aerial cover given to the armored columns advancing through Sinai.

One of the classic ways of shortening the early stages of battle is to exploit the darkness. The IDF has achieved impressive results in this field. Technical means of exploiting the night as an opportunity for assaults were developed both on land and in the air. Beginning in the 1950s, when commando units were used for nighttime reprisals, culminating in the Six-Day War with the great night offensive at Abu Ageila in Sinai, the cover of darkness has been well used by the IDF. Another characteristic of the IDF that it has developed on both the theoretical and operational levels is a doctrine of warfare to counter the Soviet strategy employed by Egypt and Syria. IDF experts have thoroughly studied Soviet theories and know their weak points. Training installations in Israel have been built according to the Russian doctrine, and armored and infantry units are familiarized with Soviet tactics.

The IDF doctrine of warfare just described applies to battle in which conventional weapons are used. The introduction of nuclear weapons into the Middle East will change the entire picture, and new strategies will have to be devised. Yet the principles mentioned in this chapter were in effect without change until the Six-Day War, after which the geostrategic changes that resulted from that conflict occasioned some modifications, although the basic tenets remain.

At the same time, the improved level of Arab military performance must be taken into account. The need for a preemptive attack on threatening enemy concentrations still appears to be essential, and the IDF has not forsaken the principle of transferring the war onto enemy territory. Changing political and territorial realities, however, require constant revision in tactical planning. And Israeli strategists still live with the fear that a foreign power could intervene on behalf of the Arabs, as the Soviet Union threatened to do during the Yom Kippur War.

The IDF continues to exploit its qualitative edge to compensate for its disadvantages. The decisive factor is not the number of men or soldiers but the national standard; not individual weapons but weapons systems that the nation can successfully produce and operate. Israel is unique in her ability to achieve the maximum mobilization of her national potential for the army and civil defense. This extends to the mobilization of men and women for emergency economic measures. Because of her paucity of resources, she cannot maintain a large standing army. Instead she must make do with a small regular nucleus and consolidate the bulk of her power in reserve forces. It is vital, therefore, that the large reserve army be properly organized, well-trained and capable of rapid mobilization. Yigael Yadin, the IDF's second Chief of Staff, studied the Swiss reserve organization and adopted its system for the IDF in an extended and improved form. Israel can assemble the bulk of its reserves within twenty-four hours and then transport these fully equipped units to the front within another forty-eight hours. Each unit summons its men by means of slogans broadcast over the radio or by unit runners. The men report to assembly points and are taken to the unit's emergency stores, where they are equipped and then transported directly to the front.

By this means, and with the help of the nucleus of a relatively small regular army, Israel has succeeded in establishing the largest per capita army in the world. It is estimated that out of a population of some three million, the IDF can field an army of half a million men. Although caught by surprise with the Yom Kippur War, Israel was able to mobilize quickly and turn the tide against the Egyptians and the Syrians. The organization of the standing army has been developed especially to enable it to face regular armies and to maintain a high level of preparedness. A major role is accorded to the air force, which is especially large and is based primarily on regular units that are capable of immediate action at full capacity. Emphasis is also placed on a sophisticated Intelligence service that can alert the militia army in time to respond effectively.

The fact that the IDF is a people's army influences the choice of the weapons systems used by the reserves, which train only once a year. Certain sophisticated weapons systems, for example, are operated by the regular army only. To bridge the specialization gap that often exists in a militia army, the IDF insists on a thorough population mix in all its units. By distributing Israel's technological and cultural elite throughout the army, the IDF achieves a higher than average level of quality within each unit and avoids social disparity between officers and enlisted personnel. Thus a professor of philosophy may serve as a sentry or driver, with the rank of private. Israel's academic community has attempted to abolish this custom, but the IDF has remained adamant, although, of course, scientists with strategically valuable skills are appropriately employed. The principle of equality has thereby been maintained in the army, contributing to high morale and raising the average level of all the units.

The IDF General Staff is an integrated and centralized structure without separate staffs for the air force, the navy, or the land forces. The Chief of Staff acts as the Supreme Commander, and in wartime the air force and navy commanders serve as his advisors. This centralization and unification of command has repeatedly proven its efficacy.

Notes

1. As demonstrated at the United Nations during the Yom Kippur War, when the Soviet Union moved in the Security Council for a cease-fire only when it was clear that Egypt was losing.

2. Allon, *Masach shel Hol,* p. 68.

The Six-Day War

T HE CAUSES of the Six-Day War had long been brewing
just below the surface in the Middle East. But despite the ongoing antagonism between Israel and the Arab states this war
might well have been averted had the sides not let events get out of
control. Egypt's President Nasser became so enthralled by his own
belligerent rhetoric that in May 1967 he closed the Straits of Tiran to
Israeli shipping and ousted the UN Emergency Force from Sinai even
though he had hoped to humble Israel without resorting to war. In
letting his exuberance run away with itself, Nasser failed to understand that he had placed Israel in an intolerable position while pressing toward a war for which he himself was unprepared. In the process
he also dragged King Hussein into the adventure—which cost Jordan the West Bank.

One of the factors behind the war was an ongoing drama far from
the Egyptian border having to do with the exploitation of water from
the Jordan River. In 1953 Israel wanted to begin diverting water from
the Jordan to the Negev for irrigation purposes, but found herself
forced to postpone the plan because America objected that the water
was to be drawn from the demilitarized zone. President Eisenhower
sent Special Ambassador Eric Johnston to the area to hammer out a
plan for dividing the Jordan's resources between Israel and the Arab
states involved, and even though Israel felt deprived of her fair share
of water she accepted the 1954 Johnston Plan and began to construct
its National Water Carrier.

Meanwhile King Hussein began to divert some of the waters of
the Yarmuk River (which flows into the Jordan) for his own country's use. And while the Israeli government pledged to draw only what
had been allocated to Israel by the Johnston Plan, the Arabs were not

appeased. In June 1961, with the construction of the National Water Carrier well advanced, the Arab Defense Council passed a fateful resolution declaring that the Arab states would mount a joint military action against Israel as soon as the water carrier was completed and began diverting the Jordan's waters to the Negev. As the date for inaugurating the system drew closer, however, Nasser realized that he was not prepared for the war he had promised his people and his allies, and he would have to find some way out of it.

To save face with his followers the Egyptian president came up with a new proposal: instead of attacking the Israeli conduction facility the Arabs would enter into a project of their own to divert the headwaters of the Jordan, thereby depriving Israel of the water altogether. In January 1964 the first Arab summit conference convened and resolved to divert of headwaters of the Jordan, located in Arab territory. Two bodies were established that were to have a lasting effect on the history of the area: the Joint Arab Command (which would be responsible for defending the diversion project), and the Palestine Liberation Organization. Six months later Israel inaugurated its National Water Carrier and began irrigating the fields of the Negev with water pumped down from the Galilee.

Nasser had tried to assuage the ferment among the Palestinians through the creation of the Palestine Liberation Organization but they were not subdued easily. A Palestinian group known as Fatah, led by Yasser Arafat, came to the conclusion that since neither Israel nor the Arab states were interested in fighting a war, it would have to act independently to make such a clash inevitable. Thus at the beginning of 1965 the Fatah began to carry out sabotage operations in Israel, with its very first action directed against the National Water Carrier.

The Fatah found a patron in Syria, the only Arab state, incidentally, that persisted in its resolve to divert the headwaters of the Jordan. While Lebanon was soon dissuaded from participating in the project, for fear of Israeli reprisals, the Syrians doggedly kept at their excavation work. Before long Israel responded to the Syrian bid by taking military action to foil the diversion scheme; and even though the Israelis were scrupulous never to send troops over the border, the violence of the clashes escalated until it climaxed in an air battle on April 7, 1967 in which seven Syrian MIGs were brought down.

Less than half a year earlier, November 4, 1966, Syria and Egypt had signed a mutual defense pact; and as the clashes with Israel grew sharper, the Arab press began to ask why Cairo was not sending troops to Syria's aid. A similarly provocative incident had occurred on November 13, 1966 when an Israeli armored force mounted a raid on the Jordanian West Bank village of Samua in broad daylight, demolishing about forty buildings in retaliation for actions perpetrated by the Fatah. According to the guidelines of the Joint Arab Command the Egyptian Air Force was supposed to provide the Jordanians with air support whenever they requested it; Jordan asked, Egypt did not comply.

The consequent criticism of Egypt was inordinately sharp, and after the April 7 incident it seemed likely that Nasser would resort to some act of bravura. Back in 1960, at a time when tension along the Israeli-Syrian border was running particularly high, Nasser had deployed three divisions (one armored) into Sinai near the Israeli border to serve as a deterrent and ease the pressure on Syria. Israel's government, then headed by Ben-Gurion, responded with sangfroid. The truth of the matter was that neither side wanted war and on March 1, as soon as Nasser decided that the show of strength had served its purpose, he ordered his troops back to their positions west of the Suez Canal.

The face-off of 1967 would not be a replay of 1960, however, for too many circumstances changed in the interim. One stemmed from the involvement of the Russians, who were prompting Nasser to come to Syria's defense. The Damascus regime was closer to Moscow than any other Arab government, and the Soviets were glad of the opportunity to stir the Middle Eastern cauldron. When Israeli Chief of Staff Lieutenant General Yitzhak Rabin declared that Israel would have to act against Syria if she continued to support the infiltrators who were committing sabotage, Moscow floated a false rumor that Israeli forces were massing on the Syrian border. Following the air battle in April Radio Moscow charged that American pilots had taken part in the dogfights and even claimed that one of them had been taken prisoner. Then the Russians claimed that Israel was planning to use gas warfare on Syria and massed thirteen brigades along the border. Israel invited United Nations observers to check out the situation on her border with Syria, and UN Secretary-General U Thant subsequently announced that to the best of his knowledge from the observers' reports no Israeli forces were concentrated where the Russians claimed.

Israel made it known to Nasser through trusted intermediaries that the Russians' contentions were not true. The message reached Nasser, but it did not prevent the situation from deteriorating further.

Nasser had already resolved to send forces into Sinai in the belief that Israel, led by Levi Eshkol (who came across as being considerably weaker than Ben-Gurion), would back down from taking any action, handing Egypt a bloodless victory. So it was that on May 15 the Egyptian war machine went into action. The intervening three weeks until the outbreak of fighting on June 5 became known subsequently as the "waiting period," a time in which both the UN and the big powers exhibited total impotence. A new war was taking shape right before their eyes, but not only did they fail to prevent it, they indirectly contributed to it.

The Egyptian forces began moving into Sinai in the most conspicuous manner possible, as if the point of the move were to attract attention. If Nasser had confined himself to this display of power he surely would have been treated to a sharp dose of criticism from the rest of the Arab world. But on May 16 he went a step further by having the Egyptian Chief of Staff demand that the Commander of the United Nations Emergency Force (UNEF) in Sinai and the Gaza Strip remove his troops from the vicinity of the border and concentrate them instead in three Sinai and Gaza Strip sites. U Thant then responded in a way that only compounded Nasser's mistake, for he publicly declared that the UN was unwilling to withdraw a part of its force; either all the troops remained in place or the whole force would be withdrawn. Challenged by that choice, Nasser opted for a complete withdrawal. On May 19 the UN flag was lowered in the Gaza Strip and Palestine Liberation Army soldiers took over the position vacated by UNEF.

That was when the race to mass forces began. Israel stepped up the mobilization of its reserves, while the Egyptians rushed every available unit into Sinai and even ordered their forces in Yemen (which had been involved in the civil war there for a number of years) to speed up their withdrawal and return home as quickly as possible. Nevertheless, a war might still have been avoided had Nasser not taken yet another imprudent step. On May 20 he ordered his forces to capture the Straits of Tiran, but Israel continued to believe that the Egyptians wouldn't dare close the straits to free shipping. After all, upon the IDF's withdrawal from Sinai eleven years earlier President Eisenhower had made a solemn pledge to Israel that freedom of shipping would be safeguarded in the straits, and Jerusalem wanted to believe that the memory of that public guarantee would make Nasser stop short of doing anything rash.

But while Israel placed its trust in the effect of the big power's influence, Nasser was looking over his shoulder at a different arena, again proving unable to stand up to the challenge to his prestige here either. The Arabs were inciting him from every quarter to attack Israel, and Jordanian state radio even tried to provoke him with taunts that he didn't have the courage to close the Straits of Tiran. The ploy worked, for in the early morning hours of May 23 Israeli Prime Minister Levi Eshkol was awakened with the news that while on a visit to his units in the field Nasser had announced the blockade of the straits to Israeli and Israel-bound shipping. "Today Israel doesn't have Britain and France [by her side], as she did in 1956. We stand face to face with Israel [alone]," Nasser jeered. "The Jews are threatening war, and we say to them *Ahlan u-sahlan!* [welcome]."

Israel had another disappointment awaiting her, further proof that she could not rely on outside commitments in matters of security. The international guarantees of free shipping through the straits proved to be worthless. First France and Britain announced that the Tripartite Declaration of 1950 opposing the use of force in the region and guaranteeing the existing borders no longer held. Rather than expressing her support for Israel, France—widely considered Israel's closest friend—declared that the issue of shipping through the Straits of Tiran was no more than a complex legal problem. The statements coming out of Paris only left Israel feeling increasingly isolated, and on May 24 Foreign Minister Abba Eban embarked on a tour of Western capitals for meetings with President de Gaulle, British Prime Minister Harold Wilson, and President Lyndon Johnson in the hope of culling international support for Israel's plight.

President de Gaulle, who just a few years earlier had clearly declared that Israel was France's ally, now told Eban that circumstances had changed since the Tripartite Declaration and that Jerusalem must appreciate that no guarantee is absolute. His best advice to Israel was not to respond with force to the blockade of her shipping or the massing of Egyptian troops. Yet de Gaulle did not stop at giving advice; on June 3, two days before the outbreak of the war, he ordered an embargo on arms to the Middle East. Since France's principal client in the region was Israel (the Israeli Air Force, for example, was overwhelmingly French-equipped), the implication of the embargo was embarrassingly clear, and it is easy to understand why the French reversal was taken as perfidy. Eban found a more supportive atmosphere in London, but Prime Minister Wilson made any possible

British action conditional upon the stand taken by the United States.

Washington did not deny its commitments regarding freedom of shipping, but President Johnson's advice was to wait until an international maritime force could be assembled to break the blockade. Some in the United States intimated that Israel's best course would be to exercise restraint, and the U.S. would cover the difference in cost of shipping oil to the country's Mediterranean ports rather than Eilat. At this stage the blockade became a secondary issue, even though Israel regarded it as a *casus belli,* for a more immediate threat had arisen in Sinai. The concentration of Egyptian forces in the peninsula had reached some 100,000 troops and 1,000 tanks, augmented by token forces from Algeria, Sudan, and Kuwait. At the same time Syria declared a state of alert, and Jordan began moving its armored forces toward the Israeli border, while Iraq announced her intention to dispatch forces of her own into Jordan.

A week before the outbreak of fighting the Israeli government deliberated its options, with the vote on whether to go to war a tie: nine ministers in favor, nine against. The General Staff pressed for action but the Cabinet decided to accept President Johnson's appeal and wait until a multinational effort could be mounted against the blockade. While the point of this maneuver was to avoid violence, the deference of the Cabinet only seemed to spur the Arabs on.

Nasser now made a new demand: that Israel evacuate the city of Eilat and the region of Nitzana on the Egyptian border. The next day Palestinian forces in the Gaza Strip shelled an Israeli settlement. Sensing Israel's diffidence, Iran was quick to deny that she was selling oil to Israel. And within Israel itself, a fear for the worst began to spread through the population. There was widespread feeling that for the second time within a generation a noose had been slipped around the neck of the Jewish people—and this time the Jews must respond vigorously and without delay. Soon the public began to clamor for the replacement of Eshkol as Minister of Defense and for the establishment of a Government of National Unity. Most of the IDF's reserves were mobilized by then, and Israel could not long sustain such a posture for obvious economic reasons.

At that stage two disparate events joined to accelerate the drive toward war. On May 30 King Hussein suddenly turned up—uninvited—in Cairo. The relations between Egypt and Jordan had been tense for a number of years, but now Hussein feared that when the Arab camp went to war he would be left out in the cold. Seizing the

unexpected opportunity Nasser had the king sign a military agreement with Egypt on that very day. Hussein then returned home with
two guests aboard his plane: Ahmed Shukairy, the head of the PLO
and a long-time opponent, and the Egyptian General Abdul Moneim
Riad, Chief of Staff of the Joint Arab Command, who had in effect
been assigned to take charge of the Arab Legion. Two days later two
battalions of Egyptian commandos were flown to Jordan. It also came
out that an Iraqi division had begun moving toward the Jordanian
frontier and that Iraqi combat planes had been restationed at airfields
close to Jordan. From Israel's standpoint this shift of forces was an
additional *casus belli,* in that she regarded the Jordanian border as her
most sensitive frontier, repeatedly warning that she would not tolerate the presence of any other Arab army on Jordanian soil.

The other factor that narrowed Israel's options was the conclusion reached by the head of the Mossad, Meir Amit, during his talks
in Washington. He had been sent there to clarify the prospects of
American aid and establish whether there was a point in waiting any
longer. He cabled home that his interlocutors no longer believed in
the likelihood of a serious international effort to open the straits,
making it quite clear that there was no point in waiting for such an
action to materialize. In fact there was a risk that if Israel did not act,
the U.S. might begin to waver in its support for the justice of her
cause. When Amit's cable reached Israeli Foreign Minister Eban he
went to the offices of the Israeli General Staff and conceded that the
diplomatic effort had run its course and that the only consideration
now was Israel's security.

On June 4 the Israeli Cabinet—reconstituted as a Government of
National Unity, with Moshe Dayan as Minister of Defense replacing
Levi Eshkol—voted to go to war. At 7:10 the next morning the first
wave of Israeli planes took off for their targets in Egypt; fifty-five
minutes later Israeli armored units crossed the border into the Gaza
Strip and Sinai.

The assumption of the Israeli General Staff going into war was
that the IDF would be able to act freely and forcefully for two or
three days before restraints were imposed from the outside. Therefore the operation would have to be conducted in such a way that
most of the military achievements could be attained in the first days
of battle. Although Washington would not commend Israel on its
decision to go to war, after having recognized the Egyptian blockade
as an aggressive act they would probably maintain a neutral stance

and prevent the Soviets from intervening. The General Staff also was confident that the Soviets would not be able to react quickly and efficiently because of the distances involved. By the time they could mobilize their forces the conflict on the battlefield probably would be resolved. At worst their navy might send some of its ships in the Mediterranean toward the Israeli coast as a show of intent. In the end what prevented them from intervening in the fighting was the swift defeat of the Arab armies within six days.[1]

It was the fear of Russian intervention that spawned Dayan's plan to befuddle the enemy. On the assumption that pressures on Israel would increase as it became clear that the IDF was winning, Dayan decided to ban announcements of Israeli victories and otherwise withhold or obscure information coming in from the fronts as a way of staving off that pressure—even if it led to confusion within Israel and consternation among world Jewry and other friends abroad. The Arabs unwittingly lent a hand by proclaiming victories that in fact had not occurred. Indeed, they fell right into the Israeli trap and drew the Soviets in with them. Eight hours passed before the Egyptian commanders notified Nasser that their air force had been destroyed. The Arabs announced their conquest of Israeli territory with Israeli forces already deep into Sinai. These announcements misled their Eastern bloc and Third World friends, even the Soviet Union. Worse yet they also confused their own officials. The Egyptian delegate to the United Nations Security Council adamantly opposed a resolution to demand a cease-fire because he was convinced that Egyptian forces were racing toward Tel Aviv. When he learned the truth several hours later he burst into tears and sued for an immediate halt to the fighting.

The Israeli war plans focused primarily on the Egyptian front, with the IDF's forces on the Syrian and Jordanian fronts assigned a defensive role. It was unclear whether Jordan would join in the fighting, but Israeli troops stood in ready of that eventuality. In response to the arrival of Egyptian commandos in Jordan and the movement of Iraqi troops toward the Jordanian border, the IDF had placed Central Command's armored brigade on reserve for a counterattack and moved two armored brigades up to Northern Command (whose southern sector bordered on the Jordanian front).

Even after fighting broke out on the Egyptian front Jerusalem still hoped that Hussein would refrain from anything more than a token involvement in the conflict. As Major General Uzi Narkiss, the chief of Central Command, subsequently recalled, "We assumed that Hussein would make do with something like a salutatory salvo and thereby fulfill his obligations to inter-Arab unity and his defense pact with Egypt."[2] As for the Syrians, the General Staff assumed that unlike their conduct in 1956, this time they would come to Egypt's aid. Still the IDF concentrated its major effort on the Egyptian front and planned to deal with any other belligerents who might join in during a later stage of the war. By exploiting her relatively short lines of communication, Israel was able rapidly to transfer units from one front to another and deploy them efficiently so as to surprise the Arabs, who were indeed astonished at the size of the forces advancing toward them.

That no prior thought was given to the conquest and occupation of Arab territories is attested by both alternative war plans. The first or "small" plan—presented to the Prime Minister on May 23—was of modest scope and spoke to a desire for a limited war that would keep Israeli casualties to a minimum. It called for Israel to break into Egyptian territory at only one location, keeping the fighting to northern Sinai and advancing only as far as El Arish. While armored units moved into the Gaza Strip and proceeded toward El Arish, infantry was to be landed by sea, paratroops from the air. The sole aim of the plan was to overcome the Palestinian units in the Gaza Strip and the Egyptian troops in northern Sinai.

Occupying this small patch of territory was to be something of a tit for tat for the closing of the Straits of Tiran and the ejection of UN forces from Sharm el-Sheikh. As the waiting period dragged on, however, and the concentration of Egyptian forces continued, the small plan was discussed less often. Divisional commanders on the southern front pressed for a bolder approach, and once Dayan was appointed Defense Minister they got it.

It became clear to the Israelis as the number of Egyptian troops and tanks in Sinai mounted that the straits could not be opened until the Egyptian Army was defeated. From a political standpoint it was better for Israel to show the world that she had opened fire in response to an incontestable act of aggression, namely, the blockading of an international waterway. But from a military point of view limiting her response to that particular area presented tactical difficulties. Therefore the preference was to open the straits by smashing the Egyptian Army in Sinai. After that it would be possible to "pluck" Sharm el-Sheikh like a ripe peach.

Thus the alternative, broader plan was to conquer all of the Sinai Peninsula, penetrating through the center of Sinai (to an area defined by Jebel Libne, Bir Gafgafa, and Bir Tamada) in order to engage and destroy the Egyptian Army. Dayan specifically instructed his commanders not to reach the Suez Canal, recalling the international pressures that had been brought to bear on Israel in 1956. Thus when the reconnaissance forces that moved along the northern axis in Sinai reached the canal, they were ordered to turn back. But then Dayan's order was rescinded because the defeat of the Egyptian Army was so rapid and total that in the absence of resistance Israeli tanks reached the canal before they could be stopped. The canal was taken in a hasty, disorganized fashion, and the IDF did not reach as many places as it could have. In the north, at the entry to the canal from the Mediterranean, the town of Port Fuad was not taken and was the only point (a six-mile sector) at which the Egyptians were able to keep control of both banks of the canal. Later, in 1969, this permitted the Soviet Navy to bring warships into the harbor of Port Said.

Three IDF armored corps, under the commands of Major General Tal in the north, Major General Yoffe in the center, and Major General Sharon in the southern sector, broke into Egyptian territory at two points. Tal's forces entered the Rafiah salient between Gaza and Sinai, moved first toward El Arish, and from there to the center of Sinai. Another secondary force took control of the Gaza Strip. Sharon's forces made a second breakthrough at Abu Ageila, and some of Yoffe's forces moved through this passage leading to the center of Sinai. The plan to drop paratroops near El Arish was cancelled, and the paratroop unit was later sent into action in Jerusalem. An additional force supplemented by dummy wooden tanks was stationed on the more southerly sector facing Quntilla for the purposes of deception, and the ruse succeeded beyond all expectations. Just before the war the Egyptians had transferred a large tank force to face the Israeli decoy because they mistakenly believed that this was where the IDF would attempt its major breakthrough.

Although the Israeli breakthrough plan was based on a frontal attack, the IDF nevertheless achieved surprise at some points by using an indirect approach. An armored brigade under Major General Yoffe infiltrated Sinai by night along an obscure ancient Roman road. They met with no resistance and constituted the first thrust into the heart of enemy territory. Yoffe's second armored brigade broke into Sinai by way of Abu Ageila. While Sharon's forces were hammering the main defenses of Abu Ageila Yoffe's men surprised the Egyptian rear-guard forces and so aided in their collapse.

Israeli tanks penetrated to the heart of Sinai along the same three axes on which they had driven toward the Suez Canal in the Sinai Campaign. The rate of advance was speeded up by parachuting fuel and water ahead. In fact the advance was so rapid that most of the missions fell primarily on two armored brigades, which moved in the classic armored-breakthrough pattern: pressing straight forward without taking notice of what was happening on the flanks.

While fighting continued along the first Egyptian line of defense, orders were given to proceed to the Mitla and Jiddi passes to cut off the retreat of the Egyptian forces. The unit of Israeli tanks that pushed forward frequently ran into Egyptian convoys traveling along the same road, but the Egyptians did not open fire because they wanted to retreat unhampered. And the Israeli tanks refrained from engaging the enemy in any skirmish not connected with the urgent task imposed on them.

The force that moved toward the Mitla Pass consisted of nine tanks, but four of them broke down and were towed by the others. On arrival at the pass the disabled tanks were stationed in dug-in emplacements and exposed on an open field. The capture and holding of the Mitla Pass was representative of the combination of classic armored strategy and daring improvisation that characterized the Israeli campaign.

In analyzing the Israeli victory one must begin with the observation that for the Egyptians, the great quantity of modern equipment proved to be an impediment. They had a hard time extracting the full benefit the equipment offered, and in the end they were defeated by it. These weapons grant their users greater speed, greater rate of fire, and greater mobility. But speed necessitates that command decisions be made at a rate faster than the movement on the battlefield. A high degree of integration and exactitude in staff work is required, and this is precisely what the Egyptians lacked. The Israeli commanders assumed this lack in advance and knew they would have to do everything possible to bring the Egyptian units into a battle of rapid movement.

The Soviets did not make things easier for the Egyptians by burdening them with their doctrines of warfare that were quite unsuitable for the Egyptian Army. Equipment and weapons were transferred to Egypt according to the table of organization of Soviet divisions without first checking whether this equipment, which was designed for use in Europe, was suitable for desert conditions. Among the considerable loot abandoned in the Sinai, Israeli experts were surprised to find amphibious tanks and equipment for chemical warfare, which only weighed down the Egyptian units.

Defeat was inevitable from the moment Israeli armor succeeded in breaking through to the heart of the Egyptians' deployment. The only questions were how long the battle would take, and the price Israel would have to pay. Even if the Egyptians had attacked first it is doubtful that their columns would have succeeded in penetrating, at best, beyond the town of Beersheba in the Negev. The Egyptians left some 15,000 dead, and almost all their equipment on the sands of Sinai. More than 12,000 soldiers were taken prisoner (among them nine generals) and the remainder were permitted by the IDF to cross the canal. For her part, Israel lost 275 men from her land forces on the Egyptian front.

From a numerical point of view, the two armies confronting each other on the Egyptian front were almost equal, each being about 100,000 strong. The Egyptian Army was organized into five infantry divisions, each with its own tank unit, as well as two additional armored divisions. The fighting force of the IDF was organized into three divisions, with a few secondary units. Egypt had the advantage in weapons, primarily artillery, but she did not make proper use of it even in defense. The Israeli artillery was outnumbered but had the advantage of being self-propelled, while the Egyptian guns had to be towed. In the final analysis, however, the decisive factors were not the quality or quantity of weapons but better organization, bolder tactics, and superior strategy.

The Israeli commanders knew how to engage only part of the Egyptian Army while avoiding the whole reservoir of Egyptian weaponry. Immediately following the initial Israeli breakthrough the attack centered on the Egyptian rear. The pressure, which can be understood in terms of the domino effect, compelled Egyptian units to retreat without fighting and therefore without any losses to Israeli forces. After the war Egyptian generals complained that they had been withdrawn from battle without having fought at all. The Russians, however, claimed that if every Egyptian tank and gun had been fired just once the results of the war would have been dramatically different.

From the outset fictitious reporting, the traditional bugaboo of

Arab armies, was rampant. As stated earlier, the Egyptian General Staff failed to report the results of the Israeli air attack to Nasser for eight hours. As false reports piled up, the operational reporting system broke down altogether. Commanders in the field fabricated successes or, in order to justify failure, exaggerated the size of Israeli forces. From experience Israeli Intelligence knew that the longer the battles continued the worse the Arab Command would entangle itself in a vicious circle wherein field commanders refused to obey orders because they knew they were based on misinformation received from the field. Officers would deliberately avoid carrying out orders and try to act independently according to information that seemed to them to be correct. Incompetent reporting and inept reconnaissance precluded effective Egyptian measures.

In summing up the elements of victory against Egypt, Major General Yishayahu Gavish, who was overall commander of the southern front, numbered the following:

(a) The concentration of our forces, speed of movement, and maintenance of the momentum. We concentrated most of our force so as to create favorable balances of force in all the arenas of the battle when and where it suited us. We maintained the constant impetus and fought day and night without stopping. We gave the enemy no rest, and we did not break off contact with him for even an hour.

(b) The Command led in battle. A high proportion of our casualties were officers who moved at the head of their units.

(c) The morale of the fighters derived from the recognition that this war was for the nation's existence.

(d) Unconventional tactics. We made unconventional penetrations to bring about a rapid decision, by isolating the enemy, and by restricting his ability to maneuver and to reinforce his besieged forces.

(e) A rapid and flexible maintenance system. This gave the ground forces independence for at least seventy-two hours, and they needed reinforcement only at the end of the battle.

(f) The decisive contribution of the air force.[3]

The Israeli attack on Egypt was led by the air force, which caught most of the Egyptian planes on the ground. Not one of their airfields escaped the surprise Israeli bombings, and their runways were destroyed by special bombs. The Israeli Air Force carried out a plan it had rehearsed for many years, and when the first wave of aircraft returned it was clear that the blow sustained by the Egyptians was devastating. After the second and third waves there was no doubt that the air war was over and that the Egyptian land forces had lost their air support.

One of the most notable aspects of the Israeli air strike was the rapid turnaround of the aircraft. The time devoted to arming and re-fueling a plane from the moment it returns from one sortie until it takes off for the next is an important factor. The operational output of each aircraft is expressed in the number of sorties carried out by the air force during the war. Turnaround efficiency reached its peak when aircraft were ready to take off for a second sortie within seven minutes with a freshly briefed pilot in the cockpit. Often pilots were ordered to move a combat mission from one front to another after they had already taken off. Rapid turnaround and split-second deci-sions led the Arabs to believe that Israel was operating many more than the 200 planes she actually had.

On the first day of war the Israeli Air Force destroyed some 350 Arab aircraft. Seventeen airfields were attacked in Egypt (300 planes destroyed), five airfields were attacked in Syria, two in Jordan, and one in Iraq. In the short space of two hours and fifty minutes the Egyptian Air Force ceased to exist. For another hour the Israeli Air Force worked over Jordan and Syria, and by noon Israel had gained aerial supremacy in the Middle East. Most of the aircraft were then directed to ground-support missions. The Arab air forces lost 452 air-craft in all, seventy-nine of them in aerial combat. Israel lost a total of fifty aircraft of various types, mostly from ground fire; twenty Israeli pilots were killed.

Over the exposed wastes of Sinai and the roads between the sand dunes, the task of ground support was exceptionally easy. Egyptian armored and transport vehicles were a convenient prey for Israeli planes. Israeli pilots foiled Egyptian counterattacks before they could be launched while Fouga trainer aircraft attacked concentrations of Egyptian artillery. When the Egyptian retreat began, Israeli pilots be-gan their hunt of Arab convoys. At first they strafed vehicles at the head of the convoy, then those at the rear. The vehicles trapped in the middle caught fire and could not escape in the sand. The mauve and white *wadis* of Sinai were specked by burning convoys. On the third day of the war the aircraft were ordered to stop attacking con-centrations of transport and armor abandoned in Sinai. Israel wanted to lay its hands on the Egyptian equipment intact.

Israel was reluctant to wage war on the Jordanian front because the going assessment was that war on two fronts—Egypt and Syria—

was a heavy enough burden, and also because the Jordanian border was particularly dangerous, touching as it did on most of the concentrations of the Israeli population. The border cut through Jerusalem, running close to government ministries and the Knesset. Jordanian artillery could easily hit the suburbs of Tel Aviv, and many towns and settlements as well, and was within range of three Israeli airfields.

On the first morning of the war Israel asked the UN truce observers' Chief of Staff to convey the message to King Hussein that if he refrained from opening fire, Israel would do likewise. The message was delivered, but events developed otherwise. Jordanian artillery opened fire all along the front and unleashed an especially heavy bombardment on the Jewish section of Jerusalem and the road into Jerusalem. Jordanian aircraft attacked various targets in Israel.

On the first day of the war a Jordanian force seized the hill in the no-man's-land where UN headquarters had been located. It gave the king's troops a commanding advantage over a wide area. Up to that point Israeli commanders had considered knocking out Jordanian artillery batteries only to prevent the shelling of the Ramat David Airfield in the Jezreel Valley. When the UN hill was captured, Israel decided to take it and to break through to Mount Scopus, which had been an Israeli enclave since 1948 and was the first site of the Hebrew University. Israeli armored forces then entered Jordanian territory and climbed the mountain slope toward Ramallah, north of Jerusalem, as Jordanian artillery shelled the Tel Aviv area, and Egyptian commandos unsuccessfully attempted to reach Lod Airport.

The next day seven Jordanian infantry brigades were stationed on hilltops that provided wide firing range, while in the rear two armored brigades waited in the Jordan Valley. One brigade of the Iraqi Expeditionary Force that had moved across Jordan also reached the valley and took up a position on the east bank of the river. The Jordanians waited with their armored forces in the valley in the belief that the IDF would break through from north to south along the valley, with the intention of cutting off the whole of the West Bank. The IDF had created that deceptive impression on purpose. In the end eight Israeli brigades, three of them armored, broke into the West Bank at six points, and although the Jordanians fought courageously they were unable to stop the Israeli forces pouring in from all sides. Their armored units were forced to a standstill by Israeli jets before they could even reach the battle zones. The armored battles were fought mostly in the northern sector of the front, where the Arab inhabitants were astonished at the sight of the IDF in their towns. In Nablus the crowds waiting in the streets for the Iraqi units to arrive applauded the Israeli tanks, believing them to be Iraqi, and were dumbfounded when the crews began talking to them in Hebrew.

After considerable hesitation, out of fear of an adverse American reaction, Israel decided to take the Old City of Jerusalem. On the morning of the third day of fighting Israeli soldiers reached the Western Wall, which Israel had lost together with the Jewish Quarter of the Old City in the War of Independence. The nation trembled with emotion at the news. With the declaration of cease-fire, IDF forces controlled the whole of the West Bank.

Developments on the Syrian front were different. It was Damascus that had fanned the flames of war and drawn Nasser into actions that Israel regarded as clear-cut aggression. But when fighting broke out on the Egyptian and Jordanian fronts, the Syrians did not lift a finger. Midway through the first day of the war, the Syrians fell silent and thereby proved the value of military alliances in the Arab world. (Damascus had behaved similarly in the 1956 war.) After the Egyptian defeat, however, the Syrians began a heavy bombardment of Israeli settlements in Galilee, and their forces attempted to overrun two settlements in a number of assaults, but were driven off without great difficulty.

The Syrian failure to attack at the outset of the war was a convenient development for the IDF, which could thereby devote its full attention to Egypt and Jordan while keeping a wary eye on the Syrian Golan Heights. The Syrians had six infantry brigades stationed in the Golan, each reinforced by a battalion of tanks. Behind these were positioned another two armored brigades as well as two mechanized regiments. Until the third day of the war the Israeli Command was more concerned with blocking this force than assaulting it, especially since most of the forces of Israel's Northern Command were engaged in fighting on the northern sector of the Jordanian front. The war was coming to an end on the other two fronts, while on the Syrian front the sides made do with an exchange of artillery fire.

It was ironic that the extremist Syrians, who in a way were responsible for the war, were to remain untouched. This was the only instance in which the Israeli civilian population actually demanded that the IDF enter enemy territory and extend the war. When the attack did not come, a delegation from the settlements in the shadow of the Golan Heights made its way to Jerusalem to lobby the Cabinet to approve action against the Syrians. Its members, some from kibbutzim that had suffered repeatedly from Syrian artillery bombardments over the years, insisted that the IDF climb the heights and put an end to their vulnerability once and for all.

But Defense Minister Dayan objected to action against Syria at that stage. He did not want to open another front before the war with Egypt and Jordan was over. He apparently also did not want to strain the patience of the Soviet Union, which was especially sensitive to the fate of the regime in Damascus. The General Staff did give an order to the Northern Command to prepare for battle, but action was postponed because of low clouds that interfered with air activity. It was not until the morning of June 9, the fifth day of the war, that Dayan suddenly changed his mind and instructed the IDF to invade the Golan Heights. Meanwhile, two armored brigades from the Northern Command had completed their missions on the Jordanian front and began to move northward toward the Syrian border.

The war on the Syrian front lasted only twenty-seven hours but it was a hard and bloody confrontation. The terrain imposed difficult conditions, for the Syrians sat on high peaks, which in a number of places rose above Israeli territory like sheer walls. The Syrian emplacement system was especially strong and their concrete bunkers could not be breached by the many bombs dropped by Israeli aircraft. The main Israeli objective was made especially difficult because of terrain, in that the Israelis assumed that the Syrian troop strength would be weakest there.

The attack developed in stages because the IDF could not concentrate all its forces on the front at the start; the only road passing along the Syrian border was subjected to heavy Syrian fire, which interfered with Israeli preparations. Two IDF armored brigades arrived from the Jordanian front and a third came up from the far south. In addition, a paratroop unit, part of which had also fought on the Egyptian front, reached the Northern Command. At the height of the attack, on the second day of battle, the IDF had at its disposal eight brigades, including three armored.

On the first day four breaches were made in the Syrian line by Israeli forces assisted by heavy bulldozers. The advance drew to a halt at nightfall, but the escarpment was in Israeli hands in a number of places. At dawn Israeli pressure increased and new units broke into two other points on the heights. On the first day the Syrian Army had fought splendidly in hand-to-hand combat, but on the second day the rout began. At noon on Saturday, the town of Kuneitra fell into IDF hands. That left the road to Damascus open, and according to the estimate of Major General David Elazar, chief of the Northern Command, thirty-six hours would have been sufficient to reach the Syrian capital, only thirty miles away. But then the Soviets began issuing menacing threats, and Israel decided to rest content with the capture of the Golan Heights.

At 6 P.M. on Saturday June 10, the sixth day of the war, guns fell silent on all fronts. Israel had lost 803 men in this short war, not an intolerable number perhaps, considering the total victory, but a hard blow in terms of the percentage of casualties to the population as a whole. (It would be comparable to the United States losing some 80,000 men in a short war.) The senior command of the IDF, although confident, had estimated before the war that Israel's losses would be substantial. After the war Chief of Staff Rabin said, "I thought we would have thousands of dead and tens of thousands wounded."[4] Mass graves had been prepared in Tel Aviv's parks in anticipation of massive bombing losses, and children were instructed at school in civil-defense procedures in case of air raids and gas attacks.

Twenty-one brigades—nine armored, three mechanized, three paratroop, and six infantry—had made up Israel's order of battle in the Six-Day War. On the Egyptian front in Sinai ten of the brigades were organized into three divisions under major generals Tal, Yoffe, and Sharon. Four of the twenty-one brigades saw service on more than one front. Vessels from the Israeli naval station at Eilat took part in securing the Straits of Tiran, and frogmen penetrated Alexandria Harbor to sabotage Egyptian vessels.

At one point, however, a grave incident in the Mediterranean Sea led to a sharp rise in tension between Israel and the United States. Before hostilities broke out, the U.S. had sent an electronic-espionage ship named the *Liberty* to the area, but when the fighting began the Sixth Fleet command cabled the ship not to approach the shore. However, for some reason this cable—like other, similar ones—never reached the ship, and the *Liberty* entered the combat zone that the Egyptians had declared a closed area. For her part Israel had asked the U.S. to inform her of the location of U.S. ships in the area because Israel had every intention of attacking any ship with hostile intentions. After the *Liberty* was spotted by Israeli planes on the morning of June 8, and as the result of a chain of errors within the Israeli Naval Command including mistaken identification, it was designated Egyptian and an order was issued to attack it. First it was hit by four planes, then three torpedo boats joined the assault. By the time the Israelis realized their mistake, they had caused heavy damage to the *Liberty:* thirty-four American sailors and espionage specialists died either as a result of being hit by Israeli fire or by drowning in cabins that had been sealed off to contain damage. Israel apologized for the incident and subsequently paid reparations to the families of the dead and wounded. After extended negotiations she also agreed to compensate the United States for the damage to the ship, even though she had initially refused to concede that the incident was solely her fault.

What dictated the results of the battle in advance was the Intelligence gap between the sides. The Arab Intelligence services knew little about the IDF, and what they did know—be it the size of forces, or strategy—was evaluated incorrectly. As Dayan commented later:

The Arab [response at the] opening of the war was slow, and they did not make use of the potential force that could be decisive in the first blow. Another mistake was that Nasser overestimated Egypt's military prowess primarily because of the way he regarded the equipment. He saw a lot of sophisticated equipment and became rather intoxicated by it, or confused the equipment with the Army and misjudged its power because he saw it all as one massive weapon.[5]

On the other hand Israel was very well informed about developments in the Arab armies. Israeli Intelligence knew such technical details as where the Arab planes were stationed, even which planes were dummy aircraft. "It was like a game of chess in which, thanks to good Intelligence, we knew the other side's moves in advance,"[6] was how Major General Gavish, the IDF's Commander of the Egyptian front, characterized the Intelligence advantage. Evidence of how far Israeli Intelligence had penetrated was the taping of a conversation on the first day of the war between Hussein and Nasser in which Nasser, quoting false information, tried to draw Hussein into the fray. Israeli Intelligence made the conversation public a few days later, causing considerable embarrassment to the Arabs.

Israel's biggest mistake was the failure to formulate strategic and political objectives before going to war. All efforts were aimed at destroying the menacing concentrations of Arab armies—and no more. No contingency plan existed for establishing a Palestinian state on the West Bank and in Gaza, which would have gone a long way toward defusing the basic issue of the Middle East conflict. Deputy Prime Minister Yigal Allon admitted after the war that it had been a mistake not penetrating far enough into Syria to bring about the establishment of a sympathetic Druze state in southern Syria (including the Golan Heights), which would have provided a buffer between Jordan and Syria. A Palestinian state and a Druze buffer were but two of postwar political possibilities. The gap between the political and military leadership in the preparation of war plans was noticeable in every field. While the army had planned its moves in terms of exact strategy years before, the politicians trailed behind developments on the battlefield.

The Six-Day War changed the face of the Middle East, and the shock of defeat that overcame the Arabs was greater than any setback they had experienced since the beginning of the Arab-Israeli dispute. After their defeat in 1948 the Arabs contended that they had been betrayed by certain rulers who were linked with foreign interests and out for themselves. They clung to the belief that the Israeli victory was not definitive, and the day was not far off when Israel would be routed. The Egyptians explained the subsequent defeat of 1956 by claiming that it was not Israel that had beaten their army, but France and England that made Egypt retreat from Sinai. Yet now a full evaluation was in order.

The capture of the Golan Heights, the West Bank, and the Gaza Strip also changed Israel's strategic situation radically. Until the Six-Day War most of Israel's population centers had been within artillery range of the Arab states; enemy forces could hit vital targets within Israel and disrupt the mobilization of her reserves without even setting foot over the border, and Arab planes could reach the Israeli heartland within minutes as well. After the war the situation was practically reversed: now Cairo was only sixty miles from the Israeli lines in Sinai, with other Egyptians cities within range of IDF artillery, and Israeli forces were located only thirty-five miles from Damascus. Yet rather than having a daunting effect, this realignment of power gave the Arabs an even more pressing reason for war with Israel: the Egyptians and Syrians now felt that they were fighting to defend their native soil and liberate their homeland from Israeli occupation. The War of Attrition following shortly after the Six-Day War, and the Yom Kippur War coming six years later, were proof that the stunning Israeli victory of 1967 had only broadened the circle of hostility. The new territories in Israel's hands may have appeared to enhance her defense posture, but they also provided another reason for waging war against her.

At first many Israelis assumed that the conquered territories would be used as a bargaining card in negotiations with the Arabs, following the formula that Israel would exchange territory for peace. The proposal of Deputy Prime Minister Yigal Allon to relinquish most of the West Bank but retain the Jordan Valley (and agree to an autonomous administration for the Palestinian inhabitants in heavily populated areas) was not even deliberated by the Cabinet. Instead new Defense Minister Dayan confidently announced that Israel was waiting for a telephone call from King Hussein. The call never came; and as if the message weren't clear enough, the Israelis were further disabused of their illusions when the Arab states resolved at their Khartoum Conference not to negotiate with Israel.

That left about one million Palestinians—a significant portion of that nation—under the rule of Israel's military government. Theoretically the new situation opened up opportunities for a different type of dialogue between the two peoples; in reality it soon became clear that instead of entering into a dialogue, the Israelis and Palestinians had merely escalated their level of mutual hostility. The Palestinians quickly organized to renew their terror actions within Israel, and along her borders, and Israeli rule on the West Bank and Gaza Strip took on the character of a classic occupation regime. What's more, as the occupation dragged on a rash of new Israeli settlements began to spring up in the territories, with Arab land expropriated for the purpose. Liberal though its original intent may have been, the military government created a regime very different from the spirit and style of rule in democratic Israel. The Six-Day War had fundamentally altered the crux of the Israeli-Palestinian conflict—and to a large degree had turned it into an internal Israeli problem.

Notes

1. Rabin, in *Ma'ariv,* June 2, 1972.
2. Previously unpublished interview with author, after Six-Day War.
3. Interview with author, originally published in *Ha'aretz,* April 7, 1970.
4. Rabin, *op. cit.*
5. Lecture at IDF Command School, July 19, 1967.
6. Previously unpublished interview with author, 1967.

The Israeli Air Force

THE REPUTATION of the Israeli pilot far precedes him, and for much of the world he symbolizes the Israeli fighter more than any other soldier in the IDF. Due to the quality of its pilots the Israeli Air Force has become its country's major deterrent. Little wonder then that the training methods, instruction, and tactics of the air force have aroused interest among its counterparts the world over.

One key to understanding the uniqueness of the Israeli pilot is found in the personality of Ezer Weizman, one of Israel's first combat pilots and the man who more than any other officer shaped the Israeli Air Force. Weizman commanded the air force for eight years, from 1958 to 1966. During that time he taught his men to excel in aerial combat and imbued them with the conviction that their objective must be attained despite all obstacles: antiaircraft fire, enemy aircraft, or bad weather.

As a former RAF pilot, the slim, tall, glib Weizman stood out among the first pilots, becoming a model for the new men entering the force. During World War II he volunteered for the RAF along with several other Palestinian youth. The British initially were reluctant to assign Palestinians to flying courses, so Weizman served as a driver; later, however, he was one of the first sent to Rhodesia for flight training. On completing the course he was assigned to a British fighter squadron at Fayid, an Egyptian airfield that was captured by Israeli pilots more than twenty years later during in the Six-Day War. During the War of Independence Weizman was one of four pilots—two Israelis, and two Jewish volunteers from the United States and South Africa—who flew Israel's first fighter planes. The planes were Messerschmitts purchased from Czechoslovakia, and they first saw action in the May 19, 1948 attack on an Egyptian column that was approaching Tel Aviv from the south. This mission, in which the South African lost his life, was crucial to the defense of the young state. The astonished Egyptians, who hadn't dreamed that Israel possessed fighter planes, stopped dead in their tracks and never advanced any further northward.

About a year and a half later on January 7, 1949, the last day of the War of Independence, Weizman took part in an air battle with British fighter planes. Units of the British Army were then stationed in the Suez Canal Zone, and a few days earlier Britain had issued an ultimatum to Israel (through the American government) demanding the withdrawal of Israeli forces from Sinai. Britain claimed that according to the terms of the Anglo-Egyptian agreement of 1936 she was obliged to come to Egypt's defense. In the January 7 engagement over Sinai, five British planes were downed in combat or by ground fire. The battle put the finishing touches on the Israeli victory in the War of Independence by displaying the IAF as a force whose pilots did not shrink from battle with the glorious RAF, and were even capable of besting it.

Israel's first day as a sovereign state, May 15, 1948, began with an Egyptian bombing raid on Tel Aviv plus Iraqi and Syrian sorties against settlements in various parts of the country. The Egyptians bombed Tel Aviv sixteen times during the war. At first the Yishuv was at a loss as to how to cope with the Arab air forces; when hostilities broke out in Palestine it had a total of eleven light aircraft and four licensed pilots. Within months of the establishment of the state, however, the number of light aircraft grew to twenty-nine, pilots fifty.

A tremendous effort was made to acquire combat planes wherever they could be found, and for the most part these purchases were made against the laws of the countries involved. Some rather unexpected aid came from Czechoslovakia, whose Communist government agreed not only to train the first Israeli pilots but also to sell Israel arms and old Messerschmitts. An Israeli base was set up near the Czech city of Zatec from where transport planes laden with arms took off for Israel. Israel paid top dollar for the armaments purchased from Czechoslovakia, but they were crucial for her war effort. The four fighters that stopped the Egyptian advance toward Tel Aviv, for example, had come through the Czech connection. Two were lost during the first sorties, but with their aid an Egyptian air attack on Tel Aviv and vicinity had also been brought to a halt (after two

Egyptian bombers were downed). At a later stage Czechoslovakia sold Israel twenty-five British-made Spitfires that had been reconditioned by Czech mechanics.

Czechoslovakia also served as a way station for planes that the Israelis acquired—with the aid of Jewish and non-Jewish friends—in the United States. As a rule these planes refueled at the Israeli base in Czechoslovakia and continued on to Israel—at least until Washington began pressuring the Czech government to close down the base on the grounds that its activities were in violation of the UN Security Council resolution declaring an embargo on arms sales to the Middle East. The base was indeed liquidated, but not before B-17 bombers that Israel had purchased from arms merchants in the U.S. took off, bombing Cairo on their way to Israel. That made it quite clear to the Egyptians that the armed forces of the nascent State of Israel were not a gang of irregulars. Much to the contrary, they confronted a force that was taking shape as a powerful regular army. Later in the war the Israelis bombed Damascus and Amman too.

Yet the Israeli Air Force could not have existed were it not been for the aid of hundreds of volunteers from abroad. All told, 660 volunteers came to Israel during the War of Independence, including pilots, navigators, and mechanics who had acquired rich experience during World War II in the service of the United States, Canada, South Africa, Britain, and other countries. Most of them were Jews, but they were joined by Christians as well, many of them idealists who volunteered as their way of helping the young Jewish state and the survivors of the Holocaust who were streaming into it. Some of these men paid for their ideals with their lives; sixteen of the thirty-one pilots and other air crew killed in the War of Independence were volunteers from abroad. In fact the volunteers initially comprised a majority of the pilots and other professionals, and the lingua franca of the Israeli Air Force was English.

Toward the end of the War of Independence the Israeli General Staff already had at its disposal a bona fide air corps that was taken into account in planning the final operations. Beyond the major transport missions to the beleaguered Negev—in which thousands of men and more than 2,000 tons of arms and equipment were delivered—the IDF executed close to 500 operational sorties during the last two major operations in the Negev (Yoav and Horev).

Weizman emerged after the war as the head and unofficial leader of the Israeli fighter pilots. Once most of the volunteers had left to return to their own countries, the Israeli Air Force had to learn everything on its own. In the 1950s, before the Sinai Campaign, Israeli pilots were not generally accepted for training in other countries. But Weizman persuaded his men that they were moving completely on their own toward becoming one of the best air forces in the world, and that someday other great air forces would come calling to learn solutions that had been already worked out by the Israelis.

The Sinai Campaign

The circumstances of the Sinai Campaign did not allow the Israeli Air Force to exhibit its full capability, for both political and military reasons. The military plan, arrived at in coordination with the French, was designed to create the impression that rather than embarking on an all-out war, Israel was only mounting a large reprisal action in Sinai. Hence the air force was not allowed to preface the ground assault with a shattering blow to Egyptian airfields. Instead it was held in reserve for the second stage of the war, in case the fighting spread. Yet this approach also attested to the government's lack of confidence in the air force's ability to neutralize the Egyptian threat from the air. It was known that the Egyptian Air Force had received thirty IL-28 bombers in the Czech arms deal, and Ben-Gurion feared that they would cause heavy losses to Israel's civilian population. He therefore asked the French to provide two squadrons that would be responsible for defending Israel's air space.

The truth is that it was not only the political echelon that assessed the air force's effectiveness with a healthy dose of skepticism. The debates among the General Staff in the years preceding the Six-Day War were evidence that the commanders of the ground forces similarly failed to appreciate what could be elicited from the air branch. While the air force was demanding that it be accorded its own special headquarters, as a separate entity, the Chief of Staff insisted that it be considered a regular corps subordinate to the Operations branch of the ground forces. This attitude was also reflected in the budgetary allocations for the air force.

Economic and political constraints at the beginning of the 1950s prevented the air force from acquiring the new equipment that was vital to its growth. Forced to purchase whatever was readily available, it ended up with mostly equipment of World War II vintage that was being sold for scrap in Europe. Thus, for example, dozens of old Mosquito fighter-bombers were bought in France for less than $5,000 apiece (and two of the last foreign volunteers to remain in the air force lost their lives transporting them to Israel). The equipment situation remained unsatisfactory until the French era dawned for the Israeli Air Force.

France, in her desire to bolster Israel against the same Arab nationalism that was fueling the Algerian uprising, supplied the Israelis with modern armaments, including many planes. The Ouragan fighters that arrived in 1955 were followed by Mystères and many transport planes. On the eve of the Sinai Campaign Israel received a shipment of thirty-six Mystères, and all told the number of jet planes in Israeli hangars at the outbreak of the war was sixty, out of a total of 175 planes. The Egyptians, by contrast, already had 150 jets, mostly of Russian manufacture. Still, the total number of Israeli pilots in 1956 (210) was greater than the number the Egyptians had managed to train.

The French government complied with Ben-Gurion's request and sent two squadrons to Israel just before the start of the Sinai Campaign. Yet since the Egyptians hardly penetrated Israeli air space (the exceptions being two unsuccessful night sorties), the French pilots did not have very much to do. They took part in dropping water and equipment to a few of the Israeli columns advancing through Sinai, and joined in some of the actions against Egyptian columns in the northern part of the peninsula. However, the second French squadron stationed in Israel (which was equipped with American F-86 planes) flew as far as the Luxor Airfield in Upper Egypt, where it destroyed eighteen Egyptian IL-28 bombers.

It wasn't until the third day of the war that Israeli planes began to play an active role in the fighting in Sinai. The Egyptian Air Force could not throw its full force against the Israeli planes because at this stage the French and British had already begun bombing its airfields. This is undoubtedly the reason why only fifteen clashes were recorded between the Egyptian and Israeli air forces in 1956, and Israel had the upper hand in them all, downing seven Egyptian combat planes. For her part Israel lost fifteen planes total in the war, all but one to ground fire. On the other hand, Israeli planes destroyed hundreds of the Egyptian Army's tanks and vehicles as it withdrew from Sinai.

Of the 1,896 sorties flown during the war, 489 were assault missions in Sinai. Israeli planes also participated in the disabling of the Egyptian destroyer *Ibrahim el-Awal*, which was captured by the Israelis—and mistakenly attacked a British destroyer in the Red Sea. But most important of all, in terms of the air force's development the experiences of the war led to full recognition for the air force's power and established the fact in principle that a strong air force, guided by an aggressive approach and kept on maximum alert for sudden war, is a vital condition of victory.

Weizman had coined the slogan, "The best to aviation," and the cream of Israeli youth joined the air force. Within a few years an elite had coalesced, living almost in isolation, thinking and speaking in its own concepts and jargon. The high percentage of young people from kibbutzim and moshavim was particularly prominent among pilots and other professionals, and far above the ratio for the population at large. Being a fighter pilot was considered a glamour profession among kibbutz youth. At first the kibbutzim took a dim view of this trend for fear that the young men joining the air force would remain in the regular army and become isolated from kibbutz life. But Weizman went out of his way to persuade them that service in the air force was no less important than living in a border settlement. And many young pilots from the kibbutzim adopted his view that they were "pioneers at 40,000 feet," that in contemporary Israel working the land no longer enjoyed exclusivity as the national ideal.

Training

While many are drawn to flight training, few are accepted into the exclusive club of Israeli Air Force pilots. The computers of the defense establishment sort the cards of the eighteen-year-old candidates for the draft, selecting those who seem suitable for flight school. They are then invited to preliminary examinations—even before they are asked whether they are interested in becoming pilots. IDF fliers, like paratroopers, submariners and frogmen, are volunteers, and those accepted to flight school must serve at least five years. Even so, the number of volunteers grew from year to year, so that the selectors have been able to choose the very best out of large groups of talented volunteers.

Over the years, with the accumulation of considerable data about volunteers for the air force and flight school graduates, sociologists and psychologists have attempted to create a profile of those who stand up to all the tests of pilot training. The air force sociologists found that those with the greatest chances of success are mostly native-born

Israelis, from families of European origin. The number of pilots coming from other ethnic backgrounds is small. As yet, however, the experts do not have satisfactory answers as to why these young people are the most successful and the number of native Israelis of Oriental origin so small.

The examination and selection procedures for flight school last several weeks. After the first series of examinations, including rigorous medical checks and psychological and technical-aptitude tests, successful candidates are transferred to the flight school, where they stay for two weeks. At the end of this period only a small percentage of the candidates remain. Those who are unable to form friendships and to live in conditions demanding a communal spirit, for example, are among the first to be eliminated. The next stage of tests is intended to quickly reveal which candidates lack an aptitude for flying. A quick flying course is given in a light plane, not to teach flying but to find out whether a trainee is capable of mastering the plane's controls.

The IDF's flight school is unique in that it trains not only pilots per se, but above all superb aerial warriors. As the Commandant of the school has explained:

We are not training a pilot here but a fighter—a fighter who is also an officer and a commander. I am convinced that it is this emphasis that afterward brings about successful results in aerial encounters with the enemy. We pay special attention to what are important character traits for a warrior: honesty, comradely relationships, mutual assistance. When a pilot leaves here, I know that he'll never abandon a wounded comrade. He'll circle above him to protect him to the last, and he'll come back from an attack and report truthfully. I don't know of a single case in which an Israeli pilot has abandoned a downed comrade. They leave the area only when fuel gives out or when ordered to do so.[1]

The Israeli Air Force makes an effort to assign the best of its pilots to serve as flight-school instructors, for the air force staff insists that educating the future generation of fighters is the domain of the best of the present fighters. Outstanding fighter pilots therefore devote, by rotation, part of their service to instruction—though they still occasionally go out on operational sorties to relieve any sense of frustration.

The pilots' course is divided into five stages with a two-week leave between each stage to lighten the physical and mental pressure. (One of those weeks, however, must be devoted to attending educational lectures.) The first two stages are preparatory, with the emphasis on ground training and on physical and mental conditioning. Special attention is given to mathematics and physics, while cadets also learn meteorology, aeronautics, electronics, navigation, and law. Those who lag behind in theoretical studies are tutored, but anyone who fails a subject is asked to leave the course even if his overall qualifications are excellent.

Next comes the stage in which the hours of flight training are still restricted to light aircraft. The emphasis at this point is primarily on developing physical fitness and stamina. Cadets undergo officers' courses and are then sent to paratroop training. They conduct sea-rescue exercises and learn topography on long marches, including night treks in which each cadet must cover twenty miles alone with a heavy pack. At the end of this period there is a further sorting of cadets. Pilots and navigators, who had been studying together are separated at the beginning of the third stage.

During this third training period, called the primary stage, the pilots concentrate on flying. After a few months they solo and perform aerial acrobatics to learn how to control an aircraft in emergency situations. At the end of this stage many cadets are eliminated. The pruning process in Israel's air force is stricter than that of any other air force in the world. In Egypt and France, for example, most of the cadets who are accepted into a flight course complete it. In the United States, seventy-six percent finish, but in Israel the percentage is much lower. Israeli instructors believe that the chief cause of failure is the inability of many cadets to think properly in the air. It is often shown that a cadet who possesses the required mental alertness on the ground loses this acuity the moment he goes up. Things that he learned well on the ground are forgotten when he is airborne and under pressure.

Rejection from the course is not arbitrary or sudden, however. Every week the cadet receives an evaluation of his progress. If he is failing, the cadet is invited to interview with psychologists and senior commanders, and he is not dropped before the matter has been brought before a special committee of experts, who also offer opinions. In the final stages of the course, the school commandant must approve every cadet rejection.

The fourth stage, known as the basic stage, is the most difficult. Cadets learn night flying, navigation, and flying in formation. Final classification comes at the end of this stage. Some of those eliminated at this point remain pilots but serve in squadrons of light aircraft in communications or as backup pilots.

In the fifth stage, called the progressive stage, the cadets are organized into a sort of combat squadron. Here they are first introduced to the aircraft as a weapons system and begin to operate it as such.

At the end of the course the cadets are assigned to three groups: the best go to combat squadrons, the others to helicopter squadrons or transport planes. They then undergo operational courses and afterward are transferred to regular air force squadrons as student pilots.

There is no doubt that one of the reasons for the high morale in the Israeli Air Force is the family feeling that Ezer Weizman cultivated in the corps when he was its commander. There are those who retain their ties even years after leaving the air force, and at air force parties they can be seen scrutinizing the younger generation. The fighters of MAHAL are also drawn to these affairs. Some of these members of MAHAL come to Israel every year just for the air force's Independence Day party.

The families of Israeli pilots live in their own housing developments, in small houses surrounded by lawns and trees. Personal contacts are important for the women and children. The men go off on operations and the families live through the successes and tragedies together. The wife of a veteran pilot explained:

> The fact that we live together makes it easier for us because our anxieties are common. Sometimes we sit together, a few of the pilots' wives, and count the planes going out. We can hear the planes and see them take off, but we don't know who's flying them and what their target is. We wait in an atmosphere of tension, almost in silence, and when the planes come back we count the engines again to see if all of them have returned.[2]

Other factors contributing to the high morale are a sense of mission and strong motivation. The Israeli pilot feels that he is fulfilling a role of supreme importance in defending his country. One such pilot, twenty-one-year-old kibbutz-born Ram put it this way: "We have no alternative but to be the best. Losing supremacy in the air is the equivalent of having the nation walk into the sea. I don't think it's likely to happen."[3] The Commandant of the flight school takes a broader view and tried to put his finger on the uniqueness of the Israeli pilot in saying, "His motivation is the chief thing, the dominant factor. The main motivation of the young Israeli is a feeling of obligation, a sense of mission, his knowledge that this is a war for our very existence, and that we have no alternative."[4]

"Israel's best defense is in the skies of Cairo," said Ezer Weizman, "and this view has largely determined the tactics and strategies of the air force, as well as the strategic planning of the entire IDF."[5] It was Weizman who established as his prime objective the destruction of the enemy air forces on the ground and all efforts were directed toward this end—training, maneuvers, attack techniques, and the general frame of mind. The approach also required the cultivation of a special kind of combat leader, and Weizman took care to select promising candidates for advanced training while eliminating those who seemed to lack combat initiative.

Like the operational concept, this approach proved itself during the Six-Day War. The air force attack plan had been honed down to the last detail a few years earlier, and each time Intelligence reported a change of any kind in the targeted airfields, a concomitant change was immediately made in the attack plan. The pilots incessantly rehearsed the operational plan, which was called "Moked" (focus), and always knew when changes had been introduced in their targets. The air force command gave much thought both to the timing of the attack and whether to assail all the Arab air forces at once or concentrate first on the Egyptian Air Force, the largest and most menacing of them all. Its decision was to risk concentrating the full force of Israel's air power against the Egyptians in the first wave, on the assumption that the Syrian and Jordanian air forces would react slowly and, even though they would then be on high alert, it would be possible to defeat them at a later stage. Of the 182 fighter-bombers involved in the operation, 160 were used in the first wave of attack against Egypt. Some of the twenty-two others were grounded for technical reasons, so that while the first wave of planes wave were on their way to Egypt, only four Mirages remained behind to defend the skies over Israel proper.

The planes began taking off at 7:17 A.M. on a meticulously planned schedule. The Egyptians' morning alert came to an end at 7 A.M., and their routine operational activities were supposed to start an hour later. When the first Israeli planes simultaneously reached nine airfields in Egypt, many Egyptian pilots were in the midst of eating breakfast, while their commanders were en route to their offices. A few of the

Israeli planes dropped bombs especially developed in Israel to demolish runways. The pilots' orders were to concentrate on the enemy's planes and airfields, and not to go for missile batteries (of which Egypt had twenty-seven) or antiaircraft guns. After dropping their bombs the pilots were to carry out three strafing runs and return home immediately.

The surprise was total, for despite five Egyptian radar stations in Sinai and three more alongside the Suez Canal, none detected the scores of Israeli planes penetrating Egyptian territory. This was because the planes flew as low as possible and jammed Egyptian radar by means of electronic devices. The success of the first wave of attack planes was beyond all expectations. As the last planes of this wave were taking off, some of the first—which had attacked the closest airfields in Sinai—were already returning. The Israelis lost eight planes of various make in this opening gambit, four in dogfights. Five pilots were killed, two fell prisoner, and another three were wounded. At 9:43 A.M. it was already possible to begin the second assault wave.

About an hour and a half earlier Fuga Mystères (jets of French manufacture used for training pilots) had begun attacking targets in northern Sinai in coordination with the IDF's armored assault. Israel had forty-five of these planes and decided to use them in combat despite qualms over employing training planes that lacked ejection seats. During the second phase of the war these planes were transferred to the Jerusalem area to be used against the Jordanian Army, and at the end of the war they also took part in the assault on the Golan Heights.

Since the Jordanian, Syrian, and Iraqi air forces did not go into action, most of the second wave was again directed against the Egyptians. A total of 164 sorties were flown, but this time new targets, such as radar installations, were added to the airfields. It wasn't until 11:40 A.M. that the Syrians woke up and began sending their planes into Israeli airspace, and about an hour later Israeli dispatched aircraft to attack airfields in Syria. At the same time Jordanian planes began to assault Israeli targets in the center of the country, and at 12:45 P.M. the first Israeli planes headed toward airfields in Jordan. Finally, during the early afternoon hours, the Iraqis sent into action the planes they had stationed at H-3, an airfield near the Jordanian border. The Israeli Air Force effected two more waves of assault that day against airfields in Syria and Jordan, and H-3 in Iraq. For the rest of the war the Israeli Air Force concentrated on flying support missions, although it also attacked the missile batteries in Egypt. The only Israeli plane lost to antiaircraft missile in the Six-Day War was downed during one of these attacks.

All together the Israeli fighter-bombers executed 3,279 sorties (an average of 3.4 sorties per plane on the first day alone) and attacked twenty-eight airfields. The Arab air forces lost a total of 469 planes: 391 on the ground, 60 in dogfights, 3 to antiaircraft fire, with 15 accidents. Yet the Israeli Air Force also paid a heavy toll for its stunning great victory: 24 of its pilots were killed (8.4 percent of the total number of pilots in 1967), another 7 fell prisoner, and 18 were wounded, while 23 planes were damaged and 46 others irretrievably lost.

In summing up the victory in the Six-Day War, Ezer Weizman commented:

It's no secret that the talent of the nation is to be found in the Israeli Air Force. We are a sensible and talented people—as evidenced by our contribution to culture, science, and religion—and within the military these talents can be fully utilized. . . .

The aircraft is above all a tool of war, but one that takes considerable intelligence to use. To operate such a complex weapons system everything must be done at maximal speed. And for this the operator must have special traits and talents. I do not say we are the Chosen People; other nations also have fine air forces. But the fact is that the Israeli pilot stands out more than most others.

It was natural for a new, small state . . . to look to the United States or the Soviet Union, England or France [for direction] as countries rich in air experience, especially after the Second World War. Many of our people wanted to know exactly what the tactical theories, systems of maintenance, and operations were in these major air forces, but some of us understood the danger in this, for what's good for one country is not necessarily appropriate for another. We are able to learn from others, but we didn't copy their ways. We knew how to apply what we had learned according to our needs, although in the beginning we had an understandable tendency to copy others because of our paucity of experience.

Among the volunteers who came during the War of Independence were many who brought along a rich store of theories and experience of their own. But some of them failed to understand that systems of organization and operation derive from a nation's way of thinking. . . . The moment the volunteers began trying to forge the image of the air force, there were conflicts with the Israelis. We knew that not everything that may have been good for them, in terms of tactics or technique, was good for us, as well.

Over the years we learned to live by the maxim of quality over quantity. It was always important for us not to sacrifice standards. I remember that in 1960 I had to grant a pilot's certificate to one lone pilot. He received his wings in my office because there was no passing-out parade. I wasn't prepared to forgo standards. I preferred to have no one complete the course—or only one man—rather than lower the standard for the sake of holding a passing-out parade.[6]

The War of Attrition was radically different from all its predecessors in that the air force went into intensive action only after it became apparent that the ground forces were at a loss to stop the heavy artillery barrages coming from the other side of the Suez Canal. The Israeli Air Force had been sent into action earlier in the war, but not on the Egyptian front; instead its planes had attacked terrorist bases on the Jordanian front each time Israeli settlements were shelled. The air force did not go into action on the Egyptian front until July 20, 1969, but from then until the declaration of a cease-fire more than a year later hardly a day passed without its planes going out on operational missions. In the course of that year the air force flew thousands of sorties in its role as the IDF's flying artillery. It also participated in a number of joint operations, such as the capture and transport of a sophisticated (Soviet-made) radar facility in Egypt to Israel.

It was during the War of Attrition that the air force first contended with a sophisticated network of Soviet-made antiaircraft missiles, which were concentrated along the Egyptian front. At first they were armed with the older SAM-2 missiles, but in the course of the war the Soviet Union supplied more up-to-date systems. The Israeli Air Force had first faced Egyptian missile batteries during the Six-Day War, but the number of operational batteries then had been few, whereas in the War of Attrition there were literally batteries by the scores. In effect Egypt's airspace had become a testing ground where both superpowers were displaying enormous interest. While the Soviet Union was supplying Egypt and Syria with generous quantities of antiaircraft and other equipment, the United States had begun to supply Israel with sophisticated combat aircraft. The Israeli Air Force had begun to assimilate the first American planes after the Six-Day War, and in the course of fighting the War of Attrition it received and absorbed about a hundred aircraft each year.

During the War of Attrition the Israeli Air Force reached three new high points. The first was in coping with Soviet missiles. The Egyptians were trying to move dozens of missile batteries up to the

Suez Canal in order to protect their artillery and ground forces there, but the Israeli Air Force prevented this shift forward. In the course of its attacks on the missiles, many batteries were destroyed and thousands of Egyptians—soldiers and laborers brought in to prepare the dugouts for the missiles—were killed. The upshot was that the Egyptians proved unable to move their missiles to the vicinity of the canal until a cease-fire was called.

Another first for the Israeli Air Force was reached in January 1970 after the first Phantoms had been delivered by United States. Israel decided to initiate deep-penetration bombing in Egypt as a way of inducing Nasser to accept a cease-fire and end his War of Attrition. Operation Florescence (Pricha) began on January 7 and included the bombing of army camps and headquarters, missile batteries, radar stations, and other military targets in the Cairo region and the Egyptian heartland. On the one hand these attacks left the Egyptians deeply shaken, but ultimately they had an escalating effect for it was because of these raids that the Soviets answered Cairo's request for full missile units (as opposed to just advisors) as well as five combat squadrons. In effect they assumed responsibility for the air defense of the Egyptian heartland, though after a while they also tried to prevent Israeli planes from staging attacks around the Gulf of Suez as well. Once the Soviets had committed the forces there was no way to avert a clash between Israeli and Russian pilots.

When the inevitable occurred on July 30, 1970, in Egyptian airspace close to the Gulf of Suez, the confrontation was not accidental because the Soviet military command in Egypt was anxious to test Israel's declaration that the IDF would not be deterred if Russian soldiers joined Egyptian units in the War of Attrition. The fact is that the Soviets were looking for combat contact with Israeli pilots, and it seemed clear that had Israel backed down from a fight Russian audacity would have increased. But Israel accepted the challenge, sending crack pilots flying American Phantoms and French Mirages to attack Egyptian radar stations. The Phantoms assailed their targets while the Mirages provided cover. It was a classic trap and the Russians fell right into it. Israeli Intelligence determined that if MIGs appeared over the Gulf of Suez, they would be flown by Russian pilots, for it was known that in the division of labor between the Egyptians and the Russians the latter were responsible for the air defense of the front's southern sector.

When the MIGs appeared the Mirage pilots outmaneuvered them

handily, downing one at close range with cannon fire. A second MIG was hit in the tail by a Sidewinder air-to-air missile and plunged to the ground. Then came the turn of the Phantoms, which also downed two MIGs, again both with Sidewinder missiles. Only two parachutes could be seen after the MIGs had been hit; the two other Russian pilots had apparently been killed. At that point the rest of the Russian pilots seemed to panic; their formation was disorderly, and a minute or so later they beat a hasty retreat.

The Israelis were ordered not to pursue them, but before returning to base they still had to complete their mission: the destruction of an Egyptian radar station. An hour after the clash, when the Israeli pilots related their experience at a debriefing session, they described it as a routine aerial battle in which they had no difficulty in downing four planes. (Only later did it come out that a fifth MIG had been hit and subsequently exploded over Egypt.) They characterized the enemy planes as coming into battle ". . . like a bull charging a red rag. They were like ripe fruit waiting to be picked."[7]

As a footnote to the incident, the results of the battle prompted an ironic reaction from the Egyptian pilots. Rather than empathize with their Russian colleagues on their defeat, they reveled at the apparent proof that they were not such bad pilots after all—or at least no worse than their Russian instructors. Moreover they finally had grounds to refute the Soviet contention that Egyptian pilots were not up to flying more sophisticated planes.

Like the other arms of the IDF, the air force was caught off guard by the Yom Kippur War. Its commanders failed to foresee that the Arabs were prepared for an all-out war in 1973. Quite the contrary, the air force's victories in the War of Attrition and subsequent air battles (such as the clash with Syria on September 13, 1972, in which twelve Syrian aircraft were downed) only reinforced the appraisal that the Arabs would not go to war. On Saturday morning, October 6, when it became known that the Arabs would launch an attack that very day, the Chief of Staff proposed that the air force carry out a preemptive strike. The Prime Minister did not approve this suggestion, but in retrospect it is clear that even if it had come to pass such a move would have neither prevented the war nor altered its outcome. For it was to be mounted against the Syrians alone, and because of the cloud cover in the area of the Golan Heights it would have been confined to airfields in the heart of Syria. After the Chief of Staff's proposal was rejected, ground crews began to change the armaments on the planes—and that was when the Arab attack began. The upshot was that many planes were either unarmed at that moment or were still armed with bombs, which impeded their maneuverability as interceptors.

Turning the tables, the Arabs were the ones to launch a surprise attack in this war, and they too opened with an air strike. In Sinai the Egyptians flew 120 sorties in the initial hours of the war, while the Syrians carried out some sixty sorties over the Golan Heights and the Upper Galilee. Both caused little damage, however, and the Egyptians paid a heavy toll; among their losses were twenty helicopters carrying commandos into Sinai. From the standpoint of the Israeli Air Force, however, the main difference between the Yom Kippur War and its predecessors was that the corps failed to implement its operational plan. The prevailing assumption had been that before or immediately upon the outbreak of any war it would be possible to destroy the Arab missile systems. That would accord the air force freedom of action at the front and the ability to aid the ground forces from the very outset of the conflict. But the assumption proved to be unwarranted.

During the first phase of the Arab onslaught, the air force had to deal with the enemy's air attack. Then it was sent to hold off the Syrian armored forces, which were headed for the Jordan River, and had they not been stopped would have broken through to the Galilee. The next day when Israeli planes mounted their first attack on the enemy's missile batteries the air force commanders realized that their assault plan was no longer feasible. At first they had intended to attack the missile batteries on the Egyptian front, but because of the Syrian armored advance their attention shifted to the Golan Heights. The attack on the Syrian missiles failed, however—and at the cost of six Phantoms. In fact the Syrian missile network, which included many batteries of advanced SAM-6 missiles, was hardly damaged during the war. The air force's recovery of its effectiveness against the missiles did not come until almost the end of the war, and even then it was primarily on the Egyptian front.

The Arab air forces had made great strides since the Six-Day War and the subsequent War of Attrition, constructing hundreds of cement hangars to protect their planes and adding many new airfields to their network. Egypt alone had twenty-five airfields, each with a number of runways. In terms of Intelligence, they augmented their own information with reports from radar stations in Jordan and

Lebanon. And to reinforce their capability in combat, squadrons from Iraq, Libya, Algeria, and even North Korea were stationed in Egypt and Syria. Even greater progress had been made in their antiaircraft systems (both missiles and guns). Egypt had 150 missile batteries of various kinds, while the Syrians had thirty-six. The Egyptians fired off about a thousand missiles during the war, but they lost thirty-two of their batteries. The Syrians, on the other hand, lost only three batteries, sustaining damage to five others.

Whereas the focus of the Egyptian and Syrian air forces during the second stage of the war was on defending their airfields, the Israelis embarked upon the strategic bombing of Syria, targeting power stations, oil refineries, and the Syrian General Staff headquarters. Yet the number of sorties flown against strategic targets was barely more than a hundred—a tiny percentage of the combat sorties which numbered 11,223. Considering that high figure it should not be surprising that the Yom Kippur War was marked by an increase in the number of dogfights (117 as compared to ninety-seven throughout the War of Attrition and sixty in the Six-Day War). They resulted in the downing of 227 enemy planes at the cost of six Israeli planes and another nine lost to ground fire during these engagements. On the other hand, the Israeli Air Force lost sixty planes in the course of extending support to the ground forces. No less than thirty-one of its pilots and navigators were killed during these support missions. Altogether the air force lost 102 planes in the Yom Kippur War. This was a high price to pay for victory, but it must be said that once again the Israeli Air Force defeated its adversaries handily.

The period following the Yom Kippur War was devoted primarily to evaluating the lessons of the war and assimilating modern equipment. In analyzing its performance during the war, the air force concentrated mainly on its experience against the Russian-manufactured missile batteries. This was particularly important because after the war the Russians supplied the Arab armies with replacement missile systems, while the United States agreed to supply Israel with such advanced aircraft as the F-15 (first delivered in December 1976) and the F-16 (first delivered in July 1980), in addition to Hawkeye radar planes. The strategic balance became less clear-cut, however, when U.S. began supplying modern aircraft to Saudi Arabia, and then pledged to provide sophisticated planes to Egypt after the signing of the peace treaty with Israel. That treaty also brought about a basic change in the appraisals and deployment of the Israeli

Air Force. With her withdrawal from the Sinai Peninsula, Israel evacuated all the airfields in that area, making overcrowding at remaining air bases acute. What's more, the air force lost an important area for maneuvers and pilot training.

In addition to assimilating modern equipment, the Israeli Air Force took part in a number of impressive operations following the Yom Kippur War. On July 4, 1976 its planes transported the troops that liberated the Israelis being held hostage by Arab and German terrorists at the Entebbe Airport in Uganda. On June 7, 1981 the air force was sent on another distant mission: this time F-16 fighter-bombers set out for Iraq to destroy the atomic reactor that had just been completed. Israel was convinced that Baghdad intended to develop nuclear weapons, and the destruction of the reactor was carried out as a deterrent measure. By flying low over the Saudi and Iraqi deserts the planes were able to reach their objective undetected, and the Iraqis were so completely taken by surprise that they failed to respond.

Beginning in 1979 a series of air battles took place between the Israeli and Syrian air forces for control of the skies over Lebanon. The Israeli Air Force regularly attacked PLO targets in Lebanon, and from time to time the Syrians intervened as a sign that they were not abandoning the arena to Israel. The first time the Syrians intercepted their planes the Israelis sent up their F-15 aircraft, according them a considerable advantage; as a matter of fact, the Israelis clearly had the upper hand in all of these engagements.

The result of these clashes were merely a pale hint of the performance that the Israeli Air Force would deliver in the 1982 war in Lebanon, where it proved just how well it had learned the lessons of the Yom Kippur War regarding the necessity of overcoming Soviet missile systems. Within a matter of hours the Israeli Air Force succeeded in destroying Syrian missiles deployed in Lebanon's Bekaa Valley and along the Syrian-Lebanese border. Various kinds of planes were integrated into the attack, some activating electronic-warfare devices and others assaulting the batteries with "smart" bombs. At the same time the IDF's artillery came into play by mounting a barrage on some of the batteries. The air force also scored an impressive achievement in the air battles that developed during the assault on the missile batteries, as well as in other confrontations: while ninety-one Syrian planes were shot down in dogfights, the Israelis did not lose so much as a single aircraft.

Notes

1. Previously unpublished interview with author, 1970.
2. Previously unpublished interview with author, 1973.
3. *Ibid.*
4. *Ibid.*
5. Ze'ev Schiff, *Knafayim Me'al Suez* [Phantoms over the Nile] (Haifa: Shikmona, 1970), p. 92.
6. Interview with author, originally published in Schiff, *op. cit.,* pp. 146–150.
7. Previously unpublished interview with author, 1973.

The War Against
Terrorism

SINCE ITS ESTABLISHMENT the IDF has needed to employ two very different combat styles: the more standard approach, waged against regular armies, and guerrilla warfare. The prime military threat to Israel was obviously from the regular Arab armies. But at the same time the IDF has had to come up with an effective answer to the guerrilla warfare and terrorist activities perpetrated by the various Palestinian organizations. While terrorism and guerrilla warfare certainly are not capable of overwhelming Israel, they do place a heavy burden on the state and its citizens. Hence the IDF has devoted considerable time and energy to this subject, and many units are trained especially to perform under guerrilla-warfare conditions or to act against terrorist squads that attack civilians. Also involved in the war against terrorism are the Border Guard, the General Security Service *(Shin Bet),* and the Mossad, which is responsible for covert activities outside Israel. Working together, they have had a considerable impact in a military sense, but the Palestinian organizations scored impressive gains politically through this struggle—most importantly, perhaps, by focusing international attention on the Palestinian issue.

In flights of rhetoric Arab leaders have been known to speak of waging a hundred-years' war against Israel. In fact that war has already passed its centennial, for the guerrilla struggle against the Jewish community began long before Israel or the IDF existed, and even before the Yishuv was first organized for defense. The terrorist groups are not an innovation of the period following the Six-Day War; they have tread a well-worn path whose beginnings date back to the 1880s with renewed Jewish settlement in Palestine. Only the tactics have changed with the circumstances: at first assaults on settlements and the destruction of orchards and crops were the major perils; now the approach has changed to include hijacking or blowing up civilian aircraft, posting letter bombs, or taking athletes or schoolchildren hostage.

The first round of the war broke out when Jews began to move out of the mixed Arab-Jewish towns and established independent agricultural settlements. This migration marked the beginning of the struggle for the land of Palestine—in both senses of the term. In those early years hardly a veteran Jewish settlement escaped attack by its Arab neighbors. Petach Tikvah was assaulted by Arab bands in 1886, but the settlers managed to drive the assailants back. Other settlements were less successful in warding off their attackers, since no organized group or plan for self-defense existed, and murder, plunder, and the destruction of crops were common for these early settlers. The Jews turned to the Ottoman authorities for protection but their appeals were either denied or simply ignored. This situation gave rise to the Shomrim and Hashomer organizations (discussed earlier) and finally to the Haganah, the direct forebear of the IDF.

Between these early years of settlement and the establishment of the State of Israel there were three more outbursts of terrorism and guerrilla warfare. They took the form of flare-ups in which the fighting was haphazard and hostilities subsided before reaching any decision. The first wave, the Arab riots of 1920–21, was ignited by religious as well as political motives. Activity was directed against the Jewish communities in the major cities—Jerusalem, Jaffa, Tel Aviv—but soon spread to the agricultural settlements as well. By 1920, however, the Haganah had been established and was able to provide some measure of defense.

Eight years later a second wave of terror engulfed Palestine, and the Jews were compelled to abandon quite a few of their outlying settlements. The prime motivation for the 1929 disturbances was again religious, with the outbreak of violence running parallel to the attempt by Arabs in Jerusalem to prevent Jews from praying at the Western (Wailing) Wall. Rioting spread to Hebron, Nablus, Gaza, Tulkarem, Jenin, and Beit Shean, with Jews fleeing these mixed towns. Yet once again the violence died down as abruptly as it had begun.

It was seven years before hostilities erupted again, this time in the form of the Arab Revolt, which was considered the most serious of the pre-statehood waves of terrorism. Beginning in April 1936, it lasted until the outbreak of World War II and the advent of warfare marked by more forceful Arab guerrilla attacks, although by then the Jewish forces had also upgraded their countermeasures. Moreover, the British Army stood squarely behind the Yishuv this time, since the Arab Revolt was also directed against the British mandate administration.

The first wave of terrorism after the establishment of the State of Israel followed the War of Independence, and was described earlier. It lasted until the Sinai Campaign of 1956, after which Israel enjoyed nine years of relative quiet. But then came another outbreak of terrorism, erupting in January 1965 and reaching its climax in the Six-Day War of June 1967, perpetrated by Yasser Arafat and his comrades in the new Fatah organization. Fatah had first sent forth shoots as far back as the early 1950s when Arafat began organizing Palestinian students in the universities of Cairo and Alexandria. Following the Sinai Campaign Arafat and most of his collaborators left Egypt for Persian Gulf countries, where they found work as teachers and engineers.

The Fatah organization itself was founded in 1958. (The name is essentially an acronym for Movement for the Liberation of Palestine, but the initials are rendered backward because forward they spell the Arabic word for sudden death while reversed they spell victory.) In that same year it began to publish a journal in Beirut after some of its members resettled in Lebanon; others moved to Algeria when it achieved independence in 1962. In this formative period Fatah also became an instrument in the ongoing inter-Arab strife. Its first ties were established with Syrian Intelligence, under the control of the Syrian Ba'ath Party, which was engaged in a rivalry with Egyptian President Nasser and used his reluctance to enter into a military confrontation with Israel over the Palestinian issue as a weapon to discredit him.

In January 1965, with Syria's permission, Fatah initiated sabotage and terrorist actions within Israel. Its leaders had come to the conclusion that the rulers of the Arab states were not really interested in fighting Israel, and that the joint Arab decision to divert the sources of the Jordan River, for example, was their way of evading a war, not provoking it. By their terrorist actions the Fatah activists hoped to generate such a sharp rise in the tension between Israel and the Arab states that it would eventually explode into war. Their first act was against Israel's National Water Carrier, and when it was aborted the saboteurs retreated into Jordanian territory hoping that Israel would revert to an earlier pattern and mount reprisal actions against her eastern neighbor.

Fatah's military actions during this period for the most part were highly amateurish. Its men avoided clashing with Israeli forces and acted only against civilian targets; the consequent damage to Israel was minimal and number of casualties very low. The Israelis responded vigorously nevertheless—thereby falling right into Fatah's trap. After nine years of relative quiet, Israel feared that she was being cast back to the days of the fedayeen; unlike the situation then, however, not a single Arab state actually supported Fatah's activities. Syria's backing was essentially no more than moral support (no Syrians, for example, were allowed to take part in its activities), while the Egyptians and Jordanians in fact were working against Fatah, doing their best to prevent its members from crossing the border into Israeli territory. Even so the Jordanians were not spared Israel's wrath, which mounted until an armored force dispatched against the Jordanian village of Samua in November 1966 blew up dozens of houses and the nearby police station. At the same time Israel lured the Syrians—known to be encouraging Fatah—into punishing aerial battles.

So it was by petty guerrilla acts that Fatah succeeded in drawing Israel and the Arab states into the Six-Day War. Until that conflict the members of Fatah spoke in terms of a popular war of liberation, comparing themselves to the fighters of the Algerian FLN and the Viet Cong. The analogy was specious, however, if only because the Arabs in Israel itself did not rise in revolt. And although Fatah fighters made no military gains to speak of, they managed to heat up the atmosphere in the region because Israel's hypersensitivity and speed the deterioration toward war.

The Fatah achieved its objective in 1967, but the outcome of the war it sparked was very different from what Arafat had in mind. Rather than overrun the State of Israel the Arab armies were roundly defeated—and the entire area that had been British mandate Palestine prior to 1948 fell under the control of the State of Israel. Yet this turnabout created the conditions for a different type of guerrilla war against Israel. For the first time since the inception of the Israeli-Palestinian conflict, Israel controlled the whole of Palestine and thus a major part of the Palestinian people. Fatah could operate among these hundreds of thousands of Palestinians to recruit a broad-based membership; its leaders envisioned establishing bases in the mountains of the West Bank and taking cover among the masses of refugees in the teeming camps of the Gaza Strip.

After the ignominious defeat of the Arab armies, the new generation of fedayeen were looked upon as the heroes of the Arab world. As the first to act against the IDF—albeit in extremely modest operations—Fatah and the other Palestinian organizations that emerged over the years agitated among the Palestinian masses and enlisted many Palestinians living outside Israeli-controlled territories (e.g., in Jordan and Lebanon) in their ranks. From a relatively small and marginal group, Fatah grew into a mass movement with its own military branch; and in 1969 Yasser Arafat rose from leader of a band of saboteurs to head of the Palestine Liberation Organization (after Nasser enabled him to wrest control of that most important of Palestinian forces).

The Arab countries began to supply Fatah with an abundance of arms, and funds flowed into its coffers (and those of the other Palestinian organizations) from the oil states, sometimes as a way of buying insurance policies to forestall terrorist actions against their leaders or regimes. These funds were one of the primary factors behind the founding of new Palestinian groups, as existing organizations split into ever smaller factions and new ones sprang up like mushrooms after rain. As their ties with the Eastern bloc (and particularly the Soviet Union) grew stronger they received arms from that quarter as well. Still, only a few of these movements actually sent their people out to fight the Israelis, while the stream of funds corrupted many leaders, who camped in luxury hotels rather than on the battlefield. Slowly these organizations also were drawn into the endless inter-Arab squabbles, on which their leaders wasted much of their time.

As forces conducting a war of liberation based on guerrilla tactics and clandestine activity, the constituent organizations of the PLO were unlike any similar movement in the past. From 1967 onward they hardly wanted for anything and certainly could not be characterized as collections of destitute guerrillas: their stores were filled with the most advanced weaponry, and they had an ample reservoir of manpower once the Palestinians began taking pride in the fact that they finally had an organization that was prepared to act. Conditions were to the PLO's advantage from a geographic standpoint as well, for the Arab states were willing to grant them bases on their territory as long as they obeyed the laws of the land. Naturally the Palestinian leaders pledged to do so, although it soon emerged—especially in the countries with weaker governments—that their promises were worthless. Egypt and Syria usually prevented the Palestinians from carrying out operations over their borders, but in Jordan and Lebanon the Palestinian organizations behaved as they pleased. They also benefited from the fact that Israel chose to pursue a liberal policy by keeping the bridges over the Jordan River open to traffic. It was possible to smuggle arms via this route, send trained fighters into Israel, and convey orders to cells in the territories.

Despite these advantages the military achievements of the Palestinian organizations were dubious. Certainly they fell far short of constituting a genuine military threat to the state (the number of Israeli casualties from the Palestinian guerrila and terrorist actions was less than five percent of the casualties from traffic accidents in Israel), but they cost Israel financially and created a certain degree of discomfort.

The reason for this mediocre performance was above all the fact that for all their efforts, Fatah and the other organizations failed to establish a broad base for action within the territory controlled by Israel. The guerrillas hiding in the caves and gullies of the West Bank were quickly flushed out and overwhelmed by Israeli forces. Units of this kind were incapable of surviving in the field for more than a few days or a week at most, and consequently they were more preoccupied with establishing means of escape than with taking rigorous measures against Israeli targets. (Yasser Arafat was himself active in the West Bank for a short while after the war but then was forced to flee to Jordan.) The fact that the West Bank is a relatively small, unforested area, and that Israeli forces were able to become thoroughly familiar with it very quickly sealed the fate of the battle. Once Israel transferred a number of IDF training bases to the West Bank there were always soldiers training in open areas, further limiting the movement of Palestinian squads. In the Gaza Strip actions were even more difficult to stage because of the even smaller area involved and also because the strip no longer bordered on an Arab state (the whole of the Sinai Peninsula being in Israeli hands).

The Palestinian organizations were therefore forced to change their tactics and place the emphasis on building clandestine cells among the population in the occupied territories. This strategy was predicated on the assumption that the members of the cells would receive their training and equipment from across the border and that from time to time squads of Palestinian fighters would steal over the frontier and find cover among local residents. Yet cell organizers came up against great difficulties at this stage too. Most residents of the West Bank and Gaza, although willing to enlist in cells, were not prepared to actually fight. Fewer still were willing to put their lives on the line in spectacular operations or direct attacks on vital Israeli targets; their actions tended more to take the form of planting bombs in public places, such as supermarkets and movie theaters, or just depositing them on heavily trafficked streets.

What proved to be the ruin of these terrorist cells was not just inexperience with the rigors of clandestine life but the readiness with which so many supplied their interrogators with information when caught, and the ease with which they betrayed their comrades. It was enough for the Israelis to latch on to one short loose end and promptly unravel an entire secret network. Too, the cells often were imprudently large, so that the arrest of one member immediately led to the exposure of many—sometimes dozens—more. Typically the lifespan of these cells was short, so short in fact that sometimes they were exposed while still organizing, before even receiving arms or embarking on sabotage missions.

The percentage of terrorist acts traced to their perpetrators was very high (far higher, for example, than the percentage of common crimes solved by the Israeli police), and the Shin Bet arrested (or at least traced) the culprits relatively quickly. To avoid being caught, most members of the terrorist squads would flee over the border after a few actions, successful or otherwise. As a result the pool of trained manpower operating in the occupied territories was depleted in almost no time.

Once the Palestinians shifted the center of their military effort outside territory occupied by Israel, within they began to stress demonstrations and strikes, which were sometimes more trying for Israel than Palestinian military exploits. For such civil unrest focused international attention on the Middle East and it was one of the reasons for the reversal of the clichéd David-and-Goliath equation so frequently applied to Israel. Rather than being perceived as the weak but plucky little state braving the threat of annihilation, Israel found that her defeat of the Arab armies and control over hundreds of thousands of Arab civilians deflected public sympathy to the newly weak and oppressed party: the Palestinians. At the same time, the disorders in the territories created a sense of discomfort and political ferment among the Israeli public—a feeling that likewise penetrated the ranks of the army, although it was not expressed in any special show of protest such as resistance to the draft or insubordination. There was a widespread feeling that what was initially referred to as the benevolent occupation of the West Bank and Gaza Strip would inevitably debase the moral fiber of Israeli society. Perhaps for this very reason, Israeli combat personnel generally refused to accept posts in the military government.

The seat of Palestinian military activity had shifted to Jordan by the end of the 1960s, where despite the opposition of the authorities many of the Palestinian fighters set up bases along the cease-fire line with Israel while others established camps in the heart of the country, even headquartering at Amman. From these bases they began to shell Israeli settlements, mine roads near the border, and dispatch sabotage squads into the West Bank. The IDF's countereffort, primarily aimed at thwarting the infiltration of these squads into the area under Israel's control, was based on a defensive network of barbed-wire fence, mines, outposts, and special "smudge paths" along the length of the frontier with Jordan. Bedouin trackers recruited into the IDF readily picked up the trail of anyone who crossed those paths, while elite paratroop units stationed in the Jordan Valley—working in collaboration with the trackers and with the aid of helicopters—developed tactics for hunting them down. The infiltrators' objective was to cross the Jordan River and the security fence at night and reach the mountainous area of the West Bank, there to melt into the local population. Yet only a handful of the squads managed to evade the Israeli patrols; countless others were hunted down and captured or killed. The Palestinian losses along the Jordanian frontier were enormous for negligible military gains.

The Jordanians paid a high price too, for Israel did not stop at defensive measures within her borders or the territory under her control; she lashed out at the Palestinian bases in Jordan with both ground and air attacks. The Jordanian Army was forced to respond to these incursions, and as the fighting spread the farmers of the Jordan Valley abandoned their homes and crops, leaving this flourishing area—which had been designated as a development zone—to deteriorate into a wasteland. One of the larger Israeli raids was executed in March 1968 by a combined force of armor and paratroops that attacked the large Palestinian concentration in the town of Karameh. Hundreds of people were killed or taken prisoner, but the IDF paid dearly too: twenty-nine of its men were killed, mostly by Jordanian artillery fire.

On the surface it appeared that the Jordanians and the Palestinians were working in concert, at least from a military standpoint. Yet a clash was inevitable. The larger their military presence in Jordan grew, the greater the sheer impudence of the Palestinian organizations toward the Jordanian government. It was easy to see that they were building a state within a state, and King Hussein feared that left to their own devices they would topple his regime and usurp his country altogether. After four hijacked American and European jetliners had been flown to northern Jordan and blown up by Palestinian terrorists, bitter fighting broke out between the Jordanian Army and the Palestinian irregulars. These battles escalated into a full-blown civil war in September 1970 in which the Jordanians (whose ranks included many Palestinians) crushed the insurgents in a series of battles that cost the Palestinians thousands of lives. In an ironic twist, scores of surviving Palestinian fighters escaped over the Jordan into Israeli-held territory and surrendered to the IDF.

The one state that took measures on behalf of the beleaguered Palestinians was Syria, which moved more than four divisions into northern Jordan. But they too were blocked by the Jordanians and quick to retreat when they discovered that Israel was massing forces on their flank. The move had been made at the request of the White House, conveyed to Israel by Henry Kissinger with the explanation that it had already been coordinated with King Hussein and that the United States would take it upon herself to defend Israel in the event that the Kremlin intervened. The episode showed just how complex the weave of subtle and often shifting interests really is in the Israeli-Arab conflict and how some of Arab players can reverse roles and even obliquely cooperate with Israel or draw upon her strength.

The Jordanian civil war ended in a stunning defeat for the Palestinians and the expulsion of thousands of their fighters, with others leaving of their own volition. Most went to Lebanon, where they established new bases and began to build yet another state within a state. From then on their terrorist activity was directed against Jordanian personages as well as Israeli. Under cover of a new organization called Black September, Palestinian terrorists murdered Jordanian Prime Minister Wasfi Tel while he was visiting Cairo. Tel's assassination sent tremors through the Jordanian regime, and one result was Jordan's willingness to cooperate with Israeli security in pursuing

Palestinian terror squads and liquidating their commanders at various locations outside the Middle East.

The defeat of the Palestinian organizations on the battlefield incited them more and more to classic terrorist actions. They resorted to terror not, as many experts claim, as the "weapon of the weak," and they did not exercise it solely against Israel (as that claim implies). Rather, many of the victims of Palestinian terror actions were other Arabs, including Palestinians. In the absence of a tradition of democratic decision making in Arab society, there evolved a convention of settling issues by other means, namely, naked violence. Palestinian society was especially noted for this trait, and it seemed to come out most prominently against the background of its struggle with the rival—Jewish—national movement.

As far back as the 1930s, thousands of people had been murdered in the course of the ideological debate between the two main Palestinian camps (the Husseini and Nashashibi families, and their supporters). For decades thereafter the Palestinians continued to bring enormous damage upon themselves by resorting to terror. This tradition of self-abuse peaked with the murder of leading personages (such as King Abdullah of Jordan and Wasfi Tel), but it was no less operative in the liquidation of Palestinian figures considered to be too moderate in their attitude toward Israel or Israelis (including such PLO leaders as Said Hammami, Issam Sartawi, and Fahed Kawasmeh).

Palestinian terrorism confronted Israel with a number of fundamental as well as moral problems. First, the indiscriminate assaults on civilians, the planting of explosives in public places, and the execution of hostages, including children, raised the question of imposing the death penalty on the terrorists who adopted these methods. While many Israelis support the institution of the death penalty—which Israel does not apply for criminal offenses—successive Israeli governments have opposed it on the grounds that it is not a deterrent at any rate, that its adoption would only exacerbate the enmity between Israel and the Palestinians, and that it would inevitably create a gallery of martyred heroes for the Palestinian national movement. There was also the consideration that exercising the death penalty would further imperil the lives of any Israelis who might be taken hostage by Palestinian terrorists in the future.

The decision not to impose the death penalty, even on terrorists responsible for the massacre of innocent people, did not make life any easier for Israel's leaders: incarcerating terrorists only encouraged Palestinian organizations to take hostages as a card to play for their release. More than once Israel was forced to yield to this demand, although at a very early stage a number of principles were established for handling incidents involving hostages. If terrorists took hostages within Israel, the principle was that everything possible must be done to avoid complying with their demands, and if they refused to surrender the army must act in a way that would obviate the question of what to do with the captured terrorists.

Hence most of the terrorists who succeeded in taking hostages within Israel paid with their lives while their victims were saved—as in the case of the Sabena Airlines plane hijacked in May 1972. Once the plane landed in Lod Airport the hijackers demanded the release of Palestinian prisoners who had been convicted of brutal acts of terrorism. Instead, the hostage passengers and crew were freed in a lightning military action that cost the lives of one passenger and two hijackers. Still, there were incidents that ended tragically, like the attack on the school in Ma'alot in May 1974, when terrorists took about a hundred children hostage and demanded the release of hundreds of prisoners in return for the children. The men of Israel's special anti-terrorist unit were sent to storm the building, but twenty-one of the children were killed before the soldiers could reach them. Earlier the terrorists had killed three members of a family in the building.

Israel could not refuse to yield to the terrorists' demands when Israeli hostages were taken outside the country. In one instance in 1972 all of the hostages in question—members of the Israeli delegation to the Olympic Games in Munich—were killed when the German police tried to free them. More than once Palestinian prisoners were released by the Israelis in exchange for Israelis who had fallen into the hands of terrorists abroad. The policy followed by the Israeli government was that in cases of this kind, prisoners who had perpetrated acts of murder were not to be released, and usually it held to it. An exception followed the 1982 war in Lebanon, when the Israeli government departed sharply from its policy and was prepared to release thousands of Palestinian prisoners of war, as well as many terrorists who had been sentenced to life imprisonment for murder, in exchange for five Israeli soldiers who had been captured by Palestinian irregulars in Lebanon.

Once the Palestinian organizations ran up against major obstacles in mounting actions with Israel, they began to transfer their operations outside the Middle East where they felt more confident about assaulting Israeli or Jewish targets. They did not have to cope with the Israeli border patrols; they could use forged passports from various Arab countries (and sometimes diplomatic passports bestowed upon them officially) to smuggle arms and explosives; and they often chose objectives that were not defended at all. What's more, it was easy to escape after an action. And if they were caught by the local police, they trusted that they would be released under pressure from the Arab states or in exchange for hostages taken by their comrades subsequently for that very purpose. In most cases the Palestinian terrorists remained in foreign jails for a relatively brief period; light pressure was sufficient to obtain their release.

This pattern was symptomatic of a deeper political ambivalence about terrorism. Although various intelligence services (including some in non-Western countries) were pleased to cooperate with their Israeli counterparts in the war against Palestinian terrorism, Israel stood almost alone when it came to cooperation from the political echelon of the international community. First, it was quickly established that Israel stood no chance of culling support or aid in the war against terrorism from the United Nations. Quite the contrary, in the wake of an Israeli reprisal action for the brutal massacre of women and children in the town of Kiryat Shmonah in April 1974 (sixteen dead, fifteen wounded), the UN censured Israel but adamantly refused to denounce the massacre of Israeli citizens. This was but one of many examples of the UN's double standard when it came to Israel and the issue of Palestinian terrorism.

Second, although Israeli spokesmen had repeatedly warned that terrorism was a scourge that, unless stamped out, would eventually spread and strike at large, their admonitions fell on deaf ears. When Palestinians struck at Israeli commercial airliners the international community reacted with indifference. Israel was expected to yield to the terrorists' demands and was denounced—the *only* side denounced—when she reacted to the assaults on her planes. Thus Israel was forced to abandon her appeals not only to the UN but usually to Interpol as well, mainly because of leaks to the Arab states that were then conveyed to the Palestinian organizations.

Those who chose to believe that Israel would remain the lone target of terrorism had a disappointment in store, for the epidemic spread both quickly and far beyond the borders of the Middle East. Other terrorist groups—many of which maintained close ties with the Palestinian organizations and were rewarded with arms, training, and hideouts courtesy of their Palestinian allies—also began to copy the methods of Palestinian terrorism. Soon organized terror had grown into an international problem, as various and far-flung terrorist organizations began to serve one another's needs. The Japanese Red Army loaned a number of hit men to the Popular Front for the Liberation of Palestine, and in May 1972 they perpetrated the massacre at Israel's Lod International Airport in which twenty-four civilians were killed and seventy-two were wounded (sixteen of the dead were Christians from Puerto Rico on a pilgrimage to Bethlehem and the Holy Land).

The Palestinians also expanded the scope of their targets to include, in addition to Israelis and Israeli institutions, avowed friends of Israel. Planes of the Dutch airline KLM and various American companies were hijacked; not content with striking down only Israeli diplomats, Palestinians massacred American envoys as well. The inevitable corollary of victimizing by association can be seen in attacks against Jews in general. During the June 1976 hijacking of the Air France plane to Entebbe, all the Israelis and Jews were separated from the rest of the passengers, who were then released. (It was chillingly symbolic that two of the hijackers with the Palestinians were German.)

With this escalation in the war, Israel too revised her tactics, and the massacre of Israeli athletes at Munich in particular changed all the rules of the game. Israel began to hunt down all those who bore direct or indirect responsibility for Palestinian terrorism and terrorists met their death in various countries throughout the world. In April 1973 three Palestinian leaders in Beirut were even struck down at home in a combined operation of elite IDF units, the Mossad, and Military Intelligence. Israel struck with every means at her disposal, not waiting to be attacked on native ground, and executing a good number of preemptive actions far beyond her borders.

Closer to home, punishing raids were carried out against Palestinian targets in Lebanon, and from time to time the air force was used against both Palestinian military targets and the offices of the PLO and other Palestinian organizations in the heart of Beirut, causing the deaths of many Palestinian and Lebanese civilians. The war against terrorism was no less brutal outside of the Middle East, although there the effort focused on individuals who were known to be associated with terrorist actions against Israelis or Jews. The waging of this war, moreover, was not the sole responsibility of the IDF; all the Israeli Intelligence services and other security branches had a share in it. One outgrowth was the founding of a Civil Guard under the Israeli Police, in which tens of thousands of civilian volunteers maintained neighborhood patrols as a deterrent to terrorist actions.

The inefficacy of the Palestinian military threat to Israel does not mitigate the real problem, however. On the contrary, from year to year the Palestinian issue is becoming increasingly more of an internal Israeli problem from both security and social points of view. It takes various forms, ranging from the unfavorable demographic trend of the high rate of natural increase among the Arabs of Israel and the territories, to the moral problem of one people controlling another and the danger that Israel may lose its democratic character.

No less alarming is the rise in extremist elements that have begun to incite and operate against Israeli and Palestinian Arabs through clandestine networks or out in the open through racist political parties that call for the expulsion of the Arabs from Israel and the territories. At the same time, a generation has grown up in the occupied territories feeling oppressed and dispossessed, already claiming that it has been deprived of land and water as well as sources of employment. In the future such disaffected youth could well succeed in inciting the Arabs of Israel to join forces in an irredentist movement and create serious civil disturbances that will be more of a threat to Israel than any Palestinian military presence across the border.

So while Israel has succeeded in neutralizing the Palestinian guerrilla war and to a large degree contained the terrorism practiced against her, she has not come to terms with the source of the problem. Even after the destruction of the Palestinian military infrastructure in Lebanon, terrorism and guerrilla warfare have not been brought to an end, and increasingly Israeli military figures have come to believe that the only solution to terrorism is the political resolution of the Israeli-Palestinian conflict.

12

The War of Attrition

DESPITE the crushing defeat of the Arab armies in the Six-Day War, it was not long before fighting against Israel was renewed. This extension of the six days of fighting into a prolonged conflict with Egypt was an arduous experience for Israel. After the June 1967 war there was talk of reducing the IDF to a minimal force. Those who argued for troop reductions contended that it would take years for the Arab armies to regain the strength necessary for a new confrontation. But even as the debate over the size of the postwar army continued, a new war had already begun.

This fourth war was known as the War of Attrition, a reference to Egypt's stated aim of wearing Israel down by hammering away at her defenses and inflicting consistently heavy losses. Israel officially dates the war from March 1969, when the initially sporadic clashes along the Suez Canal developed into daily occurrences, until August 1970 when an American-sponsored cease-fire went into effect. It started, in fact, much earlier.

The Arab states convened in Khartoum, Sudan, in September 1967 and adopted a resolution based on three no's: no peace with Israel, no negotiation with her, and no recognition of her. The outcome of the meeting was a deep disappointment to the Israeli public, which had hoped that the military victory of the previous June would naturally and necessarily be followed by a peace agreement with the Arab states.

The implications of the Khartoum decision became evident on October 21, 1967, during a routine patrol of the Sinai coast. When the destroyer *Eilat,* flagship of the Israeli fleet, approached too close to Egypt's Port Said at the entrance to the Suez Canal, a Russian-made Ussa missile boat stationed in the port suddenly launched three missiles and sank the *Eilat*. Of the 200 crew members, forty-seven were killed and ninety-one wounded. Israel was suddenly made to face the reality that despite her great victory in 1967 the war was, in fact, not over. The Arabs had been defeated, but not dissuaded from pursuing the war. Israel retaliated four days later when her artillery struck oil refineries in the Egyptian town of Suez, setting them ablaze.

September 1968: The War Spreads

The new, small war soon spread to the Jordanian and Syrian frontiers, where the Palestinian organizations launched an effort to establish bases in Israeli-occupied territories or close to Israel's borders. The IDF responded with punitive expeditions and aerial attacks. Though they were aimed at the fedayeen, there was no way of avoiding clashes with the Jordanian and Syrian armies as well. Then, in September 1968 Israeli forces on the Suez Canal were bombarded by Egyptian artillery. Within a few hours hundreds of Egyptian guns rained down more than 10,000 shells on the Israeli positions along the entire front. They inflicted severe casualties on Israeli soldiers who took shelter in emplacements and bunkers only to find that they failed to provide adequate cover against heavy shells and direct hits. The Egyptians demonstrated their advantage in fire power produced by an overwhelming number of guns used in a static battle, and seven weeks later they repeated the exercise, again causing serious casualties in a heavy bombardment.

The IDF was presented with a new military challenge. "The first barrages shook us," said the commanding officer at the Egyptian front, Major General Yishayahu Gavish. "The Egyptians then had 150 batteries of artillery. They fired delayed-action fuses in order to penetrate the bunkers."[1]

Again, as it had after the sinking of the *Eilat,* the IDF sought a retaliatory strategy. This time it chose an indirect approach far from the front: an airborne raid deep into Egypt, in the course of which an electric transmission station on the high tension line between the Aswan Dam and Cairo was blown up. The air force also damaged a bridge over the Nile and the Naga Hamadi Dam in Upper Egypt. These incursions convinced Nasser that his hinterland was not yet prepared for war. The strategy was successful inasmuch as the massive Egyptian activities of the War of Attrition were again postponed for a few months.

The War of Attrition confronted the IDF with military problems it had never before known, or had ignored since the War of Independence. Since the 1948 war the IDF General Staff had stressed offensive planning. Plans, operations, and energy had always been directed toward an offensive mode. The military thinkers devoted little time to defensive maneuvers, for their rule of thumb was that war would have to be resolved by rapid offensive and forward movement. A whole generation of commanders and soldiers had based themselves on this approach, so much so that the study of defensive strategy and "digging in" had been deliberately neglected. However, as the situation emerged after the Six-Day War, the IDF was compelled to concentrate on defensive planning. It was feared that since the IDF had for years been geared to advance, assault, and rapidly resolve a battle, the new routine of defense would change the character of the Israeli soldier. Previously known for his initiative and aggressiveness, would he now be stymied by defensive thinking?

For the first time in its history the IDF was compelled to wage war from static lines. IDF General Staff had always avoided such confrontations. In fact, since the mid-1950s the IDF had barely held troops in border strongholds; the defense of the borders had been based on small mobile units patrolling the frontier, while the bulk of the IDF's force was in training in rear camps and other nonstrategic points. But in 1968 a large proportion of the regular army and many reserve units were compelled to take up positions along the borders in emplacements and fortresses on permanent defense lines.

Digging in became of necessity the central task of the Israeli Army. The IDF had never used as much barbed wire, mines, shelters, and strongholds as it did in the War of Attrition. This signaled a major change in attitude from the prevailing doctrine of the 1950s when it was believed that fences and mines would not stop infiltrators from crossing borders. They were stopped instead by the deterrent power of the IDF and the Arabs' knowledge of what to expect if their people did cross. Under the heavy Egyptian bombardments, however, sandbags did not provide adequate shelter for the Israeli soldiers. So army engineers began constructing bunkers and trenches, pulling up railroad tracks that crossed the Sinai for heavy-duty metal to reinforce these new concrete emplacements. Ironically, Soviet field manuals provided the best instructions on the proper construction and reinforcement of bunkers.

The search for new strategies also found expression in the essential question of how to defend the Suez Canal line. The choice was between a defense based on a fortified line along the banks of the canal or by mobile forces stationed in the rear, out of range of light weapons and mortars but ready to push back any force that crossed the canal. The supporters of mobile defense, among them Major General Ariel Sharon, contended that the strongholds along the waterline would not serve as a delaying factor or even as invulnerable firing positions in the event of a general attack but merely as convenient targets for the Egyptian artillery, which would inevitably increase Israeli casualties. Those who thought differently contended that if the IDF did *not* hold the waterline, small Egyptian units could cross the canal and dig in on the Israeli side, which would result in a chain of battles that were not inevitable.

The decision adopted in 1969 was something of a compromise between the two approaches. It called for constructing a fortified line along the canal that became known as the Bar-Lev Line, after then IDF Chief of Staff Lieutenant General Chaim Bar-Lev. Unlike the Maginot and Mannerheim lines, which were continuous defensive chains, the Bar-Lev consisted of thirty-one fortified positions linked by a road. Armored reconnaissance units patrolled between the positions and armored striking forces were distributed behind them so that within minutes they could reach any point along the canal. One of the IDF commanders in Sinai commented that while the fighting that took place along the canal was not best suited to the character of the IDF, "We tried to wage this static war in the most mobile way possible. And we depended greatly on the initiative and independence of commanders in the lower echelons."[2]

The Egyptians enjoyed a number of advantages in the War of Attrition. Because it was a static war the Egyptians were less vulnerable to the command weaknesses that had been exposed in the highly mobile war of 1967. Furthermore, their land forces had superior fire power. This was especially clear in terms of artillery: the Egyptians had nearly twenty times as many guns as the Israelis, thanks to continued Soviet arms shipments, and these guns fired ten times as many shells as did the Israeli artillery.

Until the Six-Day War the Israeli artillery had been of secondary importance in General Staff plans. The fact is that at the end of the War of Independence, the standard artillery piece in the IDF was a 75mm gun (a 1906 Krupp model) and in the 1956 Sinai Campaign Israeli artillery consisted mainly of British 25-pounders and a few French

155mm guns. The Six-Day War found Israeli gunners with very few self-propelled 155mm artillery pieces. The War of Attrition was the turning point for Israeli artillery, which has since become almost entirely self-propelled. To make up for its handicap the artillery succeeded in concentrating its forces although the number of guns at its disposal was small. The Israeli gunners, moreover, excelled in rapid action and communications while moving from position to position under fire.

Another Egyptian advantage lay in their ability to sustain casualties. The Egyptians, both as soldiers and civilians, tend to accept tragedy fatalistically. This is far from the situation in Israel. It seems that there is no nation more sensitive to the loss of life than the Jews of Israel, who are still burdened by memories of the Nazi Holocaust. The Egyptians, with Nasser at their head, were well aware of this sensitivity. Thus, in speaking of the War of Attrition the Egyptian President once said: "I cannot conquer Sinai, but I can grind Israel down and break her spirit."[3] Egyptian commentators explained that cutting down seven Israeli soldiers every day on the Suez Canal would be enough to bring Israel to her knees.

The Egyptian General Staff also believed it could achieve local aerial supremacy in the Canal Zone because of the arms embargo imposed against Israel by France after the Six-Day War and the fact that U.S. Phantom aircraft had not yet reached the IDF. With control of the skies in their hands, after systematic artillery pounding and inflicting many losses on the IDF, the Egyptians believed that their army could cross the canal and seize control of all or at least part of the waterway.

Nasser's assessment of Israeli sensibilities was accurate. There was nothing more painful than the photos published daily in the newspapers of Israeli soldiers who fell in the War of Attrition. Nothing affected the morale of the Israeli public more in those days than the sight of those young faces. No less painful was the feeling that the war was pointless, since it did not seek to defeat the enemy's army. The feeling of frustration grew when the Russians deepened their military involvement on the side of the Egyptians. Throughout Israel the question "Where will it end?" was asked with greater frequency. Defense Minister Moshe Dayan attempted an answer in a speech delivered in August 1969:

This question was born with the first Hebrew—with Abraham our father. Jewish anxiety throughout the ages has been a double anxiety: fear for the

Woman on watch at fence-and-watchtower
settlement, 1936. (*Haganah Archives*)

A mixed signal corps unit in 1973 Independence Day parade. (*Israeli Army*)

Middle Eastern Airlines plane, one of thirteen blown up in December 1968 at Beirut airfield in retaliation for fedayeen attacks on El Al planes.

David Ben-Gurion (*center*) visiting an IDF base on the eve of the Six-Day War. (*Israeli Army*)

Israeli position on the Bar-Lev Line.

Helicopter photo of Syrian tanks caught in an Israeli anti-tank ditch. Two Syrian-built bridges are visible in the background. (*Israeli Army*)

Fedayeen captured by an Israeli patrol.

Defense Minister Dayan visiting the graveyard of soldiers killed during the War of Attrition.

The gunboats of Cherbourg: French sympathizers sailed these boats out of ports under cover of night in defiance of de Gaulle's arms embargo against Israel during the War of Attrition.
(*Israeli Army*)

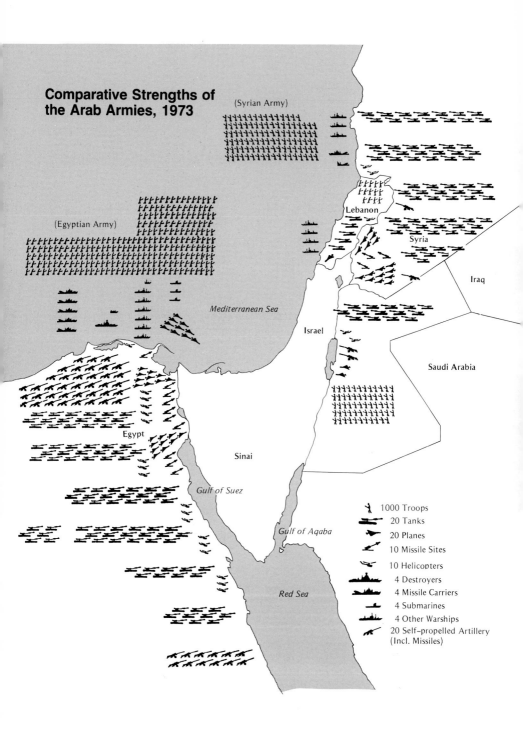

Comparative Strengths of the Arab Armies, 1973

(Syrian Army)

(Egyptian Army)

Lebanon

Syria

Iraq

Mediterranean Sea

Israel

Saudi Arabia

Egypt

Sinai

Gulf of Suez

Gulf of Aqaba

Red Sea

1000 Troops
20 Tanks
20 Planes
10 Missile Sites
10 Helicopters
4 Destroyers
4 Missile Carriers
4 Submarines
4 Other Warships
20 Self–propelled Artillery (Incl. Missiles)

June 5, 1982. Ariel Sharon (*right*) watching Israeli soldiers crossing the border into Lebanon.

Sharon (*center*) and General Amir Drori (*right*), overlooking the POW camp Anssar in Lebanon.

Yasser Arafat (wearing *kefija* headdress, *center right*) evacuating Beirut with his men. The picture was taken by an Israeli sniper. The order from the Israeli government was not to shoot Arafat as he departed Lebanon.

individual—the Jew—and for the entirety—the nation; anxiety for the physical fate of the Jew and the spiritual continuity of the Jewish people. For these, we have been condemned to struggle through all the generations. When the Lord said to the Jewish nation: "Fear not, O Jacob, my servant!" he did not give us an insurance policy. He meant that we are condemned to constant struggle and must *not* fail because of cowardice.[4]

During the War of Attrition the IDF set up the most intensive military medical system of any army and one that was without precedent in its proximity to the front lines. The achievements of this system were reflected in the diminished death rate among casualties. But Israel still paid a heavy price. The total number killed in the War of Attrition was no less than in the Six-Day War. From the end of the 1967 war until the cease-fire of August 7, 1970, 721 Israelis were killed in battle and terrorist attacks, 594 of them soldiers and the number of wounded reached 2,659. The highest casualty rate was at the Egyptian front, where 367 Israelis were killed and 999 were wounded.

The Arabs also paid a heavy price, for their dead numbered many more. Among the Palestinians alone the dead totaled, according to the IDF's calculations, 1,828, while the heads of the Palestinian organizations contended that their losses were even greater. To these must be added 2,500 of their personnel caught and imprisoned in Israel. The Egyptians did not publish casualty figures, but Nasser admitted in a letter to the President of Iraq that close to 100 Egyptian soldiers were killed weekly. At the peak of the War of Attrition, when Egyptian missile units were being bombed, the Egyptian Chief of Staff admitted that the death rate was at least 300 a day. Aerial photographs of Egyptian cemeteries in the Canal Zone alone showed 1,801 graves in this period. Among the casualties was Abdul Moneim Riad, the Egyptian Chief of Staff, who died of wounds received in an artillery barrage at the canal. What's more, Egyptian towns along the canal were almost totally destroyed and some 750,000 residents were evacuated. Important industrial plants were wrecked and with them the refineries and oil port of Suez. (Inhabitants of border villages in the Jordan Valley where the Palestinian fedayeen organizations had their bases also suffered from Israeli retaliation.)

The IDF's losses on the canal are what prompted the decision to put the Israeli Air Force into action, thereby escalating the War of Attrition. A raid by Egyptian commandos on an Israeli tank unit at the Port Taufik jetty on July 12, 1969 was the turning point. The unit suffered heavy losses, and so the government finally agreed to make use of the air force against the Egyptians. At first the air strikes were sporadic actions, but as the war spread, the activities of the Israeli Air Force intensified.

Israel's flying artillery cut down Egypt's advantage in fire power considerably and changed the situation on the front line. Israeli casualties dropped from month to month. At the same time the IDF increased its incursions into Egypt, beginning with commando raids deep into Egypt and moving to shorter penetrations near the front line.

One of the most impressive raids was the armored "excursion" of September 1969. Israeli landing craft deposited a column of tanks and half-tracks on the Egyptian coastline in the Gulf of Suez. The column consisted of Soviet armored vehicles that had been captured by the IDF in the Six-Day War and reconditioned for battle. It moved up to a main artery, started southward, and for nine hours moved forty miles from one Egyptian objective to another, destroying everything in its path—guard posts and camps, coastal positions and radar stations. The Egyptians were baffled about what was happening, and it was only a news agency report from Tel Aviv about penetration of Egyptian territory that awakened Nasser and his General Staff. Egyptian cars drove serenely past the armored column, which seemed Egyptian in every detail, only to be destroyed by machine-gun fire and artillery. The Egyptian Commander of the Suez Gulf area was killed in one of these cars. A senior Russian military advisor was also killed during the incursion. Some 150 Egyptian soldiers lost their lives and much equipment was destroyed.

The Egyptians were stunned and Nasser was outraged, removing his Chief of Staff and the Commander of the Egyptian Navy. Earlier, after two Israeli Mirage aircraft had buzzed his own home outside Cairo, Nasser had fired his Air Force Commander and Aerial Defense Commander. A few days after the Israeli raid in September 1969 the Egyptian President suffered his first heart attack, which was kept secret. He died of a second attack a year later.

Three months after the armored raid, the IDF's planners of special operations again demonstrated considerable boldness: an Israeli force, landed inside Egypt by helicopter, dismantled and flew off with an entire radar installation. The captured Russian P-12 radar, which was effective in all weather against low-flying aircraft, provided the IDF with valuable new technological information. Captured Egyptian operators and technicians were brought to Israel, interviewed, and given various aptitude tests by Israeli sociologists and psycholo-

gists, in order to compile a representative profile of the Egyptian soldier and analyze what changes had occurred over the years, especially
since the Egyptians had begun to recruit university graduates. The
results were reassuring to the Israelis, for they showed that the Egyptians had not managed to narrow the gap in the professional level of
the two armies.

In January 1970 the War of Attrition reached a turning point that
indirectly prompted Russian military involvement. Israel began deep-
penetration bombing in Egypt, mostly around Cairo and in the Nile
Delta. As the War of Attrition wore on some Israeli strategists wanted
to exert heavier pressure on Nasser's regime in an effort to bring the
war to an end. The first signs of this kind of thinking could be detected in Moshe Dayan's remarks in the summer of 1968: "If we want
to and have to, we can undermine them through the civilian population. Our presence in Sinai permits us to strike terror in Arab cities
if we really need to. This means that we could break the Arab will to
fight."[5]

It was undoubtedly the arrival of Phantom aircraft in Israel that
impelled the decision to bomb deep inside Egypt. On September 6,
1969 Israel announced that the first Phantom aircraft had arrived from
the United States. From that point on the Israeli Air Force would
have a tool of technological ability far greater than it had ever known
before: the plane's unusual load capacity, its abilities in aerial combat, and its long-range, electronic instruments that permit the rapid
identification of targets and help assure accurate hits.

In December 1969 a convenient diplomatic climate existed for Israel's decision to undertake penetration bombing. The United States'
anxiety over the Middle East and Nasser's extremism were growing.
A shift to radicalism was making itself felt throughout the Arab world.
In Libya, King Idris had been deposed by Colonel Muammar Qad-
dafi. In Saudi Arabia, a plot had been uncovered against King Faisal,
and Lebanon was in the throes of conflict with its Palestinian population. The Israeli-Arab dispute served as a convenient lever for the
Soviets, and Nasser held one of the handles. It was clear to Israel that
the Nixon Administration would prefer to see Nasser struck down.

The hints dropped to Israelis were less than subtle. At a Washington cocktail party one of the heads of the State Department remarked to an Israeli diplomat, as if in passing, that the United States
objected to Israeli activities against Jordan and Lebanon but had never
said anything about bombing Egypt. In the same month, Yitzhak

Rabin, Israel's Ambassador in Washington, returned home and reported that Israel was not making use of the options the new circumstances afforded her.

While the American position was more or less defined, how the Russians would react to bombing deep in the Egyptian heartland was in question. Israel became increasingly willing to test the Soviets and assume the risks involved, having concluded that they were more tolerant of Israel's forcefulness than had previously been thought, and that the Russian bear in fact was very limited in his reactions. The question was just how far this game could go. Israeli strategists set themselves two limits: Israel would have to avoid hitting the Arabs so hard that the Soviets would have no alternative but to save them, and Israel would have to act in such a way that the Soviets would deem it not worthwhile to react against Israel and risk American involvement.

Thus on January 7 Israel opened a new stage in the War of Attrition by sending her aircraft against two new targets, both in the area of the Egyptian capital: an army camp where Egyptian commando headquarters was located, next to Inshas, and an army camp near Hilwan. These were formidable targets: the center of Egypt's scientific research is in Inshas and it is there that Egypt's atomic reactor was being planned, while Egypt's military factories are in Hilwan. Israeli Phantom aircraft pounded at these and other targets not far from the suburbs of Cairo daily, inflicting heavy damage both physically and psychologically. Egypt's planes were incapable of shooting the Phantoms down and the Egyptian pilots could not counter the Phantoms, leaving their country highly vulnerable, and each week brought nasty surprises. The damage was extensive because every Phantom carried from four and one-half to six tons of bombs on each sortie. The targets chosen were all military, but on February 12, an accident occurred. A Phantom that meant to hit a military camp hit a pipe factory adjoining the camp by mistake. Hundreds of workers were employed in the plant and seventy were killed. Among the bombs dropped on the plant was one with a delayed-action fuse that was due to explode a day later. When the pilot's mistake became known, Israel informed Egypt through the Red Cross of the bomb's presence, advising that it would be wise to prevent access to the site.

The increased penetration-bombing and Israel's capture and occupation for a few days of the island of Shadwan at the southern entrance to the Gulf of Suez were the proverbial last straw. Nasser left secretly for Moscow and informed the Kremlin that he was incapable of thwarting the Israeli aircraft, and had no idea how far Israel would go. Effectively admitting the failure of his War of Attrition, the Egyptian President demanded direct Soviet assistance, and the Kremlin agreed to block the penetration raids.

A Soviet airlift to Egypt transported sophisticated SAM-3 missiles, antiaircraft guns with their crews, and new radar along with radar technicians. These were the vanguard of a complete system that would soon include modern fighter planes and Russian pilots. For the first time complete Russian military units reached Egypt; until then they came as experts, advisors, and instructors working as individuals in the Egyptian General Staff, training bases, or the various units of the Egyptian Army. Now the Soviets were bringing in whole units. What's more, they quickly built missile bases around the port of Alexandria, Cairo, and the Aswan Dam. Egypt was soon covered by eighty batteries of missiles. The number of Russians stationed in the country grew monthly and reached 15,000 by mid-1970. Israeli bombing in the heart of Egypt slowly dropped off until it stopped completely in mid-April 1970.

But this was only the first stage of Soviet involvement. Before long the IDF began to detect their presence in the Canal Zone. Russian advisors were taking part in the management of the war and encouraged the Egyptians to intensify their attacks. This evidenced both a desire to convince the Egyptians that Soviet military doctrines were valid in confrontation with the Israelis, and a personal interest in proving that their presence improved the performance of Egyptian units. Egyptian planning was routine in character and always lagged behind developments in the field. It did not provide answers to the tactical challenges presented by the IDF. But because of the Russians, who began to intervene in every plan, operation, and shooting schedule, reactions from the Egyptian side of the front were faster. The Israeli Army could tell that somebody endowed with better reflexes was at the helm. But overall implementation remained in Egyptian hands.

On Saturday April 18, 1970 it became clear that the Russians had made a step forward and taken upon themselves the defense of Egypt's skies—at least in the central and inland regions. Israeli aircraft flying near Cairo on reconnaissance and photography missions were intercepted by MIG-21 fighters bearing Egyptian markings, but their pilots conversed among themselves and with the control towers in Russian. The first confrontation with the Russian pilots was kept secret by Israel, though the United States was informed. To Israel's surprise, American officials suggested that Israel publicize the presence of Soviet fighter pilots in Egypt, for it was likely to help the Nixon Administration convince the American public that the Soviet Union was organizing a general offensive and jeopardizing positions essential to the West. Although the American proposal was in conflict with the previous Israeli decision, it was nevertheless decided to leak the information.

Israel made it clear that she would not shrink at a fight with Russian pilots if the latter attacked or attempted to prevent Israeli aircraft from operating in the canal area, but her planes halted their penetration raids because the tactic had failed to create the conditions for Nasser's overthrow.

Nevertheless, the Soviets defied Israel's warning and brought their fighter planes forward over the front line of the Suez Canal. On July 25, 1970 MIGs flown by Soviet pilots attempted to shoot down Israeli aircraft flying over the canal. They fired on the Israeli planes and pursued them beyond Suez probing to see just how far they could extend their military intervention without getting involved in a Mideastern-style Vietnam.

This aerial battle with Israel on July 30 (described in an earlier chapter) showed the Soviets that their pilots were inferior to the experienced Israelis fighting close to home. The Russians realized that if they really wanted to beat Israel they would have to bring hundreds of thousands of soldiers into the area. That aerial battle led Moscow to increase its pressure on Egypt to accept a cease-fire and later to warn its Egyptian clients against breaking the cease-fire. With Russian help, however, the Egyptians moved missile batteries close to the canal and downed some Israeli jets with their SAMs. Electronic warfare was playing a far greater role than ever before.

In August the United States got Israel and Egypt to agree to a cease-fire as part of an overall plan for an Israeli withdrawal from part of Sinai in return for Egypt's participation in negotiations on a final peace settlement. The talks never got going, but the cease-fire remained in effect from August 7, 1970 until October 6, 1973. Almost immediately, however, Egypt violated the standstill provisions of the cease-fire agreement by moving SAM missiles forward to close gaps in her air-defense system near the canal. Israel complained to the

United States, which was slow to accept the validity of her claims. Nevertheless the cease-fire held and arguments over Egyptian violations were obscured in 1970 by other events: the wholesale hijacking and destruction of European and American jetliners by Palestinian terrorists, the civil war in Jordan between Hussein's army and the Palestinian fedayeen, and Nasser's death at the end of September, all of which served to further change the complexion of the Middle East.

Israel welcomed the cease-fire, for although the Egyptians had been hard hit, the IDF found itself in danger of conflict with Soviet forces. The cease-fire prevented that and two years later the Egyptians would ask the Russians to remove their units and advisors.

The War of Attrition exacted a heavy price from Israel and necessitated a constant state of military preparedness. Compulsory service for men was extended after the war from the previous two and a half years to three years, and reservists, almost all of whom had been called up during the War of Attrition, had to serve as much as two months a year after the war. Israel's defense budget also grew. In 1966–67 the defense budget had reached 10.7 percent of the gross national product, but in 1968–69 it rose to 18 percent, and in 1971–72 it climbed even further to 24.7 percent.

Israel's losses in the War of Attrition were heavy, but at least she preserved her military achievements from the Six-Day War. Although the Arabs had been able to inflict bitter casualties on the IDF, and despite increased Soviet military involvement, Israel had stood the test in another episode of the ongoing Mideast War.

Notes

1. Previously unpublished interview with author, 1970.
2. *Ibid.*
3. From *Al Ahram,* quoted in Schiff, *op. cit.,* p. 22.
4. Lecture at IDF Command School, August 1969.
5. Lecture in Tel Aviv, July 1968.

Military Intelligence

I NTELLIGENCE has played a major role in the Jewish struggle
for Palestine and the subsequent Israeli-Arab conflict—certainly no
less and perhaps more than whole arsenals of weaponry. For without good Intelligence the Jewish minority in the region would not
have stood a chance of emerging victorious against the combined
power of so many Arab states, their supporters, and the Arab terrorist organizations. Israeli Intelligence, and the Intelligence service of
the organized Jewish community in Palestine before it, made it possible for the Jews to know their enemy better, while the Arabs not
only failed at this task but came to perceive Israeli Intelligence as
something of an omnipotent monster. A well-known Arab military
analyst once stated that since Jewish Intelligence preceded the State
of Israel, in order to understand the latter one must thoroughly study
the growth and development of the former from its inception.

He was certainly right about one thing: the activities of Jewish
Intelligence in Palestine long predated the establishment of the State
of Israel. There is striking symbolism in the fact that the first contact
between the Children of Israel and the Promised Land was made
through spies, or so the Bible tells us. While the Children of Israel
were in Sinai, Moses sent twelve spies to reconnoiter the Land of
Canaan; and just before they crossed the Jordan, Joshua dispatched
two men to spy secretly on the land he intended to conquer, particularly Jericho. In its modern incarnation, from the moment the Jewish community of Palestine began to extend its hold over the country
it engaged in organized Intelligence activity. One of the better-known
examples was Nili, a group of Palestinian Jews who worked together
during the First World War to aid the British against the Turks
through espionage activities—with the expectation that after con-

quering Palestine, the British would reward the Jewish community there with a political quid quo pro.

Once the Haganah was organized, Intelligence received a respected standing therein. The Yishuv's Intelligence service was known by the acronym SHAI (for *Sherut Yediot,* or Intelligence Service), and all the branches of the Israeli Intelligence community were subsequently built on this foundation. The SHAI acquired much valuable experience, and considering the fact that it was the intelligence network of an underground its achievements were impressive. Extending its focus beyond the Arab-Jewish struggle, it also concentrated on amassing information on the British regime, its military branches, and changes in its policy on Palestine. As the struggle against the British mandate authorities gathered force, the SHAI also extended its work beyond the borders of Palestine, among other things so as to aid the illegal immigration of Jewish refugees from postwar Europe. Thus the SHAI had operatives working in two spheres—Arab and British—and early on it began to engage in eavesdropping and code-breaking work.

By 1947 the Haganah was running a course for Intelligence officers, and well before the outbreak of the War of Independence the SHAI, aided by reconnaissance teams from the Palmach, had begun to prepare dossiers on every Arab village in Palestine. A so-called Arab Platoon was established as part of the Palmach, even before state agents had been planted in a number of Arab countries. At the time they were concerned primarily with maintaining contact with local Jewish communities, with the goal of organizing emigration to Palestine; yet some of these agents stayed on and continued their covert activities in Arab countries after the establishment of Israel.

On one level the transition from the SHAI to the Intelligence service of the State of Israel was a mere formality that belied a natural continuation of work begun so many years earlier. On June 30, 1948 the SHAI was disbanded and the IDF published an official order formally establishing the Military Intelligence Service under the command of Isser Be'eri. At about the same time a classified Political Department was established within the Foreign Ministry, headed by Boris Guriel, and an Internal Security Service was founded under the direction of Isser Halperin-Harel. At first Military Intelligence was not accorded the status of a separate branch in the IDF's General Staff, remaining instead a subdivision of the Operations branch. Yet in addition to responsibility for field intelligence, electronic surveillance, and military censorship, it was charged with such tasks as counterespionage, a responsibility it was not relieved of until a later reorganization when counterespionage was transferred under the jurisdiction of the General Security Service (Shin Bet, or SHABAK).

This move was the purely organizational aspect of the shift. At another level the transition from an underground organization to the official Intelligence service of the young state was occasionally a painful adjustment. The need to operate within the constraints and rules of a democratic state, under full civil supervision, led to some friction. David Ben-Gurion, the state's first Prime Minister and Minister of Defense, was scrupulous about toeing the line: in matters of internal security he readily authorized the surveillance of political figures from the leftist parties; but when it came to the limits to be observed by Military Intelligence he was an absolute stickler, and Isser Be'eri was dismissed over just such an issue.

Two unfortunate and highly serious incidents occurred in Military Intelligence during the first month of its existence. In the first Ali Kassam, an Arab informer in Israeli pay, was eliminated without his executioners having received authorization to act. During that same month Meir Tubiansky, an engineer and captain in the IDF, was court-martialed on suspicion of relaying information to the British in Jerusalem—information that ultimately reached the Jordanian Arab Legion. His interrogators, including the head of Military Intelligence and some of his aides, served as self-styled prosecutors, judge, and jury. The so-called court-martial was held on July 1, 1948, and Tubiansky was executed that very same day. Six months later, Isser Be'eri was himself court-martialed for the incident and found guilty. He was relieved of his post, stripped of his rank, and sentenced to one day's imprisonment, while Tubiansky was posthumously exonerated. The outcome of this deplorable affair showed that the secret services of the young state were not above the law, and that they would not be allowed to become drunk with their power even though they were on the front line of this difficult war that had been forced on Israel.

The second Chief of Military Intelligence, Chaim Herzog, was a native of Ireland (besides being the son of Israel's Chief Rabbi), and unlike his predecessor he had acquired Intelligence experience in the British Army during World War II. Herzog had been the Intelligence officer of a British armored brigade during the invasion of Normandy and was, in fact, one of the few Palestinian officers to have served in British Intelligence. Abba Eban was another, but Herzog had seen duty in a combat unit and therefore brought valuable experience to the IDF. During his first term (he was again called upon to head the Intelligence branch some ten years later), Herzog laid the foundations for the growth of technical intelligence and the activities of the military attachés. He was also responsible for the establishment of a special department to survey the profusion of publications coming out of the Arab world.

It was finally during Herzog's term (and that of his successor, Benyamin Jibli) that the Israeli Intelligence community underwent an official division of labor that remained in force for many years. The Intelligence community encompassed four separate organizations: Military Intelligence, the Institute for Intelligence and Special Duties (Mossad), the General Security Service, and the Research Department of the Foreign Ministry, whose name was changed in the 1970s to the Center for Research and Strategic Planning. In 1950 a Committee of Service Chiefs was established to coordinate between the various Israeli Intelligence agencies and set priorities for their work. In addition to the heads of the Mossad, Military Intelligence, and the Shin Bet, the Director-General of the Foreign Ministry and Inspector-General of the Police were co-opted on to this committee. During the period in which the Prime Minister had a special advisor on Intelligence, he too participated in the committee's meetings. Reuven Shiloah was the committee's first chairman, and he was succeeded by the Chief of the Mossad, Isser Halperin-Harel. Ever since then the custom has been to have the Chief of the Mossad serve as the committee's chairman.

As long as the Israeli Prime Minister was also the country's Defense Minister, the state's three principal Intelligence services remained under the control of a single man. From 1967 onward, however, since these two posts have been held by separate ministers, the Mossad and Shin Bet have been under the supervision of the Prime Minister and Military Intelligence has been under the jurisdiction of the Defense Minister, through the aegis of the Chief of Staff. This division of jurisdiction militates against an overconcentration of authority in the sensitive sphere of Intelligence and indirectly contributes to better supervision of the Intelligence services.

While the division of ministerial responsibility was rather straightforward, the situation was less clear-cut regarding the jurisdiction and relative status of the various services. It was understood that the Shin Bet would focus exclusively on matters of internal security, but jurisdictional disputes—especially regarding the control of agents and operations behind enemy lines—broke out between Military Intelligence and the Mossad. Questions such as who was responsible for controlling Jewish and Arab agents created such friction that special committees were established to look into the division of authority. What finally determined the priority status of Military Intelligence was not its superior authority over agents in the field but its responsibility for research and assessment. Initially IDF Intelligence limited its inquiry to strictly military affairs, but it soon became clear that a comprehensive strategic assessment could not be arrived at without delving into the political and social spheres, the economic structure and natural resources of the Arab states, and the involvement of the big powers in the Middle East. Hence, as time went on Military Intelligence broadened its research endeavors, especially during the tenure of the fourth Chief of Military Intelligence, Yehoshofat Harkabi.

It was only natural that Military Intelligence would be charged with preparing and presenting the comprehensive national Intelligence assessment to the Prime Minister. For years the work carried out by the Research Department of the Foreign Ministry steadily diminished, so that eventually Military Intelligence remained in a class by itself in terms of its research capability. At the same time Military Intelligence had its standing upgraded within the General Staff as well. In 1953 it was promoted from a department within the Operations branch to a branch in the General Staff, with its jurisdiction expanded.

The work of Military Intelligence during and following the War of Independence was considered good. Among other things Intelligence succeeded in getting hold of the officers' book of the Egyptian Army, which contained the biographies of all its officers; and its listening experts, led by a young Iraqi-born Jew by the name of Shaul Shamai, managed to break the codes of the Egyptian Army and other Arab forces. Yet those achievements were offset by a number of conspicuous setbacks during the second half of the 1950s, one of which again culminated in the dismissal of the Chief of Military Intelligence.

The hapless operation that led to the dismissal of Benyamin Jibli, the third Military Intelligence chief was referred to euphemistically as unfortunate business and it subsequently sparked the notorious Lavon Affair. It occurred in the summer of 1954, when there was no longer any doubt that British forces stationed in Egypt were about to be pulled out. Within the confines of Military Intelligence the idea was floated that Israel should act to forestall the British withdrawal and postpone the signing of the Anglo-Egyptian defense treaty, which more than anything else spoke to Israel's lack of self-confidence and fear of being left to face Egypt alone, without the presence of foreign forces in the area. The suggested course of action was to perpetrate acts of sabotage in Egypt that presumably would show the Egyptians to be incapable of ruling their own country after the departure of the British. Toward this end it was decided to activate an existing network of agents in Cairo and Alexandria. Composed wholly of Egyptian Jews, most of whom had been trained in Israel, this network had been established for the purposes of espionage but on this occasion was to be used for sabotage work. The commander of the network was an Israeli agent named Avraham Zeidenberg Elad.

The agents began to carry out acts of sabotage on July 2, 1954 but they didn't get very far. At first they struck in a highly amateurish fashion, using incendiary bombs, at the USIS libraries in Cairo and Alaxandria. (This was the period in which the Eisenhower Administration had contributed to heightening Israel's political isolation by supporting the Baghdad Pact. Washington also backed the British withdrawal from Egypt and the transfer of British Army camps along the Suez Canal to the Egyptian Army.) Because of a technical mishap (one of the bombs exploding on his person), a member of the network was caught and arrested. After the rest of the network was exposed (the only person who managed to evade capture was its Israeli commander), Military Intelligence became deeply embroiled in a dispute about who had given the order to execute the operation. Feelings were running particularly high after two network members were sentenced to death and hanged, and another Israeli not directly connected with the network was arrested in Egypt and committed suicide in prison. The Chief of Military Intelligence, Benyamin Jibli, claimed that he had received approval for the operation from Defense Minister Pinhas Lavon (who had replaced Ben-Gurion), but Lavon countered that the activities had been initiated before he had authorized the operation, and that at any rate American targets were not included in the action he had approved. The plot thickened considerably when an investigation of the affair revealed that the documents cited that placed the blame on Lavon had in fact been forged.

Intelligence Chief Jibli was dismissed from his post, Defense Minister Lavon resigned, and Ben-Gurion returned to conduct the country's defense and security affairs. Military Intelligence suffered a severe blow to its reputation in the process and it would be years before faith in it was restored. The commander of the network, Avraham Zeidenberg Elad, was arrested three years after the fact on charges of having maintained contacts with Egyptian Intelligence, which led to the suspicion that he had betrayed his comrades to the Egyptians. He was brought to Israel, tried, and sentenced to twelve years' imprisonment for his ties with enemy Intelligence.

The execution of the two Jewish agents in Egypt was only one of the reasons for the further decline in relations between the two countries. By this time Israel was engaged in a program of forceful reprisals against the Egyptian Army—on the grounds that Egyptian Intelligence was behind the murder and sabotage being perpetrated by the fedayeen. This was also the time of the first disclosures of the major Egyptian arms deal with Czechoslovakia, and the first time that the Soviet Union had penetrated the area strongly with its massive infusion of arms. Israeli Intelligence found itself confronted by two knotty problems: the first, how to deal with Egyptian Intelligence, which was behind the fedayeen actions (or at least had been ever since the start of the Israeli reprisal actions); the second, how to keep a close watch on Egyptian-Soviet military ties, which could well upset the balance of forces in the region and touch off a second round of fighting at Egypt's initiative.

Together with the reprisal actions, Israeli Intelligence was interested in striking directly at the man responsible for the fedayeen activities, Colonel Mustafa Hafez, who headed the Palestine Department of Egyptian Intelligence. Hafez's headquarters were in Gaza, so a trap was set for him using a Gazan Arab named Muhammad Tallaka who was in the pay of Israeli Intelligence but was known to be an Egyptian "plant" controlled by Colonel Hafez. Since Hafez's main rival in Gaza was the city's Chief of Police Lutfi el-Akawai'i, during one of the meetings with Tallaka the double agent was asked to send the Chief a gift through the mail in Gaza. The Israelis naturally assumed that before carrying out their request, Tallaka would first consult with Hafez, and that Hafez, delighted at the discovery that the Chief maintained ties with Israeli Intelligence and eager to obtain proof of his rival's treason, would open the package.

That is precisely what happened. After crossing back from Israel, Tallaka made directly for Hafez's headquarters in Gaza. The package contained a book in German on Field Marshal Karl von Rundstedt that was packed with a deadly charge of explosive. Hafez opened the package and was killed instantly in the blast. The blow to Egyptian Intelligence was exacerbated two days later when the Egyptian Military Attaché in Amman, who was responsible for the fedayeen activities over the Jordanian border, was likewise killed by the explosion of a package (another book) that he had received through the Jordanian mails. This did not bring the fedayeen actions against Israel to a halt, however; that would take a full-scale military operation against the Egyptian Army's bases in the Sinai.

Chief of Staff Moshe Dayan had been pressing for such an operation from the moment he realized that the Israeli reprisal actions were not, in fact, mitigating the fedayeen problem. Dayan's chief argument was that the Egyptian army would have to be defeated before it had a chance to absorb the staggering amounts of arms purchased from Czechoslovakia. The Soviet penetration of Egypt and the integration of Russian advisors into the Egyptian Army placed new challenges before Israeli Intelligence. Not only did it have to keep close tabs on Soviet activities in the region, Intelligence experts would have to develop competencies that before had either not existed or had received scant attention. It was necessary to develop the technical side of intelligence, to better understand the makings of the Russian weapons systems, and to master the Soviet doctrine of combat that the Egyptian and Syrian armies had begun to embrace as their own. However, fearing that his people might focus too rigidly on technical matters, Intelligence Chief Yehoshofat Harkabi repeatedly stressed that it was not the strictly mathematical intelligence that would supply answers to what was happening in the Arab states, so that the emphasis must continue to be on human intelligence.

Regarding Egypt's war plans, Military Intelligence contradicted the view—advanced by Dayan—that Egypt was assimilating the influx of Russian arms quickly and would be ready to launch a war against Israel in a year or two. As matters turned out its evaluation proved to be accurate, although the proof did not come until the Sinai Campaign was well under way. Still the war was very successful for Military Intelligence. It began with a major coup, a diversionary ploy concocted on the eve of the war to create the impression that Israel was about to attack Jordan because of continued fedayeen actions originating in Jordanian territory. The fact is that not only the Jordanians and the Egyptians were taken in this ruse, but even Eisenhower was led to believe that Israel's objective was Jordan, and not a few IDF officers were convinced until almost the last minute that the feverish preparations were for a military action against Israel's eastern neighbor.

The Sinai Campaign also provided gains for Military Intelligence, from the opportunity of interrogate thousands of Egyptian POWs to the Egyptian documents that fell into Israeli hands and helped to expose Egyptian agents, among other things. However the magnitude of this success, which included the eradication of the fedayeen units, in no way stood Harkabi in good stead two and a half years later when he was dismissed for a technical oversight—a mobilization exercise that caused a flurry of panic in Israel because it had not been coordinated in advance with the Defense Minister or even the Chief of Staff.

More striking yet was the Intelligence failure of February 1960 that led to a revamping of the corps' early-warning system. In the wake of a military incident between Israel and Syria Egyptian President Nasser ordered his army to move into Sinai. (After the Israeli pullback from Sinai in 1957 the peninsula was unofficially but effectively demilitarized.) This movement of Egyptian troops was effected without any publicity, so that suddenly Israel was surprised to find two Egyptian infantry divisions deployed along her border and a third, armored division situated in the heart of Sinai. Military Intelligence had not warned of this development early enough, so that when it was discovered there were only twenty or so Israeli tanks deployed on the border.

For Army Intelligence this was considered a near disaster (which has been referred to ever since as Exercise Broom), and Chief of Military Intelligence Chaim Herzog ordered the early-warning system checked thoroughly. Moreover, with the approval of the General Staff and the Cabinet great pains were taken to improve this system, and the results were clearly felt when Nasser again massed his army in Sinai on the eve of the Six-Day War. In 1960 Nasser's gambit came to its conclusion a few weeks later when convinced that he had deterred Israel from attacking Syria he withdrew his troops from Sinai. In 1967 he tried to repeat this ploy, but a series of miscalculations led him into a disastrous war instead.

Nasser's efforts to boost Egypt's military strength had Israeli Intelligence quite concerned. In July 1962 the Israelis had been caught off guard by Egypt's testing of surface-to-surface missiles and the exhibition of new locally developed weaponry in a military parade in

Cairo. Before long the Israelis discovered that the powers behind the development of the missiles were German scientists, some of whom had previously been actively involved in this technology during World War II. But whereas Military Intelligence contended that the chances of Egypt developing missiles that would actually constitute a threat to Israel were slim, the Mossad portrayed the threat to Israel as very grave indeed—especially if the missiles were fitted with warheads containing radioactive materials. It even instituted a campaign of intimidation against the German scientists and was not above resorting to violence. Chief of Mossad Isser Halperin-Harel also suggested that Ben-Gurion pressure the German government to recall the scientists from Egypt and end the involvement of German institutions in the Egyptian military effort. So strong were Harel's feelings on this issue that he wanted the government to launch a political campaign against Germany, even at the risk of sparking a crisis in the relations between the two countries. When Ben-Gurion rejected these suggestions, Harel felt compelled to resign and he was replaced by the incumbent head of Military Intelligence Meir Amit.

The 1960s were a fruitful time for deepening Israel's familiarity with the workings of the Arab armies. Under the command of Aharon Yariv, Military Intelligence succeeded in amassing highly detailed information about the enemy's disposition that served the IDF in constructing its operational plans. Without doubt this information was one of the principal factors behind the Israeli Air Force's success in destroying the air forces of Egypt, Syria, and Jordan within hours of the outbreak of the Six-Day War.

During that same period, however, an old enemy returned to the scene in a somewhat different form, and Military Intelligence found itself devoting much time to this latest challenge. This new incarnation was known as Fatah, which initiated sabotage actions in Israel in 1965. Once again Intelligence had to deal with an underground guerrilla organization. However, this time much like other agencies that were monitoring developments in the Arab states and among Palestinians in the latter half of the decade Israel failed to perceive that the renewal of Palestinian guerrilla activity was more than just a military matter. In essence, it signaled the genesis of a political and ideological phenomenon that would gain both considerable momentum and timeliness in the future.

In its assessment for 1967, Intelligence forecast that war was not in the offing that year. Since part of the Egyptian Army was tied down in Yemen, where it had intervened in the civil war, Intelligence understandably predicted that the Egyptian Army was not in a position to go to war, and it was doubtful whether Egypt's leaders would feel confident enough to take Israel on before 1970. What it failed to take into account was the possibility of a deterioration in the situation to the point where both sides would lose control of events. What ultimately occurred was a snowball effect triggered by Nasser that climaxed in a full-fledged clash which Nasser himself did not want.

The speed with which the deterioration occurred caught even Military Intelligence off guard, but from the moment fighting broke out Intelligence branch put in a truly impressive performance. First, even before the actual initiation of hostilities, it succeeded in deceiving the Egyptian command about the possible direction of an Israeli attack. Consequently, the Egyptian command diverted its units in Sinai southward, thereby easing the way for the IDF to break through the Egyptian lines in northern Sinai and the southern Gaza Strip. While the fighting raged, Israeli Intelligence broadcast false orders to Egyptian units, misleading and confusing their commanders. Even the Soviet press reported on an incident in which the Israelis contacted an Egyptian MIG pilot named Mortaji while he was on a combat mission, spoke of his wife and two daughters by name, and suggested that he drop his bombs over the sea. Mortaji was so rattled that he not only aborted his mission, he abandoned his aircraft, and parachuted to safety!

Very little has been published about the work of Israeli Intelligence agents in the Six-Day War, though the Egyptian press reported that one such agent was arrested in his home near Alexandria harbor, which was attacked by Israeli frogmen launched from a submarine. Chief of Military Intelligence Yariv also disclosed that on another front Israel lost one of its most talented men, an agent who enjoyed an important position in the Egyptian Army. As Israel's armored forces were attacking an Egyptian military base in the heart of Sinai, the agent tried to turn himself over to Israeli soldiers but was shot and died of his wounds.

Inevitably, perhaps, the Israeli victory in the Six-Day War accorded Military Intelligence and its commander a great boost in prestige both within the Israeli administration and among foreign Intelligence services as well, some of which scrambled to establish ties with their Israeli colleagues as a result. One consequence of this upturn in fortunes was that Military Intelligence became increasingly more involved in political decisions, and its chief was often seen seated at the Cabinet table when policy questions were discussed. Another was that the self-confidence of the Military Intelligence soared—although in this sense it was no different from the other arms of the IDF. Admittedly it had been surprised again at the beginning of 1970 when the Soviets sent combat squadrons and missile units to defend Egypt against the Israeli Air Force, yet Intelligence still was an integral part of the Israeli establishment and was largely responsible for the establishment view that the Arabs would not dare initiate an all-out war because they knew they would lose.

Here again was an instance of the classic phenomenon where Intelligence knew countless particulars about trends and developments in the enemy's camp but this mass of information did not ensure that it would properly predict the enemy's behavior. For example, long before October 1973 Israeli Intelligence knew about an Egyptian military plan for crossing the Suez Canal. On the eve of the war, while the Egyptian and Syrian armies made their final preparations for attack, Military Intelligence received a spate of reports about unusual activity in the camp. The Syrians did not resort to any ruse at all, while Egyptian deception was painfully simple: it was built on a simulated military exercise designed to climax in a genuine attack on Israel. Yet this deception would not have succeeded had it not been for the dogmatic conception tenaciously upheld by Israeli Intelligence, compounded by an erroneous reading of the ratio of forces.

Anwar Sadat's plan was to mount a war for limited objectives on the ground. Its real aim was to jolt the political process out of its impasse, bring the "powers" into it again, and ultimately force Israel to withdraw from Sinai. The Egyptian writer and editor Hassenein Heikal has stated that when Sadat's security advisor Hafaz Ismail returned from a mission to the United States in 1972, he reported that the Americans were not alarmed by the prospect of a certain measure of tension along the canal if that was what it would take to achieve a renewal of political contacts and indirect negotiations between Egypt and Israel.

The erroneous Israeli conception was that Egypt would not go to war with Israel as long as Egypt lacked the ability to vie with the Israeli Air Force, and Syria certainly would not opt for an all-out war with Israel if she had to go it alone. Moreover, since Egypt had failed to achieve her objectives in the War of Attrition she would shun a renewal of hostilities on a limited scale. What this failed to take into account was that Israel's air superiority might not keep the Egyptians from embarking on a combination of the two options: a full-scale war, for limited aims. This would entail not the conquest of Israel or even all of Sinai but merely of the Suez Canal and a strip of Sinai to the east. Israel's error also stemmed from the fact that Intelligence failed to appreciate the extent of the risk that the Arabs were prepared to take just to terminate a situation they found so humiliating. And to all this must be added the failure to foresee the oil embargo that the other Arab states would impose during the war.

The errant Israeli conception was reinforced by other mistaken assumptions, the most influential of which was perhaps the notion that in the event of war the IDF would have enough time to mobilize its reserves. This premise was based on the understanding that Intelligence would sound the alarm twenty-four to forty-eight-hours before an Arab attack. After the Yom Kippur War Military Intelligence protested that it had never given such an explicit assurance, but the fact of the matter is that the General Staff behaved as though it had.

Since the Six-Day War, with the addition of the territories conquered in 1967 Israel's reaction margin had improved considerably in the air. But on the ground it had actually been reduced due to the relatively large Arab forces stationed along the front lines—all of them regular armies—and the fact that the shift from a routine-defense to an attack posture did not require much preparation. Another erroneous assumption taken for granted in Israel, including by Military Intelligence, was that come what may the IDF could quickly negate any Arab military gains. This can only be described as sheer contempt for the Arabs and their level of motivation. Equally serious was the fact that such cockiness fostered a climate of laxity about the IDF's early-warning capability and increased the general willingness to take risks.

Ironically, then, Intelligence's great success in the Six-Day War ultimately worked to its detriment, not least because Israel's leaders—the decision-making political echelon—developed a distorted attitude toward it. Their expectations of Military Intelligence were fundamentally unrealistic, and they treated it as if it dealt in prophecy rather than evaluation, with an answer for every contingency. Moreover, the fact that in May 1973 Intelligence correctly judged that the alert in the Egyptian Army was not leading to war actually worked to its disadvantage—and that of the entire country—again in October 1973 when its senior analysts insisted practically up to the last moment that war was not in the offing then either. (That American Intelligence did not challenge this assessment was of little consolation in view of the outcome for Israel.) Even when the Soviets began to evacuate the families of their advisors from Egypt and Syria, the heads of Military Intelligence stood fast in their prediction. Reports that clearly indicated a move toward war were put aside and not brought to the Chief of Staff's attention. The report that finally reversed the reading of the situation came not from Military Intelligence but the Mossad—and even that only at dawn on Yom Kippur, the day the war broke out. By then it was too late: the IDF rushed into war in panic and disorder, and paid heavily for all its failings.

The Agranat Commission, appointed to investigate the errors committed by the IDF as a whole and Military Intelligence in particular, recommended that the Chief of Military Intelligence Eli Zeira, his deputy for Research and Assessment, Aryeh Shalev, and two other senior Intelligence officers be relieved of their duties. It further recommended that the Prime Minister appoint a Special Advisor on Intelligence Affairs, that a special Research Department be established within the Mossad, and that the Research Center in the Foreign Ministry be revived. Some of these recommendations were adopted and carried out, while a number of changes were effected by Military Intelligence itself through a reorganization program that placed special weight on field intelligence and bolstered its capability by introducing such instruments such as drones and long-range, television-equipped observation posts. Intelligence mapped out geographic regions for study and placed emphasis on obtaining an integrated picture of the region's military, political, and social dispositions. To enable the Chief of Military Intelligence to concentrate on research and evaluation, a Chief Intelligence Officer was appointed to handle the branch's administrative affairs. Finally, postwar Chief of Staff Mordechai Gur reshaped the General Staff's approach to the whole subject of utilizing intelligence. Whereas the earlier doctrine had been to react to the movement of enemy forces and various other shifts in military disposition solely on the basis of comprehensive assessments, Gur ruled that the IDF must calculate its moves and respond according to the situation in the field, not the premises of any one conception or another.

It took a few years for Military Intelligence to recuperate from the fiasco and setback of the Yom Kippur War. Not all of its achievements in the years that followed have been made public, and again the experts found that even the best reorganization cannot promise success or ensure against failure—especially the failure to predict the actions of a single man who makes critical decisions without involving others in his thinking. Israeli Military Intelligence encountered just this type of situation at the end of the summer of 1977 when it began to draw up an assessment for the coming year. When it came to the matter of Egypt's likely moves, the experts agreed that it would be unreasonable to expect Egypt and Israel to reach another agreement on Sinai. The following year would mark three years since the signing of the Interim Agreement on Sinai, which Egypt declared would be valid for three years only, and Military Intelligence's assessment therefore was that Egypt would have no choice but to again hitch her fortunes to the wagon of war.

Yet Egyptian President Sadat opted to move in exactly the opposite direction, and in November 1977 he astounded the world with his boldness in coming to Jerusalem to address the Knesset. How could such a flagrant error in assessment have come about? Then Chief of Military Intelligence Shlomo Gazit explained it this way: "There's no question that Sadat's policy stemmed from a personal decision—a decision that was not discussed or examined beforehand or arrived at by any forum of the senior rank of government in Cairo. Neither did this decision come in response to pressure from Egyptian public opinion, and it certainly did not rest upon a broad and deep Arab consensus."[1] Gazit essentially described one of the greatest difficulties facing an Intelligence organization whose task is to anticipate the decisions made in a closed, totalitarian society whose ruling class is limited to a few people. And this is precisely the problem facing Israeli Intelligence with almost every Arab state she confronts.

Military Intelligence's apprehension that President Sadat's intended visit to Jerusalem was no more than a cover for another ruse lasted up to the moment he disembarked from his plane onto Israeli soil. Chief of Staff Gur even issued a public warning to that effect and placed the army on alert. Suspicion mounted after an intelligence drone sent from Israel to check the movements of the Egyptian Army was lost somewhere along the way. After Sadat's visit it was learned that because of that drone the commanders of Egypt's air-defense network were dismissed, and their successors placed the network on alert. Of course Israeli Intelligence took notice of this alert. It also reported the movement of units away from the Libyan border—and therefore in the general direction of Israel—without knowing what the Egyptians would reveal after the signing of the peace treaty, namely that this movement had been the result of a clash between two commanders and the simple desire to distance their units from one another. The upshot was that both sides had placed their forces on alert and were highly suspicious of each other's motives, all the while Sadat having honestly intended to launch an initiative that would lead to peace.

In the 1982 war in Lebanon, Military Intelligence suffered a reversal of a different sort: its assessments were vindicated but it came out of the war severely damaged nevertheless. The problem this time lay in a different direction. From the very start of the contacts between Israel and the Christian militias in Lebanon, Military Intelligence had been highly skeptical about the benefits to be derived from these ties. Its judgment was that they would not lead to much good because, in the final analysis, most of the Christian leaders would throw in their lot with Syria. Military Intelligence also doubted the reliability of the reports and assessments coming out of the Christian camp in Lebanon. The Mossad saw things differently, but this discrepancy probably stemmed at least partly from the fact that the Mossad was responsible for contacts with the Christian militias, and its men had developed direct and personal ties with their members, whereas the analysts in Military Intelligence were able to view the matter with a greater degree of detachment.

When Defense Minister Ariel Sharon began to plan a war in Lebanon in close collaboration with the Phalange militia, the reservations of Military Intelligence grew even stronger. Intelligence Chief Yehoshua Saguy argued that the military capability of the Phalangists was highly limited, that they would shrink from attacking the PLO directly, and that they certainly could not be expected to capture Beirut at the same time as an IDF operation in Lebanon. Even the head of the Mossad, Yitzhak Hofi, concurred with this assessment of the Phalange. But Military Intelligence went even further in its warning about the consequences of a military venture in Lebanon. Chief Saguy asserted that if the war were pursued along the lines suggested by Defense Minister Sharon and Chief of Staff Eitan, it would be impossible to avoid a clash with the Syrian garrison in Lebanon.

Every one of these assessments was borne out. Saguy's error was not one of judgment but a lack of nerve. For at General Staff meetings he repeatedly and forcefully warned that the outcome of the war would be negative for Israel. He even presented this position to the Prime Minister in closed meetings at Begin's home. But he did not air his views before the Cabinet, to whose meetings he was often invited, and under Israel's system of coalition government it is the Cabinet that ultimately decides questions of policy. The ministers consequently were unaware of his reservations, and when they voted in favor of war they did so unaware that Military Intelligence had recommended against it. It appears that Saguy was deterred from presenting his position to the Cabinet because he knew that it was diametrically opposed to that of Sharon, and to a large degree the position of Begin as well. Thus the man who was responsible for presenting the national intelligence assessment held his peace to avoid clashing with his civilian superiors.

When the Kahan Commission delved into the work of Military Intelligence with regard to the massacre of Palestinian refugees in the Sabra and Shatila camps following the PLO's evacuation of Beirut, Saguy and his men were not credited for their accurate assessments about the war and its outcome. The commission found only that Saguy had been delinquent in his duty regarding the circumstances surrounding the massacre and recommended that he retire from the army immediately, and so Saguy joined the long list of Israeli Intelligence Chiefs who were dismissed or forced to resign from their posts.

While the war in Lebanon cannot be depicted as the failure of Military Intelligence as a body, it does indicate that despite the growth and strengthening of Military Intelligence, there are clearly limits to the extent of its influence on events. Even when its assessments prove highly accurate there is no guarantee that they will sway the country's political leaders to adopt or reject a certain policy line. The position of an Intelligence Chief in Israel (military or otherwise) is therefore regarded as no less, and perhaps even more, of a high-risk job than that of a front-line combat officer.

Notes

1. Major General (Retired) Shlomo Gazit, "Intelligence Assessments—Exaggerated Expectations," *Maariv*, January 7, 1983.

The Yom Kippur War

T HE FIFTH WAR between Israel and the Arabs broke out
on October 6, 1973. It was the holiest day of the Jewish cal-
endar, the Day of Atonement, which was undoubtedly less than
fortuitous. This war marked the first time that small nations activated
immense numbers of weapons—more than 6,000 tanks, 1,500 modern aircraft, hundreds of batteries of ground-to-air missiles, and highly
sophisticated electronics systems. Missile battles were waged at sea
for the first time in history. Neither side could have used such a profusion of armaments had it not been for the assistance of the great
powers. Though the Soviet Union and the United States did not directly intervene in the fighting, they provided massive support in arms
and ammunition to the warring parties. Both powers tried out their
weapons systems in this war.

On October 24, when Israeli armored columns were within striking distance of Cairo, the Kremlin threatened direct intervention and
placed seven airborne divisions on alert. The United States replied by
placing her forces on alert, but fortunately did not have to use them.

The attack launched against Israel on October 6 was a unified and
comprehensive operation. The armies of Egypt and Syria opened the
offensive, but it was not long before Iraqi and Jordanian expeditionary forces reached the Syrian front, and they were subsequently joined
by another force from Morocco and auxiliary units from Saudi Arabia, Algeria, Libya, Tunisia, and Kuwait. Pilots from Pakistan and
North Korea also rallied to the Arab effort. Further, the Arabs utilized their oil as a political weapon by enforcing selective or full embargo on the countries that supported Israel.

In eighteen days of bitter combat the IDF lost 2,521 men, dead or
missing. The impact of these losses compares with those suffered in

the War of Independence. Both these wars were very painful for Israel, but the military achievement in 1948 was clear and tangible: the State of Israel was created in the midst of battle; the Arab armies were defeated and compelled to sign armistice agreements that indirectly recognized the new frontier lines of the young state. In 1948, Israel enjoyed the extensive support of other nations. On the other hand in 1973 Israel was all but isolated; her allies had dwindled to one: the United States. The rest of the world seemed to be divided between countries that supported the Arabs outright, and those that feigned indifference out of fear of being blackmailed with the oil embargo.

On the northern front there was a decisive military victory, with the Syrian Army being driven back from the Golan Heights and the IDF finding itself a mere twenty-two miles from Damascus when the cease-fire went into effect. Here more than 1,100 Arab tanks were destroyed.

On the Egyptian front a dramatic breakthrough was achieved. The Egyptian Army had taken control of large areas of the Suez Canal and of many strongholds on the Bar-Lev Line, but the IDF broke through in the central sector of the canal and occupied some 1,200 square kilometers in Egypt, isolated the Egyptian Third Army, and held positions within sixty miles of Cairo. Still, the military victory on the Egyptian front was incomplete and Israel again found that she could never achieve a total victory over the Arabs. Moreover, in 1973, unlike in 1967, the Russians stood ready to prevent a decision against the Arab armies.

From a political point of view Israel sustained an unequivocal defeat in the Yom Kippur War. The political and economic might of the Arab countries dictated the positions of many governments on the Middle East dispute; members of the NATO alliance, for example, were reluctant to allow American aircraft carrying armaments to Israel to land for refueling at their airports. The U.S. supplied military assistance of a scope and kind that she had never before extended, but Israel's dependence on outside aid increased even more, despite her technological progress. The IDF was facing armies supported by the logistical capabilities of the Soviet Union and the Warsaw Pact nations. Israel, in turn, had to rely on the support of the U.S. and in exchange was obliged to follow her dictates.

The Arabs failed to achieve their objectives on the battlefield, but their political and strategic success was beyond dispute.

By resorting to war Sadat succeeded in triggering the negotiation process that culminated in an Israeli pullback from the Suez Canal into Sinai. This was an objective that Egypt had failed to achieve both in the War of Attrition and following the cease-fire of August 1970. Sadat tried in vain after becoming President to draw the United States and Israel into negotiations on an Israeli withdrawal from Sinai. Even the expulsion of the Russian advisors from Egypt failed to prompt an American political initiative. At one point Sadat's Intelligence advisors counseled that Washington would object to Egypt heating up the cease-fire line in Sinai; quite the contrary, a measure of that sort was precisely what was needed to spark off negotiations between the opposing sides. In time the Egyptian President rightly concluded that the only way to induce American intervention in the Middle East conflict and bring about an Israeli withdrawal was to launch a war in which his army would recover some Israeli-occupied territory along the canal.

Thus, by resorting to war Sadat carried off an Egyptian strategic coup that changed the face of the Middle East, while American Secretary of State Kissinger quickly exploited the new situation to extend the peace process. His first step was to obtain the Arabs' agreement to convene a conference in Geneva to be attended by the two superpowers as well the parties involved the war (Syria joined the fighting during the second stage). In the field itself a separation of Israeli and Egyptian forces was achieved in Sinai, and Israeli and Syrians in the Golan Heights, along with Israel's withdrawal from territory she had occupied since the Six-Day War. Thereafter the negotiations continued between Egypt and Israel, and with Kissinger's help the two sides reached an interim agreement whereby Israel pulled back even further into Sinai in return for arms, financial aid, and various political guarantees from the United States (e.g., that Washington would not enter into contracts with the PLO unless it first recognized Israel). This was an important step on the road to the 1978 peace agreement between Israel and Egypt.

The Intelligence Fiasco

The Yom Kippur War first and foremost was marked by the failure of Israeli Intelligence to properly evaluate material it had collected. They had a wealth of information, but a series of false alarms led analysts to put two and two together and come up with nothing.

Several times since the War of Attrition the Arabs had massed forces along the cease-fire lines. In December 1972, for example, Israel strongly suspected that the Arabs were preparing for war, and as a result the decision to shorten the term of conscript service in the IDF was postponed. But nothing happened. A similar event occurred in May–June 1973—it was rather like a dress rehearsal for the Day of Atonement. In addition to massing their forces, the Egyptians moved missiles forward from the Cairo area and prepared fording equipment for action. Israeli Intelligence concluded at the time that the Arabs were not yet prepared for total war and would therefore not open fire. But the Chief of Staff David Elazar did not accept the Intelligence evaluation and extensive measures were taken to assure alertness. New units were quickly established, emergency stores transferred closer to the line. But again nothing happened. The Intelligence evaluation, countermanded by the Chief of Staff, was thus vindicated, and as a result the confidence Intelligence experts had in their own assessments grew almost to the point of arrogance.

The Intelligence blunder was all the more serious since the IDF's commanders did take the possibility of an Arab offensive into account. Following the June alert, the Chief of Staff spoke with this author about the possibility of a war:

The Egyptians have the motivation and the strategic reasons for opening fire. The Arabs have entered a stage of political stalemate, and Egypt's situation in the Arab world is not a comfortable one. Among the various possibilities that the Egyptians may choose, the most dangerous is that of total war, in partnership with Syria and with reinforcements from other Arab countries—especially in aircraft. . . . The Egyptians are likely to determine that they can attain some preliminary achievements, even if they are limited. They may believe that the opening blow will cause Israel heavy losses, after which the situation on the ground will freeze.[1]

Asked about the Arabs' ability to surprise Israel with such a move, Elazar said:

It is impossible to open a general offensive in a totally tranquil situation without us first sensing it. The reasonable assumption is that they will shift to the alert almost publicly and begin the offensive in the second stage. Yet, I assume that the Arab's first blow will not be fatal. In our present situation, a preemptive strike is not essential.[2]

The Israeli Chief of Staff had laid out an almost complete scenario in advance for the opening strike of the Yom Kippur War.

Nevertheless Israel was unprepared when the attack came. In June 1973 the Intelligence assessment of a low likelihood of war was rejected by the High Command. However, in October Elazar and Defense Minister Dayan transferred the Intelligence evaluation to the Prime Minister without comment, and in so doing became party to the evaluation. It was not until Friday, October 5, that the Chief's suspicions developed. He ordered a state of high alert in the IDF and the air force was ordered to prepare for a preemptive strike. At dawn on the Day of Atonement, the Chief of Staff finally rejected the low-likelihood assessment—but by then it was too late.

"Israeli Intelligence knew the facts, but was preoccupied with its own conceptions," Kissinger later explained. Then again, the American Intelligence services likewise failed to predict the events that followed. The CIA had been alerted ten days before the war broke out, but the overly confident Israeli Intelligence persuaded the Americans that war was not on the horizon.

Israeli Intelligence did have plentiful details; it knew the movements of almost every Arab unit. But despite this abundance of information, it made a crude mistake in its final evaluation that can be partly explained by its adherence to a well-established assumption that the Arabs wouldn't dare open fire for fear of repercussions. Again, overconfidence led the Israeli Command to come to that conclusion without considering the precise details of the situation as it stood in 1973.

On a 1960 visit to Israel English military analyst B. H. Liddell-Hart had observed that the greatest danger threatening the IDF, well known as a superior army, was the propensity of victorious armies toward overconfidence. At that time the IDF had sustained two major victories over the Arabs. Since then two more victories have been added to the scorecard: the impressive campaign of 1967, and the thwarting of Arab plans in the War of Attrition.

Indeed Liddell-Hart's warning was borne out to no small extent. The prevailing attitude in Israel, not only within the IDF, failed to take into account the import of frustration as a factor in determining Arab actions. The majority of the IDF's commanders saw what was taking place before their very eyes but surrounded themselves with an impenetrable wall. And Israeli Intelligence fell in with the process. Instead of influencing the mood of the day it was influenced by it. While serving the IDF well as eyes and ears, it was caught up in the complacency that was spreading through the entire nation. The assessments that the Egyptians wouldn't dare start a war were further validated each time Sadat promised a war but didn't start it.

Three weeks before the war, Israel first noticed that Syria had begun amassing her forces and was erecting the extremely dense network of antiaircraft missiles along the border. Israeli Intelligence interpreted this troop movement as a response to the aerial battle of September 13, in which the Syrians lost thirteen MIGs. When reports came in that Egypt was also starting to move units, Israeli Intelligence assumed that the Egyptians were merely conducting their annual fall exercises. Those predictable exercises were in fact a part of the Arab deception plan. The Egyptian General Staff acted as if it were holding an extensive exercise but was actually following a plan by which war was to begin when the exercises reached their peak. The Arabs were careful to maintain their secret well; few were made a party to it, to the point where even the senior commanders received their orders only a day before the war was to begin.

Israeli suspicions were aroused two days before the war when it was reported that the Soviet advisors and their families were beginning to leave Syria and Egypt. At dawn on the Day of Atonement Intelligence received a report that the Arabs intended to open fire that day. According to that communiqué the battle was to begin at six that evening. Even so, Intelligence stuck to its general assessment that the likelihood of war was slim. Its consistent appraisal was that as long as the Egyptians and Syrians lacked an antidote to Israel's superiority in the air they would never mount an all-out attack. The Chief of Staff did recommend total mobilization of the reserves and using the air force to strike a preemptive blow, but his requests were rejected. The air strike was to be primarily against Syria. Its purpose was to hamper the expected attack, though it would not have prevented the war at this stage. Many planes had already been armed for the strike, and after it was canceled the ground crews were still in the process of removing the bombs when war broke out. The planes consequently had to take off and drop their bombs into the sea before engaging the enemy's aircraft in battle.

The preemptive strike was turned down by the Prime Minister and the Minister of Defense because they believed that in light of the territories added to Israel in the Six-Day War, the IDF could risk holding fire until it was attacked. As for the mobilization of reserves, Moshe Dayan opposed full mobilization as a way to ensure that Israel could not be accused of provocation. Prime Minister Golda Meir, however, intervened on Elazar's behalf, and a partial mobilization was ordered. Again, it was too late. Under the best possible circumstances, Israel needed prior warning of twenty-four hours to move at least part of her reserve units to the front. The decision to mobilize the reserves was made after eight in the morning; by two that afternoon war had broken out.

In the face of all this an order was issued by the General Staff that armored forces in Sinai were not to move toward the canal, for fear that a change in the disposition of the armor would incite the Arabs to act. Israeli tanks, as a result, were not in position at the canal when the fighting began, and the main armored units were to the rear, in central Sinai.

The Yom Kippur War was the first armed conflict that the Arabs had planned thoroughly. Moreover, they had the advantage of initiative and surprise. In 1948 the Arabs initiated the invasion of Palestine, but their strategy was faulty, their military preparedness poor, and their military coordination nonexistent. In 1956 and 1967 it was Israel that opened fire. Although Egypt had created a *casus belli* for the Six-Day War by imposing a sea blockade on the Straits of Tiran and building up her forces in Sinai, Israel still held the initiative. The Egyptians admittedly began the War of Attrition, but the objectives of that primarily static confrontation were limited.

The situation was radically different in 1973. The Arabs set the date of war and enjoyed the advantage of both surprise and initiative, in addition to greater quantities of armaments and superior fire power. Their operational plan was based on two principles: the war would begin on the Arabs' initiative, and it would be waged on two fronts simultaneously. Because they understood that the IDF was highly mobile and capable of reacting quickly, the Arab leadership, adopting one of the essentials of the IDF doctrine, determined that the major achievements must be attained during the first stage of the war. Later they would shift to a prolonged war of attrition fueled by the immense quantities of armaments and manpower that were expected to flow in from the other Arab countries. In short, they counted on Arab quantity to defeat Israeli quality.

At ten minutes to two the assault began simultaneously on both fronts. The Syrians opened with three divisions and a number of independent brigades. Too, some 800 tanks took part in the first assault waves; their function was to penetrate a depth of six miles and open the way for two armored divisions, which would follow in the second stage and break through as far as the Jordan River. This represented an absolute deluge of armor operating in a relatively small area. And although Israel had reinforced the Golan Heights with an additional armored brigade on the eve of war, their contingent numbered no more than 180 tanks.

The numeric gap between the attacking and defending forces was felt immediately. In fact the speed of attack was so great that the air force found it difficult to give support. Syrian tanks approached very close to their Israeli adversaries, and Israeli pilots were unable to distinguish between the two. As darkness fell the Syrians carried on their attack, sending their tanks plunging forward with the assistance of infrared equipment and SLS starlight systems that intensify available light for night fighting. The IDF armored forces, which were spread over an extensive area, were slowly eroded, tank by tank, and after midnight the Syrian tanks surrounded Israeli headquarters on the Golan Heights. Major General Rafael Eitan, who was in charge of the blocking stage on the heights, was compelled to leave his command post as Syrian tanks approached the entrance to the bunker from which he was directing the battle. The Syrian tanks then crossed the main road and approached the B'not Yaakov Bridge over the Jordan.

The first Israeli reserve unit—a reinforced armor company—reached the heights at three in the morning and immediately went into battle. As day dawned, another Syrian tank unit approached the bridge close to the Jordan estuary at the Sea of Galilee. The Israeli forces were thinner on the southern edge of the Golan, so the work of blocking until the reserves arrived fell on the shoulders of the air force. The situation was so grave that Dayan suggested to the Prime Minister that the IDF retreat to the slopes of Golan. His proposal was rejected as more and more reserve units reached the front and joined in the blocking action.

On Monday October 8 the Syrians began a renewed offensive by throwing a division of heavy armor into the battle in the northern sector near Kuneitra. It was faced by a regular armored brigade. The attack lasted for eight hours, and at times it appeared that the Syrian tanks would succeed in breaching the front line.

The Syrians' most outstanding achievement in the first stage of war was the conquest of the IDF position on Mount Hermon. Syrian commandos surprised the position, which housed an electronic installation. Some of men surrendered after a battle, while others continued to fight from within the bunkers until they were overwhelmed. A few soldiers succeeded in escaping. Other IDF positions along the line withstood attacks because the Syrian tanks passed between them, and these strongholds were not assaulted until the second stage of the battle. Apart from one position that was abandoned, all these positions stood firm until IDF forces linked up with them.

The assault on the Egyptian front was a different nature. After a heavy but brief shelling and an attack by 150 Egyptian planes on various objectives in Sinai, the land assault began over the Suez Canal. In the first waves of the assault, ten thousand infantrymen crossed the canal in hundreds of small boats and established bridgeheads for the men and armor that were to follow. They occupied the embankment erected along the canal by the IDF and went on to attack the IDF strongholds.

By nightfall the Egyptians succeeded in transferring some 40,000 soldiers across the canal. Five Egyptian divisions in all took part in the attack wave, which was an unqualified success. A mere 1,000 Israeli soldiers faced them on the front line, several hundred of whom manned the strongholds while others commanded the few artillery batteries. About ninety IDF tanks were on the front line during the opening stage of the assault.

The Israeli Air Force could do little to help. It struck at the bridges, but had difficulty distinguishing between the attacking Egyptians and their own tanks. Its primary achievement in this stage was the downing of Egyptian MIGs and of some twenty helicopters carrying Egyptian commandos to seize the Mitla and Jiddi passes deep inside Sinai in order to delay the flow of Israeli reserves to the front. Facing the Tel Aviv coastline, an Israeli Mirage shot down a Kelt air-to-ground missile that had been fired at the city from a distance.

Although the roads to Sinai are very long, an order was issued to send tanks on their own tracks rather than on transporters to hasten their arrival at the front line. Speed was given such priority that many tanks were dispatched with incomplete stocks of ammunition and even incomplete crews. Artillery received a very low priority for transporters moving into Sinai, which proved to be one of the grave errors of the Israeli command.

In the first stage of combat Israeli armor was faced by effective Egyptian infantry equipped with anti-tank weapons. The Israeli units were insufficiently backed by artillery and mortars, and they were not prepared for that sort of confrontation. The IDF rushed to the front expecting a mobile war based primarily on tanks and artillery like that of 1967. The forte of the Egyptian infantry lay in its possession of two anti-tank weapons, mobile Sagger missiles, and RPG-7 bazookas. The Sagger has a range of about two miles. Two men are needed to fire the missile, which can be carried in small suitcases and aimed with the aid of a telescope. The RPG-7 bazooka is very light, easy to carry, and can penetrate most armor. With the help of the Sagger the Egyptian infantry had a longer reach than the Israeli tank guns. As the first night of battle passed, a considerable share of the Israeli armored force was worn down; of 265 tanks that were in Sinai at the beginning of battle, only 100 remained.

Another defect in the structure of the Israeli units likewise derived from the special priorities that carried over from the Six-Day War. That primarily mobile war relied on the tank as the primary ground weapon. To facilitate tank mobility, the IDF neglected other elements that are traditionally considered a part of the armored team. The fact that the IDF's budget was limited only served to intensify this neglect; artillery, as previously mentioned, was slighted. Also put on low development priority was the infantry, which operated out of armored personnel carriers. When the Israeli tanks were unsuccessful in opposing the Egyptian infantry the Israeli infantry was called in, but in the first part of the war there were few elite infantry units in Sinai. Fortunately for the IDF the capacity for improvisation among its junior officers is excellent, and in the midst of battle the unit commanders were able to find tactical solutions to the problems posed by the Egyptian infantry.

Within less than twenty-four hours it became clear that the strongholds of the Bar-Lev were hopelessly surrounded and cut off. One of the strongholds fell in the first Egyptian assault; six others were abandoned and the men in them extricated, although losses were heavy. Nine more strongholds fell before the war was over; only one, on the coast in the northern sector of the Suez Canal, held fast until Israeli forces succeeded in linking up with it.

The reserves that raced to the front did not succeed at first in moving over to the counterattack, for the fact that the regular army had been worn down in blocking engagements on the canal compelled the reserve units to bolster the blocking force. They arrived in a haphazard fashion, and at times the battle resembled a street fight.

Minister of Defense Dayan suggested falling back to a second line of defense in Sinai close to the Mitla and Jiddi passes, but his proposal was rejected. The military command, led by the Chief of Staff, insisted that blocking take place no further than six miles from the canal.

The Israeli Air Force encountered serious problems in the Yom Kippur War. Even though it was not taken by surprise, as was the armored force, it had to pay a heavy price for its achievements. The air force succeeded in sealing the populated area of Israel against enemy aircraft and maintained more or less clear skies over the front. Israeli pilots were victorious in ninety percent of the aerial battles and succeeded in reaching every selected target within the Arab countries. Nonetheless they had great difficulty providing support to ground forces on the front line because of the Arabs' missile systems.

With the assistance of the Soviet Union the Egyptians and Syrians had built networks of antiaircraft missiles even denser than those used by North Vietnam. They were composed of many missile batteries of different types and hundreds of radar-operated guns. Among the types of missiles was the brand-new SAM-6, which was difficult to spot and boasted electronic gear unknown in the West.

In eighteen days of combat the Israeli Air Force lost more than a quarter of its combat aircraft (104 planes of various make), most of them to antiaircraft fire and the majority to cannon fire (usually radar directed) rather than missiles (as was believed during the war). An air force spokesman noted that Israel lost only six planes in air battles. By contrast, the Egyptian and Syrian air forces lost a combined total of 456 planes in dogfights, to ground fire, or in Israeli bombing raids while still on the ground.

The only good news during the first days of the war came from the sea. The Israeli Navy, equipped with advanced weapons systems, and bolstered by twelve French-built missile boats and two larger Israeli-built missile boats, concentrated its forces in the Mediterranean Sea. Because it had not managed to launch a similar force in the Red Sea, and its contingent there was made up solely of small craft (without a single missile boat), the navy was unable to react to the closing of the Bab el-Mandeb Straits, 1,250 miles from Sharm el-Sheikh. The small Red Sea navy limited itself to actions in the Bay of Suez and the Gulf of Aqaba, most of which involved the Naval Commandos.

The navy adopted an offensive approach in the Mediterranean, and within a few days it had created a situation in which the movement of Egyptian and Syrian fleets was completely circumscribed. The supply of weapons to the ports of Latakiye and Tartus in Syria was effected in Russian ships, under their own escort. Nevertheless Israel succeeded in maintaining freedom of action in the Mediterranean. The hardest blow was sustained by the Syrian Navy, which lost eight of its missile boats, a minesweeper, and a torpedo boat. The Egyptians lost between five and six missile boats, a patrol ship, and many other vessels, including eighteen fishing boats that were armed for action in the Red Sea. In the missile battles Israeli boats held the upper hand, even though the range of their Gabriel missiles is less than that of the Russian Styx, with which the Syrian and Egyptian boats were equipped. The Israeli Navy was the undisputed victor; it lost not a single vessel in the naval battles of the war.

During the first four days of war, Command decisions were strongly influenced by the shortage of reserve forces. The High Command had to face the critical issue of how best to utilize the reserves while there was still a danger that the Jordanian Army would open a third front to the east. The question was whether to mobilize all the reserves or to wait for unexpected developments. And if the decision was to throw them all into battle, on which front—the Suez line, where the enemy was strongest and where a territorial achievement would change the political and territorial status quo; or the Syrian front, closer to populated areas in Israel, where there was also a greater chance of beating the enemy because of the balance of forces? The decision was to move forces to the Syrian front where they helped to repel the Syrians from the Golan Heights. Thus on the fourth day of war the center of gravity shifted to the north.

On the previous day an Israeli counterattack near the canal had failed after Major General Adan's division was thrown against the bridgehead of the Egyptian Second Army. This setback sealed the decision in favor of an offensive on the Syrian front, leaving a relative stalemate in the south for the time being.

After a day of regrouping Israeli forces opened a general offensive against Syria. Two divisions began the assault, Major General Eitan's on the northern road, from Kuneitra along the length of the Hermon foothills, and Major General Dan Laner's division further south on the Kuneitra–Damascus road. The Syrians had been hard hit on the two previous days by heavy strategic bombing of their Defense Ministry, military command posts, power stations, and fuel dumps.

On the third day of war the Soviet Union's involvement underwent a significant change as giant Russian transport planes began to land in Syria, and later in Egypt. The sheer speed of the Russian airlift indicated that the Kremlin had prepared considerable equipment in advance and was privy to the Arab decision to go to war. At first these planes brought antiaircraft missiles; later they began to transport other equipment—ammunition and weapons. Freighters were also hastily loaded at Black Sea ports.

Within the Soviet Union itself a large transport operation was carried out as trains moved to the Black Sea ports and airfields in Hungary and Yugoslavia. The quantities needed by the two countries were so great that it was necessary to draw equipment from the stores of the Red Army's regular units. Later, Warsaw Pact armies were asked to transfer weapons and equipment from their stores. At the peak of the airlift Russian planes were landing in Egypt every ten minutes. Scores of freighters loaded with tanks and other weapons reached Syrian, Egyptian, and Algerian ports throughout the war. Dismantled planes were transported to Syria where they were reassembled by Russian technicians and flown to forward airfields. Israel had attempted to destroy the Syrian runways on which the Russian transport planes were to land, but this was a futile race. The Syrians hastened to fill in the holes in the tarmac, and there was, moreover, a risk of confrontation with the Soviet Union.

American aid to Israel was not quite so swift. On the second day of war Jerusalem approached Washington with an urgent request for aid, especially in aircraft, bombs, and sophisticated ammunition. Two days passed before the Nixon Administration decided to supply Israel with equipment and replace those arms destroyed in battle. At first Washington anticipated that its action would not be publicized and that Israel would herself transport the considerable equipment. El Al planes and chartered aircraft began to fly the supplies to Israel, but it soon became clear that Israel alone could not handle the quantities involved. Hence it was decided to activate an American airlift to Israel (by which time the Russian airlift was at its peak). It was October 14 before the first American Galaxy C-5 aircraft landed at Lod International Airport.

The IDF had destroyed appreciable quantities of Arab arms and equipment, but even in victory the wear and tear on equipment in modern warfare is immense. Thus the quantities of replacements needed were so great that they strained even the reserves of the United States.

The Russian and American airlifts did not take place under comparable conditions. The Soviet airfields were a mere two-hours' flying time from Syrian bases; even their ships needed no more than three days to sail from the Black Sea ports to Latakiye. In addition to the relatively shorter distances, the Soviet Union had access to airfields in Hungary and Yugoslavia and was able to transfer military equipment by train through the Eastern bloc. Squadrons of Russian planes even flew over Turkey without receiving prior permission to enter Turkish airspace.

The United States, on the other hand, found herself almost isolated in her attempts to help Israel face the Arab onslaught. Her colleagues in the NATO alliance refused to play a role in the operation. Fearing an Arab oil embargo, various European countries told the United States that they could not permit American planes carrying arms to Israel to land at their airfields. The sole exception was Portugal. West Germany even protested that the U.S. was drawing on military equipment in her bases in Germany for transfer to Israel; and England declared an embargo on weapons to the Middle East.

Clearly the country worst hit by such an embargo was Israel, since the Arab states received more than ample supplies of arms from the Soviet Union. At one point medical equipment destined for Israel was held up in London Airport for a few days while bureaucrats debated whether it might not be construed as military supplies. Israeli fighter planes flew out over the eastern Mediterranean to escort the American cargo planes to Lod Airport. From the standpoint of its efficiency and scope, the American airlift proved to be far more effective than its Russian counterpart. Among the items brought by the airlift were artillery shells, air-to-air missiles, a small number of tanks, and other equipment, as well as clothing for hundreds of thousands of reservists. After the war it came out that a good proportion of the equipment requested by Israel was not actually lacking. Other than shells for 175mm guns, which had indeed run out, and certain ammunition for planes, most of the other types of ammunition were in the supply "pipeline," but the Israelis responsible for ordnance were improperly informed about what they had in stock. The U.S. also supplied a substantial number of aircraft to replace what had been lost by Israel. Among others, the aircraft brought forty Phantoms (F-4s), forty-three older model Skyhawks (I-4s), C-130 cargo planes, and helicopters. It was necessary to adapt a number of systems in the aircraft, such as the communications systems, before sending them into action; as a consequence these planes flew only 480 sorties during the war.

Russian intervention in the war extended as far as persuading other Arab states to send expeditionary forces to the front. The first to intervene directly in the battles was Iraq by sending a division of 16,000 men with 200 tanks that clashed with IDF units on Friday, October 12. This time the Israeli Air Force did not succeed as it had during the Six-Day War in locating the Iraqi force on its way to the front. The Iraqis had moved under cover of darkness. It was known that they were en route to Syria, but the IDF was nevertheless surprised by the sudden appearance of British-made Centurion tanks that Iraq had purchased in the early sixties.

The Syrian front line had been broken on the previous day, and the Syrian forces were retreating toward Damascus. Syrian President Assad hoped that while the Iraqis took on blocking tasks, his forces could erect a new defense line on the way to the capital. But the Iraqi division came into battle unprepared and was not a serious obstacle for the IDF. On that day and the following one, it was hard hit in armored battles, and on October 12 IDF units came within artillery range of Damascus. An airfield to the south of the city was shelled, but for the time being Israel decided not to strike at Damascus itself.

The very fact that the IDF was within artillery range of the Syrian capital was sufficient to rouse the Soviet Union into making threats of her own. On Saturday, October 13, the Kremlin announced to Washington that it was placing two paratroop divisions on alert, and the staff of one of the Russian advisory divisions departed for Syria. It was clear that this time the Soviets had resolved to prevent a decisive defeat to the Arab armies. The moment the tide began to turn against the Arabs, the Russians began to step up their involvement.

The Soviet Union had learned about the fallibility of Arab Intelligence during the Six-Day War and was careful not to rely solely on Arab sources. Instead they launched six espionage satellites that provided them with a source of constant and reliable information about troop movements. In addition, Soviet espionage ships in the Mediterranean maintained perpetual surveillance. On October 16 Soviet Prime Minister Kosygin arrived in Cairo himself to take a close look at the situation on the battlefield.

On Thursday, October 11, the IDF's Southern Command again recommended breaking through the Egyptian lines to the west side of the Suez Canal and continuing on into Egypt. On the previous two days a balance had been achieved as far as the Israeli armor was concerned, for the IDF had several hundred tanks in the field by then and the Egyptians had lost more than Israel had in armored battles. Southern Command had three divisions at its disposal—in the south that of Major General Albert Mendler, who had been commander of the Israeli forces in Sinai when fighting broke out; in the center Major General Ariel Sharon; and to its north that of Major General Avraham Adan. Another force, under the command of Major General Kalman Magen, was operating in the northern sector of the Suez Canal. The plans for fording the canal were presented to the General Staff and the government by Chaim Bar-Lev, who had been Chief of Staff during the War of Attrition and was Minister of Commerce and Industry in Golda Meir's government. Early in the war, Bar-Lev had been mobilized and sent to the Egyptian front. Although he was not actually appointed front commander, it was clear that he was to control the battles as an officer senior to the Commanding Officer of the Southern Command, Major General Shmuel Gonen, who had received his appointment only three months earlier.

Even though the fighting on the Syrian front was about to stabilize, the war cabinet found it very difficult to give the go-ahead for crossing the canal. Apart from determining the location of the breakthrough and the direction of operations once a bridgehead had been secured, there was another highly critical question: when to mount the crossing? On the one hand, time was pressing: as long as the war continued, the wear and tear on the IDF increased and there was a danger that the Egyptians would establish positions in Sinai. On the other hand, the Egyptians' heavy armor was still on the west side of the canal, presenting a defensive obstacle. While the debate in the Cabinet was at its height, a report came in that the Egyptians were preparing to transfer a few hundred of their tanks into Sinai with the intention of opening a new offensive to reach the Mitla and Jiddi passes. The Syrians had demanded that Cairo launch this offensive to ease the pressure on them, and the Egyptians believed that their chances of crossing the canal were better while most of the Israeli Air Force was occupied on the Syrian front. This information caused the Cabinet to delay the crossing operation until after the anticipated Egyptian offensive.

The Egyptians activated 1,300 artillery pieces in the heavy bombardment that preceded the offensive. Major General Albert Mendler was killed when his command half-track took a direct hit. Mendler reached Israel as a sixteen-year-old boy after he, his mother, and his brother had escaped from Austria after the Nazis took control. He had fought in all of Israel's wars and, on the eve of the Yom Kippur War, was about to be appointed Commanding Officer of the Armored Corps. His place as division commander was taken by Major General Kalman Magen.

The Egyptian offensive began in the early hours of October 14. The previous day hundreds of tanks of their heavy-armor divisions had been moved to Sinai. Eight hundred Egyptian tanks participated in battles all along the front, while the IDF activated 700. This was the first time that such extensive mobile battles had taken place on this front. The battle marked the first turning point in favor of the IDF. At the end of a day of combat the Egyptians had lost more than 250 tanks, while the IDF had lost only ten. The time was ripe to breach the Egyptian line and cross the canal.

The crossing operation was an audacious action. The IDF didn't return to the Egyptian front until this operation began. The place chosen for the breakthrough was at the center of the front rather than on the flank. This seam between the two Egyptian armies, to the north of the Great Bitter Lake, was a weak spot that had been noted about a week earlier by scouts from Sharon's division.

The first penetration took place before the Egyptians could discern what was happening. Without waiting for the actual bridges, which were held up at the rear of a traffic jam moving toward the canal, Sharon transferred the first force onto rafts and crossed the canal without any opposition. This force included paratroops and thirty tanks. Once on the other side, they began to hit at rear echelons, command posts, and missile batteries. They penetrated as deep as twenty miles west of the canal on the first day, but toward the evening received an order to concentrate closer to the canal bank. Once the Egyptians' original plans were upset, their reactions became slower. What's more, the commanders of the Egyptian Army misjudged the IDF's objectives. They thought that this was a small task force that would limit itself to raids in the rear and then return to Sinai; and they were convinced that their armies would be able to overcome it easily if it remained to the west of the canal.

According to the plan Sharon was to establish the bridgehead, expand and enlarge it, and then consolidate his forces while Adan's armored units were to pass through it and penetrate further into Egypt. After the first crossing, a stormy debate broke out over the continuation of the operation. It would never have developed had it not been for the fact that the IDF's bridges had been held up at the rear, both because of Egyptian artillery fire and because of traffic jams on the roads leading to the crossing point. Sharon demanded that he be allowed to continue the crossing and assault operation without waiting for the bridges to arrive. He was so eager to attack with his forces that for the meantime he wanted to transfer the armor over the canal in rafts.

Meanwhile, the task of securing of the crossing area on the east bank—the breached section of the Egyptian line—would be completed by Adan's forces, which had originally been slated to cross the canal first. Southern Command felt that his approach was too risky; it was too precarious to base the crossing of this large of a force on pontoon bridges through a narrow corridor that could easily be cut. First the corridor had to be enlarged, roads opened to it, and real bridges laid across the canal. As for Sharon's contention that this delay might cause a significant slowdown in the political timetable, Bar-Lev replied that in any case the timetable was determined by events in the field and that the Soviet Union would intervene to impose a cease-fire earlier if it noticed that the Egyptian Army was crumbling.

Bar-Lev's view prevailed and on the evening of Wednesday, October 17, after bitter battles waged by the paratroops and armor to open the roads, the first bridge was erected across the canal. A short while later Adan's tanks began to cross. It was Kosygin himself who apprised Sadat of the intelligence (obtained by Soviet satellites) that the Israeli penetration west of the canal was far deeper than the Egyptian field command had guessed. It took quite a while for the Egyptian senior command to grasp that this was not a small task force but a major move that threatened to choke off the Egyptian Army from the rear. That is when they began to concentrate scores of gun batteries against the Israeli bridgehead and send in wave after wave of aircraft on suicide attacks.

Despite the heavy fire the IDF's engineers erected another two bridges north of the Great Bitter Lake by Friday morning, October 19. A part of Magen's division also crossed the canal. While Sharon continued to hold the bridgehead and mop up to the north on both sides of the canal, Adan and Magen began a race over open, flat country. Magen at first moved west toward Cairo, while Adan's armored vehicles began an encirclement action in a southwesterly direction to cut off the Egyptian Third Army.

By the time the Egyptians saw what was about to happen to their field force it was too late. Within two days, Adan's tanks had taken up positions on the main roads between Suez and Cairo. The Egyptian forces were indeed holding a part of Sinai, alongside the canal, but there were only 150 Egyptian tanks between the IDF columns and Cairo—and on the Syrian front, the IDF was threatening Damascus. Meanwhile, despite heavy losses the Golani Brigade had retaken the Mount Hermon position from the Syrians, while a paratroop reserve unit had occupied the Syrian side of the mountain.

On October 19 Moscow announced to Washington that it was determined to bring the fighting to a halt immediately and therefore suggested a meeting with American Secretary of State Kissinger. When the United States tried to delay the meeting, the Kremlin retorted that this was a critical matter. Kissinger then decided to hold the meeting with the Russians in Moscow; in that way, he calculated, he would be able to give Israel another day to exploit its success to the west of the canal.

The Egyptian Army showed signs of collapsing on the west bank of the canal. While Sharon's forces were finding it difficult to advance through the heavy foliage toward Ismailia, the rear echelons of the Egyptian Third Army crumbled in the face of Adan and Magen's thrusts. Israeli tanks overran missile batteries, making it possible for Israeli planes to extend close and massive support. Nearly 8,000 Egyptian soldiers surrendered on the west bank alone.

On October 22 the UN Security Council declared a cease-fire, to take effect that evening. The council had previously refrained from passing a cease-fire resolution since the majority of its members, being pro-Arab, were interested in allowing Egypt and Syria to act against Israel until it became clear that the IDF would overcome them. While the cease-fire was to take effect at nightfall, the battles raged on. Israel utilized the time to complete the encirclement of the Egyptian Third Army, while Magen's tanks reached the Gulf of Suez at the port of Adabiya. It wasn't until October 23 that the battles ended on the Egyptian front. One day later the Syrians also announced their acceptance of a cease-fire.

That the IDF completed the encirclement of the Egyptian Third Army after the time set for cease-fire evoked an angry reaction from the Soviet Union. The Kremlin announced an alert in all its paratroop and marine divisions and told Washington that it intended to send forces to the Middle East. In response the U.S. declared an alert of its own. The tension lasted for a few days until it was certain that Moscow had abandoned the idea of direct intervention.

Washington, on the other hand, demanded that Israel permit the transfer of supplies and water to the surrounded Egyptian Third Army. Israel's political leaders assumed that the surrounded troops would be an important bargaining card by which they could secure the Egyptians' evacuation of the recaptured territory in Sinai. Some 25,000 Egyptian soldiers—about 2,000 of them wounded—were encircled in the desert, and Israel could pressure them at will by mounting air attacks or merely by withholding drinking water. But Washington had decided to save the Egyptian Third Army and sternly warned Jerusalem that if a clash broke out between Israel and the Soviet Union as a result of the situation, the Israelis would stand alone. Kissinger even demanded that Israel permit the immediate evacuation of the wounded and the supplying of drinking water to the rest of the beleaguered Egyptians sans quid pro quo. It was his way of bidding for Sadat's confidence, and the Israelis grumbled but yielded to his pressure.

The Aftermath

Foreign military analysts have concluded that Israel's performance in the Yom Kippur War was essentially similar in style to the Six-Day War; speed, firepower, and tactical air support were their great strengths. The IDF used battle-tested equipment, and Israeli battle performance was up to standard. Improvisational skill was amply demonstrated, but no new weapons and equipment were unveiled. The Arab forces, on the other hand, had access to much new and sophisticated weaponry and equipment that took their toll on Israel. Egypt's ability to deploy a seven-division force rapidly on the Israeli side of the Suez Canal was due largely to the new Soviet heavy pontoon bridge. The Egyptians constructed fourteen bridges across the Suez Canal and were able to keep about seven of them operational despite heavy Israeli air strikes. The Egyptians used smoke to cover the bridges, and indeed Israeli planes had trouble finding them.

The IDF ended the war with the feeling that political events had deprived Israel of its just rewards for succeeding in battle. The UN Security Council had called for a cease-fire as soon as it was clear that Egypt's Third Army was on the verge of being destroyed. After disputing the course of the cease-fire lines, Israel and Egypt, through Kissinger's mediation, agreed on a troop disengagement. (Some four months later, on May 31, 1974, a separation-of-forces agreement was signed in Switzerland.) Israel gave up the territory she had captured on the west bank of the canal and withdrew close to the Jiddi and Mitla passes in Sinai. Earlier a prisoner exchange had been effected and Israel accepted a tacit understanding that Egypt would lift the blockade at Bab el-Mandeb on the Red Sea. Preliminary peace talks opened in Geneva and were then postponed as Kissinger tried to work out a disengagement agreement between Israel and Syria.

The war and its diplomatic aftermath left the Israeli government shaken. This was reflected in the Labor alignment's poor showing in the elections and the difficulty Mrs. Meir had in forming a new government in 1974. An angry public outcry arose over the government's handling of the war. The role of Defense Minister Dayan was particularly criticized, and what is now referred to as the War of the Generals flared up as the guns fell silent. It was sparked by Ariel Sharon's charges that the High Command had unnecessarily delayed exploiting of the bridgehead his forces had achieved on the west bank of the canal. Both IDF Chief of Staff Elazar and Chaim Bar-Lev refuted Sharon and defended their decisions. This "war" only served to underscore a national sense of depression. It also provoked concern over the apparent politicization of IDF command, since Sharon was a leader of the hard-line Likud opposition.

After the Yom Kippur War Prime Minister Meir appointed a commission of inquiry, headed by the Chief Justice of the Israeli Supreme Court, Shimon Agranat, to investigate Israel's lack of preparedness for the war. The commission's report characterized Chief of Staff Elazar as overconfident, unprepared, and unresponsive to the early signs of war. Elazar was asked to resign and did under protest on April 2. Also named by the commission was Military Intelligence chief Eli Zeira and three of his assistants for their failure to properly assess and report the signs of Egyptian and Syrian mobilization that preceded the Arab attack. Shmuel Gonen, commander at the Egyptian front, was cited by the commission for his poor tactical control and faulty decisions. The commission recommended that Zeira and Gonen be relieved of their posts, a recommendation that was duly implemented.

Both Meir and Dayan were cleared by the commission, which concluded that Dayan's judgment had been limited by the information he received from the General Staff. Still, the clearing of Dayan provoked sharp criticism in the Cabinet, the Knesset, and the press until the public outcry over his refusal to resign led to Meir's own resignation and the fall of her government.

The Egyptian Army had scored a major achievement during the Yom Kippur War in crossing the canal and occupying positions in Sinai until the cease-fire. This was the first Arab military success since 1948, and it left Israel rather shaken. Furthermore, the heavy losses in the Yom Kippur War had considerably depleted the command of the IDF. Of the 2,521 Israeli soldiers killed during the war, 606 (or twenty-four percent) were officers, including twenty-five colonels and more than eighty majors. The Egyptians and the Syrians did not publish any statistics on their losses in the war, but Western Intelligence services have ventured that the Egyptians lost about 12,000 men, the Syrian about 4,000.

From a purely military point of view it seemed clear in retrospect that Israel's repeated victories over the previous twenty-five years had fostered a sense of complacency. In the aftermath of the Yom Kippur War, however, the IDF realized that the time had come to review its operative, tactical, and planning strategies.

The General Staff decided to enlarge the IDF substantially, adding a number of armored units organized according to a broader operational framework. It was felt, for instance, that in the event of a new war a strategic reserve was lacking; hence special emphasis was placed on supplementing infantry units and upgrading the arms and equipment issued to them. At the same time it was decided to acquire more up-to-date armaments that in any future confrontation would balance the odds with the much larger infantries of the Arab armies—particularly with those operating anti-tank missiles.

Another decision was to greatly enlarge the store of equipment and ammunition, for a war between armored forces consumes vast quantities of equipment and ammunition and there was a risk that Israeli stores could be depleted relatively quickly. Dependence on American airlift was both unsound as an option and politically.

Postwar reorganization reached territorial and regional defense units as well, so as to avert any situation in which it would be necessary to abandon settlements—as had happened on the Golan Heights even before fighting broke out. The Israeli Air Force was also refurbished, with a rise in the number of squadrons and helicopters (including assault helicopters) added to its store. The air force also made a special effort to prepare for a more successful contest with the missile systems possessed by the Arab armies. And finally, changes were made in the Intelligence Corps, which had failed so disgracefully on the eve of the war. For example, it was decided that the states of alert in the IDF were not to be influenced by the political situation in the Arab states but would be dictated, first and foremost, by changes in deployment and other military conditions in the field.

Notes

1. Previously unpublished interview with author, June 14, 1973.
2. *Ibid.*

Politics and the Army

ISRAEL'S EMBATTLED STATUS creates a special tension and dynamic that thrusts the military into practically every aspect of the nation's political, cultural, and social life. The army touches the life of every Israeli, for an awareness of the nation's precarious position makes the fortunes of the army a matter of concern vital to all. Most Israelis are directly involved in the IDF, either through their own service in the reserves, or through their families and jobs. The unrelieved history of war and terror against Israel coupled with the feeling that many Arabs still harbor the goal of destroying the Jewish state are indelibly stamped on every Israeli's consciousness, making garrison mentality an inevitable fact of life. Moreover a strong IDF prepared for any renewal of hostilities is the only guarantee of Israel's future. No number of guarantees from the United States or any other country can change the fact that the burden of Israel's defense rests with her own people.

These circumstances have made it possible for military interests in Israel to exercise greater influence over the country's domestic affairs than is the case in other democratic countries, and the IDF's presence in Israel's political life is particularly significant. *Bitahon*, literally meaning security, but also a byword for national security, is a term often heard in Israel. Concern for security is at times an obsession, at other times a convenient pretext for politically expedient decisions in such areas as censorship. In some ways security is sacred to this people that has known persecution throughout its history, and security at all costs may even be a logical extension of the Israeli national character. Yet the imperative of national security has sometimes been abused.

Israelis encounter security regulations established by the army wherever they turn—whether it's call-up papers for reserve service or the need to obtain a special release from such service when leaving the country, however briefly. The newspaper the Israeli reads has gone through military censorship, and although there is no political censorship in Israel per se, anything that touches even obliquely on a military subject must be passed by the army censor. If the matter in question relates to quantities of arms or equipment, or the disclosure of an army or navy maneuver, the relevance of the security issue is clear. Sometimes, however, security is evoked as grounds for suppressing reports that might prejudice the government's position in the domestic political arena. It is here that censorship impinges on freedom of expression and the Israeli press constantly battles this tendency, often resorting to fierce and formal protests in defense of the public's right to know. Nevertheless, when Israeli politicians feel pressed to justify some action or policy, they often invoke the name of security in vain.

On another level the Ministry of Defense exercises great influence over the fields of science and industry, and therefore over the nation's economic life. Its importance as an economic power base derives both from the preferential status of the IDF and from the relationship between defense and scientific research. (For example, the Ministry played a key role in building Israel's two nuclear reactors.) As Israel's defense budget is more than thirty percent of the entire national outlay, those responsible for disbursing defense funds naturally have considerable influence over the nation's economy.

The Defense Ministry is the largest of the Israeli government's offices in terms of budget and staff; apart from the tens of thousands employed in the various defense industries, such as aircraft and munitions, more still are employed directly by the IDF and the ministry proper. This means that one-fifth of the nation's labor force is connected directly or indirectly with defense work. And the growth of the aircraft and arms industries has also enabled the defense establishment to extend its ties abroad through the export of weaponry to more than seventy countries—including many that do not have diplomatic relations with Israel.

The Ministry of Defense is also deeply involved in some of the more ticklish aspects of Israel's foreign policy. It has been known to develop its own contacts and relationships with various foreign governments, often dictating policy to the Foreign Ministry. The most important contacts between Israel and France in the 1950s, for example, were conducted by representatives of the Ministry of Defense rather than professional diplomats from the Foreign Ministry. This was also the case with preliminary contacts made prior to the establishment of full diplomatic relations with West Germany.

The question of control over the military establishment and its accountability to the civilian government has long been a sensitive subject in Israel. For the first fifteen years of the state's existence, from 1948 to 1963, Israel's political and military leadership was embodied by one man: David Ben-Gurion. He exercised almost exclusive control over both spheres as Prime Minister *and* Defense Minister, and most important matters were resolved behind closed doors without the advice, consent, or even knowledge of the Knesset. Often the Cabinet was uninformed, or made privy to only select information on essential defense matters; the decision to embark on the 1956 Sinai Campaign, for example, was reported to some ministers and parliamentary leaders only after it was already a fait accompli.

In response to protests of highhandedness Ben-Gurion invoked the cause of security, claiming that he could not present such secret matters before a full plenum of the Knesset for fear of leaks. As a compromise he established a ministerial Committee for Defense Affairs, which was supposed to take part in future decisions of a political and military nature; in practice, however, the committee was wholly dependent upon on the good graces of the Prime Minister throughout Ben-Gurion's tenure.

When Ben-Gurion was on leave from the government for a brief period from 1953 to 1955, Pinhas Lavon served as Minister of Defense under Prime Minister Moshe Sharett. But Lavon complained that much vital information on military affairs was kept from him by the IDF Command and senior members of the Defense Ministry. When Ben-Gurion returned to power the portfolios of Prime Minister and Defense Minister again were held by the same man. Various quarters, including representatives of most of the parties that made up Ben-Gurion's coalition government, sharply criticized the sequestering of the defense establishment and Ben-Gurion's exclusive control over it. But he was adamant that military and defense personnel should not appear before the Knesset's Defense and Foreign Affairs Committee, and when the committee asked for details on the sale of weapons to Portugal and the reconditioning of Portuguese planes, Ben-Gurion refused to comment. In another case he refused to reveal to the committee that Holland was a market for many Israeli-made Uzi submachine guns.

Perhaps the stormiest controversy caused by Ben-Gurion's imperious ways erupted in the 1950s over the decision to build a nuclear reactor by the Negev town of Dimona. This matter of far-reaching strategic, political, and economic consequence serves as a prime example of how security decisions of the first order were made secretly. The Defense and Foreign Affairs Committee had received only a general summary on the project—and that only after it had been published in the newspapers. Even the decision to build the reactor had been kept from members of the Knesset's Defense Budget Committee, which was usually informed of fiscal matters even if they were top secret. The result was a great outcry in the Knesset, with indignant charges of concealment being leveled at the government. Chaim Landau, one of the senior delegates from the Herut Party and a member of the Defense and Foreign Affairs Committee, complained that, "The most important fact regarding the atomic reactor in Dimona was *not* made known to us, and that was deliberate subterfuge." But Ben-Gurion was resolute and again cited security as a justification.

After Levi Eshkol became Prime Minister in 1963, Cabinet ministers were better informed of defense matters. The political influence of the military elite, on the other hand, grew considerably during Eshkol's term. Chief of Staff Yitzhak Rabin enjoyed political status that had never been accorded to his predecessors in Ben-Gurion's day, and Eshkol leaned on him as though he were his Minister of Defense. The Six-Day War and its outcome were further conducive to involvement of military men in political life. The friction that characterized the waiting period prior to the war traced to the disagreement between the majority in the Cabinet and the General Staff majority over Intelligence appraisals, with the military disgruntled that the political echelon was dragging its feet about deciding to go to war. After the stunning victory the commanders became national heroes, emerging from their relative anonymity into the limelight of greatly exaggerated publicity.

Another consequence of the Six-Day War was that many IDF commanders permitted themselves certain liberties in the political arena that had previously been regarded as unthinkable. They began to intervene—directly and indirectly—in matters of political importance, ranging from the country's desired borders and settlement in the occupied territories to the proper reaction to Soviet involvement in the Middle East to talks with the United States on a settlement with Israel's neighbors. The political leadership contributed to this development by courting the military; after all, they were national heroes and therefore welcome additions to the ranks of any party. Before the Six-Day War Moshe Dayan and Yigal Allon were the only two top-ranking IDF commanders to have joined government not long after departing from military service, but after the war the shift from the army to politics became a norm. In this way Major General Ezer Weizman moved directly from the General Staff to the Cabinet as Minister of Transport, and Lieutenant General Chaim Bar-Lev stepped straight from the Chief of Staff's office into the Ministry of Commerce and Industry. Often the parties were known to be negotiating with officers while they were still in uniform: Major General Ariel Sharon moved straight from the IDF to organizing the right-wing parties into the Likud bloc, and Major General Aharon Yariv also went directly from the army into political life and was soon appointed to a ministership.

The amazing thing is that Moshe Dayan, of all people—Ben-Gurion's leading disciple—accepted this phenomenon with equanimity. Not only did he refrain from fighting it, indirectly he contributed to its development. In contrast with Ben-Gurion, Dayan as Defense Minister agreed to have the Chief of Staff become a permanent fixture at Cabinet meetings. Perhaps Dayan wanted to relieve himself of the responsibility for certain critical security matters—or at least share it with his subordinates. At any rate, once the long-standing custom was breached and the Chief of Staff became a regular Cabinet participant it was impossible to deny the privilege to other officers as well, and so they too were invited occasionally to express their views before the ministers. This remained true after the Likud formed a government in 1977.

The Yom Kippur War prompted a bitter and controversial debate not over the involvement of the military in political decisions but over the politicization of the Israeli Army. The opening salvo in this so-called War of the Generals was fired by Ariel Sharon, who in a series of interviews with foreign journalists complained that the war had been terribly mismanaged and that as a result Israel had lost her power of deterrence. Moreover, Sharon charged, "In the second phase of the war, [Lieutenant General Chaim] Bar-Lev was brought out of retirement ostensibly to coordinate the southern front. This was a political appointment. Bar-Lev came to save his own reputation and his concept of defense."[1]

Sharon, who had joined forces with the right-wing opposition

Likud bloc shortly before the war, was not only Bar-Lev's rival in terms of strategic thinking but also his political opponent, since Bar-Lev was an important minister in Golda Meir's Labor government. Needless to say Bar-Lev angrily refuted the charges, while Chief of Staff Elazar publicly rebuked Sharon for undermining army morale by his fractious attitude. He also forbade his generals to grant any further interviews. Sharon, however, was soon back in civilian clothes (he had served in the war as a reservist) and continued to press his criticism of the IDF Command.

The War of the Generals convinced many Israelis that the IDF was too political. Yet in a very real sense the weakness of the civilian leadership rather than the political ambitions of the IDF officers was responsible for that situation. As a rule the ranks of the IDF have not been open to partisan political activity; young officers have shunned the temptation to align themselves with political parties, and the Israeli Army does not—nor can it because of its very nature—cultivate military cliques. There have never been anything even vaguely resembling the development of a junta that seeks to protect the army's interests. For IDF officers (or at least most of them) service in the army is an expression of their desire to serve their country. The only other common denominator is professional and technical, certainly not political or factional.

The standing army is composed mostly of draftees—aged eighteen to twenty-one—and partly of regulars, with reservists integrated at all levels continuously. Even the regulars include a substantial number of men who have chosen to sign on for a few years, but not as a career. This is particularly true of junior officers, thousands of whom decide to devote a few extra years to the security of the state, above and beyond their compulsory service, but who fully intend to make their careers in the civilian sector. An essentially parallel process—albeit anchored in regulations set down by the IDF—occurs among the higher command ranks. All officers who reach the rank of major general know that at most they have five more years of service ahead of them. A major general usually rotates through no more than two postings at this rank; few remain for a third posting, and those who do generally are regarded as candidates for Chief of Staff. The turnover among ranking officers is high, with the result that a decisive majority of IDF officers become civilians before their fiftieth birthday; most begin their second, civilian career somewhere between the ages of forty-five and forty-eight. This means that IDF officers have their eyes on a civilian job market that must absorb them in mid-career, and middle aged.

In examining the relationship between the military and the government during Menachem Begin's tenure as Prime Minister one can see that there was a significant shift in approach between his first and second Cabinets (1977–1981 and 1981–1984, respectively). The Defense Minister in Begin's first government was Ezer Weizman, who had been considered a hawk as a military man but who turned out to be a moderate as a political leader. Weizman's first decision as Defense Minister was to effect a significant cut in the defense budget, an extraordinary move, especially in that it was contrary to both the military's position and the recommendation of his predecessor as Defense Minister, Shimon Peres.

Far more important in terms of the relationship between the military and the government were developments that took place after President Anwar Sadat's visit to Jerusalem. The issue then was whether to agree to Sadat's demand that Israel withdraw from all of the Sinai Peninsula in return for peace. The General Staff prepared a plan by which only part of the Sinai would be returned to Egypt in the first phase, with two vital areas of the peninsula remaining in Israeli hands even after the peace accord. But the generals were astounded to learn that Prime Minister Begin and Foreign Minister Dayan had essentially promised Sadat to pull back from all of the Sinai before consulting with them. In fact the General Staff's proposal was never even deliberated, and its recommendation never so much as considered. In all probability a similar situation would never have arisen under Levi Eshkol, Golda Meir, or Yitzhak Rabin—meaning that a decision profoundly affecting national security would never have been made by a Labor government without first consulting the General Staff.

Then both standards and approach changed radically in Begin's second government. His first Cabinet had boasted a number of senior ministers with military backgrounds, including two former Chiefs of Staff (Yigael Yadin and Moshe Dayan) and a former Deputy Chief of Staff and Commander of the Air Force (Ezer Weizman). When Begin took over the defense portfolio following Weizman's resignation, Mordechai Zippori, who had the advantage of a rich military background, served as his Deputy Minister. In Begin's second government, however, when he was appointed a minister in his own right, Zippori was excluded from the Ministerial Committee for Defense Affairs.

One of the main reasons for faulty civilian control over the armed forces from 1980 onward was that the ministers in Begin's second Cabinet lacked real experience in defense affairs. Though the average age of its ministers was relatively young, most of them had not served in the IDF—a very unusual phenomenon in Israel. The change began when, rather than replacing Weizman during his first term, Begin took over the defense portfolio himself. This was a period marked by ineffective civilian supervision of the defense establishment, as a result of which the Chief of Staff effectively functioned as the Defense Minister. Begin's respect for uniforms—and most everything else connected with the Israeli military—enabled this development to occur, and the fact that Chief of Staff Eitan professed extremely hawkish views set the tone.

But the real turning point in the relationship between the government and military came when Ariel Sharon was appointed Minister of Defense. All the rules of the game changed, as the 1982 war in Lebanon sadly and amply demonstrated. It was a venture that traced to a political-military phenomenon quite unprecedented in Israel's history. Israel is a thoroughly democratic country, but on the eve of the war and in its initial phases something happened that can only be described as a putsch—albeit a novel one in which control over the Israeli Army and its operations was arrogated by a single man who proceeded to flout governmental decisions in matters of crucial importance. It was not the army that engineered this sophisticated putsch but the Cabinet member in charge of the army on behalf of the civilian establishment—the Minister of Defense. Sharon acted contrary to the government's intentions and sent the IDF into action to achieve aims and serve purposes that lacked the Cabinet's sanction—sometimes because the ministers were deliberately kept in ignorance. In essence he would lay out one plan before the Cabinet and then implement a very different one—on which his mind had long been set—using the IDF as his tool. The result was that the Cabinet either had no idea what the General Staff was thinking or doing, or it received the pertinent information too late. He fully succeeded in isolating the ministers from their military.

In a very real sense Sharon manipulated the government through the medium of the IDF. He did not do so in the manner usually associated with a putsch; the army was not sent out to take over the country's democratic institutions. The Defense Minister did not seize the state television and radio stations. He did not shut down the

Knesset or arrest fellow ministers. Nor did he clamp down on the Israeli press. Sharon's method was more subtle and his putsch rather a covert one—an innovation whereby the army acted against the will and intentions of the government without being seen to challenge the country's democratic structures. Israel's democratic framework remained intact, but it was severely hobbled in its ability to function properly. Some ranking IDF officers, suspecting that the government was being manipulated, spoke out at General Staff meetings and questioned whether certain moves had been approved by the government and whether operations in the field were not in fact contrary to Cabinet resolutions. On the whole, however, the reaction of the IDF High Command was strikingly passive: given to discipline as a matter of course, the members of the General Staff outdid themselves on this occasion and their conduct led to a wave of soul searching once the full picture became known.

Sharon's departure from the Defense Ministry brought about certain changes. Actually the Sharon era in the ministry came to its end even before the Cabinet accepted the report of the Kahan Commission, which had been charged with investigating the extent of the IDF's implication in the September 1982 massacre in the Sabra and Shatila refugee camps in Beirut. In publishing its findings the commission recommended that Sharon resign or be dismissed as Defense Minister because he bore "indirect responsibility" for what happened in the camps. Before relinquishing his portfolio, however, Sharon tried to rally the General Staff behind him as a way of pressuring the Cabinet to reject the Kahan Commission's report. He wanted to create the impression that in voting for his resignation the ministers would be doing damage to the armed forces. But the General Staff demonstratively turned its back on Sharon. Chief of Staff Eitan (also rated in the report) went so far as to publish an Order of the Day—which he read personally in public—declaring that the IDF accepted the Kahan Commission report as having the weight of a court decision. The move had the potent effect of symbolically dissociating the IDF from Sharon and effectively brought his tenure in the Defense Ministry to an end.

Notes

1. Perlmutter, *op. cit.*, p. 52.

16

The War in Lebanon

THE 1982 WAR IN LEBANON, which the Israeli government dubbed "Operation Peace for Galilee," differed from all
of Israel's previous wars in being the first one not addressed
solely to the country's security problems—in this case the threat posed
to the Galilean towns and settlements by the PLO artillery stationed
in Lebanon. For the IDF's foray into Lebanon was also conceived as
a means of influencing the political processes of a neighboring state
and imposing a "new order" on Lebanon. Toward that end, for the
first time in the history of Israel's armed conflicts, the IDF was to
reach and take control of the capital of an Arab state. Those who
promoted the war and its far-reaching aims, headed by Defense Minister Ariel Sharon, contended that Israel had a vital interest in who
ruled and what was going on in the capital of every neighboring state.
The reply of those opposed to such ambitious objectives for Israel's
defense army was that while Israel indeed had an interest in the disposition of the governments in the neighboring states, this was not
a reason for going to war, and certainly not for conquering a neighboring capital.

Using the army to meddle in the political affairs of a neighboring
state was also a signal departure from the premise upon which the
IDF was built as the defense force of the State of Israel. Inevitably,
perhaps, this violation of one of the prime articles of faith of Israel's
security consensus led to a bitter controversy that reverberated even
through ranks of the army in time of war. No comparable clash of
views had ever rocked the country before; for the first time in the
state's history, in fact, the IDF had gone to war without a national
consensus on an issue as sensitive as the war's purpose. Without
question this controversy affected the course of the war, and even the

fighting man's devotion to his duty. It also explains another phenomenon exclusive to the war in Lebanon, namely that dozens of officers and men chose to stand trial and serve jail sentences rather than serve in Lebanon.

The war in Lebanon was also marked by the ouster of Defense Minister Sharon, and Chief of Military Intelligence Yehoshua Saguy due to the implication of the IDF in the massacre of hundreds of Palestinian civilians by Phalange forces in the Sabra and Shatila refugee camps in West Beirut. Ultimately, an operation slated to end within forty-eight hours became hopelessly stuck in the Lebanese quagmire. Well into war's third year, the government of Israel was still unable to extricate the IDF from Lebanon and restore even the dubious conditions that prevailed on the Israeli-Lebanese border prior to the war in 1982.

Lebanon, long considered the least extreme of the Arab countries surrounding Israel, was also the weakest. It was generally assumed therefore that her moderation notwithstanding, she would not be the first Arab country to sign a peace treaty with Israel. And as matters turned out Lebanon's chronic instability prevented her from reaching such an accommodation even after Egypt, the largest and strongest of the Arab states, had made peace with Israel. It was this same infirmity that had led Lebanon into a vicious civil war in the mid-1970s, in whose wake she was effectively partitioned between the country's various ethnic communities and their militias. The civil war also enabled the Palestinians to establish a military network in south Lebanon, whence its forces regularly harassed Israel.

To understand the background to Israel's invasion of Lebanon we must go back over a decade to the development that first marked Lebanon's transformation into a confrontation state. In 1969 the Palestinian organizations began to concentrate their forces in Lebanon near the Israeli border, and particularly on the slopes of Mount Hermon, and this came to be known as Fatahland. Following the 1970 civil war in Jordan in which the Palestinian military force was crushed, the focus of Palestinian political and military activity shifted to Lebanon. Soon the Palestinian organizations had reestablished their headquarters in Beirut and hundreds of irregulars were streaming into south Lebanon, effectively creating a state within a state.

The Palestinians behaved with little consideration for their Christian and Shiite neighbors in south Lebanon, while their harassment of Israeli settlements over the border mounted yearly. Israel responded with reprisal actions that grew increasingly more fierce and frequent. In addition to the Israeli Air Force's regular attacks against the Palestinian organizations in Lebanon, Israel also carried out three major ground operations in south Lebanon prior to the 1982 war: the first in May 1970, the second, reaching the Litani River, in September 1972, and the third in March 1978, after which the IDF remained stationed in the stretch of territory up to the Litani for almost six months, withdrawing only when it was replaced in part of the sector by United Nations (UNIFIL) forces.

The residents of south Lebanon, who found themselves in the midst of a battleground of a war not their own, loosed their resentment on the Palestinians. Israel exploited this mood to establish ties with the Christian inhabitants of south Lebanon, who proceeded to form a local militia commanded by Saad Haddad, a major in the Lebanese Army. Over the years these ties flourished, with the Haddad militia receiving aid from Israel in the form of arms and training. By 1978 the Haddad militia had gained control of an enclave along the Israeli border.

The second development took place after the establishment of military ties between Israel and the Christian militias in northern Lebanon. It is doubtful whether these ties would have developed so intensively had it not been for the Palestinian involvement in the Lebanese civil war. The PLO had joined forces with the leftist Moslem camp (headed by the Druze leader Kamal Jumblatt) against the Maronite Christians of Lebanon, thereby tilting the scales in favor of the Moslems.

Faced with the prospect of defeat, the Christian militias—and especially the forces led by former President Camille Chamoun and Pierre Gemayel's Phalange movement—felt they had no choice but to appeal to Israel for help. They approached the Israelis not only as common enemies of the PLO but also as a kindred minority vulnerable to the pressures of the Moslem world. The Israeli government responded with modest military support, but over the years these ties grew stronger and Israel's involvement in Lebanon deepened. In retrospect it appears that the PLO's prominent involvement in the Lebanese civil war may have been one of its greatest mistakes: it led Lebanon's Christian leadership to conclude that the solution to their country's internal strife lay in the expulsion of the Palestinians from their midst; it drove the Christian leaders into Israel's arms; and it caused the Palestinian people immense suffering and losses that, according to one estimate, reached as high as 20,000 dead. Most telling of all, however, the PLO's involvement in the Lebanese civil war caused the Palestinian national movement to squander its efforts and resources on aims that were merely incidental to its real cause.

The Lebanese civil war, and the Palestinian involvement in it, were also the direct causes of the third development: the Syrian Army's invasion of Lebanon in 1976. Damascus had always considered Lebanon as an integral part of Syria that had been artificially detached from the homeland during the colonialist era. (Hence, Syria does not have an ambassador in Lebanon to this day.) In addition to its nationalist ambitions, however, Syria had legitimate security interests in Lebanon, particularly in the area adjoining her border.

Damascus's aim was to keep Lebanon a united Arab state in which the non-Moslem minorities could live in peace, but the civil war— and the prospect that the coalition of the Palestinians and the Moslem Left would defeat the Christian militias—placed this vision in jeopardy. President Assad feared that a victory by the leftist coalition would lead to the partition of Lebanon and an alliance between the Lebanese Christians and Israel. Worse yet, he feared that ultimately a Christian state would arise in Lebanon and, like Israel, constitute a threat to Syria and the Arab world at large. So strange as it may have seemed to the uninitiated observer, Syria's invasion of Lebanon was initially directed against the Palestinians and their leftist Moslem allies. It engendered the first rift between Assad and the head of the PLO, Yasser Arafat—though Arafat's chief ally suffered a far grimmer fate: Jumblatt was murdered, and by all indications the Syrians were deeply implicated in the act.

To pave the way for its army to enter Lebanon (in the end its pretext was nothing less than a request for intervention from the Lebanese President), Damascus was ready to reach a tacit understanding with Israel that the latter would not intervene militarily in Lebanon. This unofficial accord was achieved through the auspices of the United States and was known as the Red Lines Agreement. Until then Israel had been opposed to the presence of the Syrian Army in Lebanon, but Rabin's government was prepared to tolerate a Syrian military presence there on condition that the Syrian forces would not introduce antiaircraft missiles onto Lebanese soil and would not move any farther south than the line running from Sidon eastward to Aishiya and on to the Syrian-Lebanese border. It was also understood that Syria would not use its air force against the Christian militias in

Lebanon. In so agreeing to these conditions Syria implicitly recognized Israel's security interests in south Lebanon.

Israel's policy at that stage was to ensure that no hostile military force would become ensconced in south Lebanon; to prevent Lebanon from turning into a confrontation state; and to neutralize the PLO's activities there—all while taking care not to be drawn into the incessant Lebanese civil war. When representatives of the Maronite Christian community met with Israeli Prime Minister Rabin in mid-1976 they asked him to intervene militarily. In essence they wanted the Israeli Army to drive the PLO and the Syrian Army out of Lebanon, but Rabin rejected the notion out of hand. He was thinking in terms of helping the Lebanese Christians to help themselves by providing them with arms, training, instruction, and the like, but certainly not of active intervention. Toward that end a permanent Israeli delegation was stationed in Beirut headed by representatives of the Mossad.

The fourth development that spurred the downhill slide toward war occurred in 1981, when a distinctive change took place in Israel's policy toward Lebanon. It began with a deliberate provocation of the Syrian garrison in April 1981: Phalangists attacked Syrians stationed near the Lebanese city of Zahle, which is on the main road from Beirut to Damascus not far from the Syrian frontier, and in response the Syrians began to shell the city heavily. When appealed to for help, Israeli Prime Minister Menachem Begin, who had vowed that Israel would not permit the Syrians to annihilate the Christian minority in Lebanon, approved an air strike against Syrian helicopters presumably involved in the attack on Zahle—in violation of the 1976 understanding.

Begin was of course unaware that the incident had been provoked by extremist elements in the Phalange who wanted to draw Israel and Syria into a military clash in Lebanon—and how well they succeeded. Israeli Intelligence opposed the air action, but Begin overruled its counsel, and the Syrians responded precisely as the Intelligence people had predicted by introducing surface-to-air missiles into Lebanon. This brought an end to the so-called Red Lines Agreement, and Israel, now headed by the Likud government, was determined to remove those missiles one way or another. Initially, however, she did not resort to military action.

The situation took another turn for the worse in July 1981. In the wake of Israeli air activity against Palestinian targets in south Lebanon and the bombing of Palestinian headquarters in Beirut, an exchange of artillery fire broke out between Israeli and Palestinian forces over Israel's northern border. The volleys lasted for days, with many Israeli settlements sustaining hits, and soon residents of Kiryat Shmonah began to flee the border town. The residents of the Galilee had become hostage to the PLO's artillery, whose power was growing apace. Obviously it was impossible to put the entire population of northern Israel in shelters, so the only way to protect civilians was to drive the PLO's artillery back out of range. The cease-fire reached begrudgingly between Israel and the PLO through American mediation only aggravated the situation, for it was clear that Begin's government could not live for long with an agreement that might foster the development of a relationship, however indirectly, between the American government and the PLO. After the artillery exchanges of July 1981 war seemed a foregone conclusion; only its timing and scope remained to be seen.

Those last two elements were decided as the result of another change that occurred in 1981. In the summer of that year the Likud again won the Israeli elections, and Ariel Sharon was appointed Israel's new Minister of Defense. It was Sharon who brought about the fourth development by completely revamping Israel's policy toward Lebanon. Until his installation in the Defense Ministry, the Rabin and subsequent Begin governments maintained much the same policy toward Lebanon—although during his first term as Prime Minister Begin promised the Lebanese Christians full protection against the Syrians. But it was Sharon who decided on a completely different tack. He contended that Israel had made a great mistake in agreeing to a Syrian military presence in Lebanon, and he took measures to end it. At the same time he completely revised the nature of relations between Israel and the Lebanese Phalange, and in so doing set down new objectives for Israel that found expression in the aims of the war he was planning.

Sharon established three direct aims months before hostilities broke out in June 1982. The first was to evict the PLO's military and political organs from Lebanon. Not content with destroying the Palestinian military network in south Lebanon, Sharon planned to purge it from the entire country. His attendant indirect aim was to send a sobering shock through the Palestinian public and leadership in the West Bank and Gaza Strip. For he was convinced that the destruction of the PLO's political and military capability in Lebanon would bring out moderate leaders in the occupied territories who were amenable to the limited form of autonomy proposed by the Likud government.

The second aim was to engineer the election of Bashir Gemayel as the new President of Lebanon, for he was sure to block the return of the Palestinian organizations to Lebanon and sign a peace treaty with Israel.

The third was to bring about the withdrawal of the Syrian Army from Lebanon. For as long as the Syrians remained there, they were likely to foil Bashir Gemayel's election as President and prevent the expulsion of the PLO.

These aims would obviously make it necessary to extend the war beyond south Lebanon. To achieve them would require the IDF to reach Beirut and draw the Syrian Army into battle—as indeed happened in June 1982. Yet these were not the war aims authorized by the Israeli Cabinet at its meeting on Saturday night, June 5, when it voted to send the IDF into Lebanon to lift the PLO's threat from the Galilean settlements. The Cabinet's decision on the war, worded by Prime Minister Begin, addressed itself, inter alia, to the aims: "To charge the IDF with taking all the northern settlements out of the range of fire of the terrorists concentrated . . . in Lebanon." But it noted specifically that "in the course of implementing this decision, the Syrian Army is not to be attacked unless it fires on our forces."

A few of the ministers had debated the actual range of the PLO's artillery and whether or not the city of Sidon, for example, would fall into the sphere of the IDF's ground action. Prime Minister Begin translated these issues into numerical values in noting in a letter to President Reagan that the IDF intended to operate in an area of up to forty kilometers from the Israeli border. One would assume that the Prime Minister would not have committed himself in such definitive terms had he not been sure about the distances involved.

Washington had known for a number of months that an Israeli invasion of Lebanon was to be expected, though the American Administration, like the Israeli Cabinet, had a very different war in mind. As far back as December 1981, at a meeting held at the Foreign Ministry in Jerusalem, Ariel Sharon had spoken with Special Ambassador Philip Habib of his intention to solve the Palestinian problem by military means. To Habib's amazement, which was shared by the American Chargé d'Affaires in Israel, William Brown, Sharon disclosed many details of his military plan; and immediately upon leaving the meeting Habib dispatched a detailed report on the talk to American Secretary of State Alexander Haig.

Two months later Haig personally received a special emissary from the Israeli government, Intelligence Chief Yehoshua Saguy, who spread a map out before him and spoke of mounting a major ground operation in south Lebanon. Haig's reservations about such a plan were confined to the nature of the provocation that could serve as a pretext for such an Israeli action, and he spoke of the need for a flagrant provocation that international public opinion could not ignore.

Three months later, in May 1982, Ariel Sharon repeated his warnings to the Secretary during a visit to the United States, this time hinting quite clearly at the possibility of a clash with the Syrian Army. Yet Haig said nothing about sanctions should Israel decide to embark on a military venture. He left it entirely up to the Israelis, moreover, to decide what provocation would be deemed sufficient to justify going to war. Therefore, when Sharon returned to Israel, Begin justly concluded that Washington had given Israel the green light for a limited military operation against the PLO in south Lebanon.

Paradoxically, even though the Cabinet ministers believed that Israel was entering into a limited war, many members of the Israeli General Staff understood that the war could not be confined to south Lebanon. Intelligence Chief Saguy made it clear to his colleagues that a broad military action against the PLO would of necessity draw the Syrian troops in Lebanon into a clash with the IDF, especially if Israeli forces advanced through the Shouf Mountains to the Beirut–Damascus highway along the flank of the Syrian forces in the Bekaa Valley. Similarly, the participants in a war game conducted by the head of the Training Department of the General Staff, Major General Uri Simchoni, concluded that extending the war in Lebanon could well have negative political ramifications and leave Israel hopelessly entangled in a debilitating situation.

For quite a while Israeli officers who had visited the Phalangist forces in Lebanon—including the head of Northern Command, Major General Amir Drori—had been reporting that the Phalange could not be relied upon as a military ally and that it was indeed doubtful whether they would participate fully in the war against the PLO. But these reports and the General Staff's reservations about the upcoming operation were not made known to the Cabinet, and this mutual isolation of the military and the elected policy-making body was one of the gravest errors of the war.

Inevitably the desire to extend the scope of the war without the Cabinet's knowledge wreaked havoc with the IDF's war plans. Because it was necessary to conceal from the Cabinet that the army's ultimate destination was Beirut, the IDF could not follow the best course from a purely military standpoint. Instead of heading directly for more distant targets in the vicinity of Beirut and the Beirut–Damascus highway during the initial stage of the war, so as to outflank the enemy on the north while closing in from the south, the IDF was forced to make a frontal advance from the south alone. The idea of landing forces amphibiously and by helicopter to the enemy's rear in the port of Junieh, the north of Beirut, was rejected out of hand. Thus against its better judgment the IDF was forced to take on both the Palestinian forces and the Syrian Army with a directness and ponderousness that were uncharacteristic of its style.

The war broke out officially on Sunday June 6 at 11 A.M., when the IDF's divisions began to cross the Lebanese border and head for their targets. However, it had been clear since the previous Friday morning, following the assassination attempt on the Israeli ambassador in London, Shlomo Argov, that a war was unavoidable. That morning the Cabinet decided to have the air force bomb various Palestinian targets in Beirut, and the Palestinians responded immediately by shelling Israeli settlements in the Galilee.

On Saturday night, while the Cabinet was still deliberating the prospect of a full-scale ground operation, tanks, field guns, and paratroops were being loaded on landing craft that were immediately sent out to sea. The commander of this force, Brigadier General Amos Yaron, still did not know where it would set ashore, but the head of the Northern Command Drori was convinced that the landing would take place at the estuary of the Awali River, north of Sidon and more than forty kilometers beyond the Israeli border. Drori also believed that after landing, Yaron's paratroops would be ordered to continue northward to the town of Damur and on toward Beirut. However, first they would have to receive their APCs (armored personnel carriers), which were to be delivered by the armored brigade moving up the coast road. This amphibious landing was the only outflanking movement undertaken in the war.

The most important operational decision made at the war's outset was to send an armored division up the central axis skirting the Bekaa Valley to the east. The division's orders were to advance through the Shouf Mountains to the Beirut–Damascus highway. Upon reaching that main east-west axis, it was to turn east toward the mountain pass known as Dahr el-Baidar, thereby closing in on the rear of the Syrian forces stationed south of the highway in the valley. The clear implication of this plan was to draw the Syrians into the fighting, for there was no question that outflanking the Syrian garrison in Lebanon and threatening it from the rear would precipitate a clash. The assumption that the Syrians would prefer to withdraw quickly rather than engage in battle was totally unfounded; even Israel's Military Intelligence argued that the Syrians would not readily retreat.

Hence the dispatch of Brigadier General Menachem Einan's division up the central axis became the focal move of the Lebanese venture and turned that road into the pivotal axis of the war. If Einan's force had reached its destination quickly it would have placed the Syrians in a difficult position: the Syrian brigade in Beirut would have been cut off from the rear, and the Israelis could choose whether to advance into the northern part of the Bekaa Valley or to turn east toward the border and Damascus. The problem was that Einan's force did not get anywhere quickly; in fact, its movement all along the way was agonizingly slow. It received low priority in the initial penetration of Lebanon, and instead of thrusting forward immediately, it was placed behind a long column of troops heading for the Nabatiye highland and on to Sidon. That placement alone cost Einan's division almost a day. Afterward it was delayed again at the Basri River, in the meantime the Syrians had grasped where it was headed and dispatched armored forces from the vicinity of Beirut to block the central axis.

In the end Einan's force failed to reach the Beirut–Damascus highway during the critical first week of the war, so that the Syrian force in the valley was not cut off. Einan's tanks were halted on the third night of the war a mere ten kilometers short of the main highway, in the Druze town of Ein Zehalta. The battle there lasted from after midnight on Wednesday June 9 until the first cease-fire went into effect on Friday afternoon June 11. Despite the fact that the Syrians sustained heavy losses in tanks, equipment, and men, their line held firm, and Einan's force made no further progress at this stage.

The heaviest fighting with the Syrians took place further to the east in the Bekaa Valley and on the slopes of the Anti-Lebanon range, where the Syrians had stationed two armored divisions, mechanized infantry, and commando forces. They also had nineteen surface-to-air missile batteries in the valley, most of which had been brought into Lebanon back in 1981. South of the valley in Israel proper the IDF had massed a multidivisional force under Major General Avigdor Ben-Gal, a former chief of Northern Command. Additional forces had been concentrated on the Golan Heights in case the war with the Syrians were to spread, but also as a means of exerting psychological pressure on the Syrians.

On the first and second days of the war the IDF confined itself to a shallow penetration into the Fatahland and refrained from attacking the Syrians outright. The wording of the Cabinet's Saturday-night decision left no doubt that it had no intention of ordering an attack on the Syrian Army. Neither would public opinion in Israel have accepted such an attack unless the Syrians clearly provoked Israel. Moreover, had the IDF mounted a simultaneous attack on the Palestinians and the Syrian garrison, it was reasonable to assume that Moscow would have been immediately summoned to Syria's aid while Washington would have taken Israel to task for overstepping the bounds of a raid against the terrorist concentrations in south Lebanon.

Besides, the Syrians—far from provoking Israel—did everything possible to avoid a showdown in Lebanon. They confined themselves to a few sorties of small aerial forces—and lost many of their planes in the process. They did not send reinforcements into the Golan Heights even though Israel had. Initially they demonstratively refrained from reinforcing their troops in the Bekaa—even after the operation had begun against the Palestinian strongholds in the western sector of Lebanon—and when Syrian reinforcements were sent to the Bekaa they were small units dispatched only after Einan's division had begun to move up the central axis. All this leads to the conclusion that in the opening stage of the war the Syrians still believed that Israel did not intend to attack their forces.

By the third day of the war, however, that assessment changed radically. For in addition to the movement of Einan's force (which had begun to alarm the Syrians), Special Ambassador Philip Habib arrived in Damascus that day carrying an ultimatum from the Israelis. It demanded that the Syrians order any Palestinian forces located behind their lines in Lebanon and within forty kilometers of the Israeli border to withdraw northward, and that the Syrians pull back the reinforcements sent to the Bekaa Valley, as well as the batteries added to the existing missile system in Lebanon.

Syrian President Assad flatly refused. He might have consented to the withdrawal of Palestinian forces under his wing, but he certainly had no reason to recall his own forces when Israeli units were streaming northward along the central axis in a move to outflank the Syrians in the valley. To make matters worse, on Tuesday, June 8, the IDF began attacking Syrian positions in the town of Jezzin, just off the central axis. Ironically, the attack on the Jezzin began just as Begin was addressing the Knesset, calling upon Assad not to attack Israel's troops and publicly pledging that the IDF would not attack Syrian forces if the Syrians did not open fire first. Unbeknownst to the Prime Minister, however, matters were being handled quiet differently in the field.

Philip Habib was still in Damascus the next day, waiting for Assad's reply to the Israeli ultimatum, when the Israeli Cabinet approved Sharon's request to attack the missiles in the Bekaa. The result was seven batteries destroyed, two more damaged, and twenty-nine Syrian planes downed in dogfights over the area. The destruction of the missiles was a dazzling achievement, the climax of years of diligent and painstaking preparation. Since the Yom Kippur War the Israeli Air Force had dedicated a vast amount of time and energy to the problem of neutralizing surface-to-air missiles, and its victory now over the Soviet-made system was absolute and devastating—although undoubtedly it came at the cost of disclosing technological secrets. After the war experts questioned whether it was truly necessary to reveal the possession of such technology in the context of the Lebanese operation, suggesting that it may have been wiser to save such potent weaponry for a situation in which Israel truly found herself in jeopardy.

Be that as it may, on Wednesday, June 9, Israel faced a different question. Her forces had already succeeded in overrunning the forty-kilometer security belt (at the cost of twenty-five dead, ninety-six wounded, and seven missing in action), and she had satisfactorily established that the Syrians would not intervene on behalf of the PLO even if Israeli forces reached the outskirts of Beirut. Thus the war definitely could have been limited to an operation against the PLO. Even if Israel had wanted to jolt the Syrians with an aerial blow, she could have contented herself with the destruction of the missiles and with the aerial battles against the Syrians—in which ninety Syrian planes had been downed without a single Israeli loss (later in the war, one Israeli plane was shot down by antiaircraft fire)—but spared herself the trouble of the far more costly ground battles.

That, however, was the road not taken, and immediately following the successful strike against the missile batteries Ben-Gal's divisions began moving northward. Not that there was a consensus for
this move within the army. At a meeting of the Northern Front command, the retiring Deputy Chief of Staff, Yekutiel Adam (who was
killed the following day), questioned whether the Cabinet had indeed approved this major assault on the Syrian Army, and his successor Moshe Levi, remarked to Sharon that from an operational
standpoint the move had come as a surprise to even the IDF.

Like Einan's division, Ben-Gal's forces were supposed to reach the
Beirut–Damascus highway; and especially after Einan was blocked just
a few kilometers short of this goal, the High Command urged Ben-
Gal to make a frontal advance. Ben-Gal had a large force (the ratio
of forces being conspicuously in his favor) but little time at his disposal (as matters would turn out, less than two days before a cease-
fire would go into effect). Nevertheless it did not appear that his
commanders were touched by a sense of urgency. For one thing they
failed to exploit the cover of night to move quickly, and their advance suffered extensive delays. The Syrians, on the other hand,
withdrew slowly, and although they made mistakes and lost many tanks
they staged an orderly retreat, putting in a far better performance than
in the past.

So it was that the IDF's second thrust for the Beirut–Damascus
highway turned into a grueling frontal attack during which, in addition to battling the Syrians, the IDF suffered many casualties from
its own ground and air forces. Although the Syrian First Division
was repulsed and effectively destroyed as a fighting force, the Israeli
advance was nonetheless blocked in the early hours of Friday, June
11, when an Israeli armored battalion unwittingly drove right into a
Syrian fortified locality at Sultan Yakoub. When day broke it turned
out that the unit was trapped, and only after an exhausting effort
costing many casualties, with eight tanks and a number of men left
behind in the field, did the battalion finally extricate itself.

Meanwhile the lead units of the Syrian Third Armored Division
had already reached the area, but their advanced T-72 tanks were repulsed—some falling to tank-hunting helicopters, others to Israeli armor or anti-tank units.

As Ben-Gal's drive through the Bekaa came to a standstill, on the
political front Reagan was adamant that Israel honor the cease-fire
slated to take effect at noon on Friday, June 11. The IDF, conse-

quently, did not manage to reach the Beirut–Damascus highway until the second and third weeks of the war—and even then only in the western sector just outside Beirut. The Syrian Army was not driven out of the vicinity of Zahle and Rayak, further down the road to the east, and it maintained its positions in the northern Bekaa Valley. Sharon's grand design was foiled by his own web of deceit, and because he had to conceal his true aims, the IDF had to forego the most effective strategy and thus lacked enough time to achieve its objectives.

The war with the Palestinians was a completely separate operation that took place mostly along the coast—a flat plain whose villages are surrounded by citrus groves and heavy vegetation. The area also boasts two cities, Tyre and Sidon, and most of the fighting in this sector raged in built-up areas among a civilian population (more Lebanese than Palestinian). Israeli Intelligence estimated the number of Palestinian fighters in south Lebanon, including the Fatahland, at about 6,000 men: most were organized in quasi-regular brigades equipped with a few dozen antiquated T-34 tanks, scores of field guns and Katyusha rocket launchers, antiaircraft guns, and an abundant supply of anti-tank weapons. They did not want for arms.

From an ordnance point of view their strength was equivalent to that of a infantry division, with enough weapons in their stores to arm another unit of equal size. The quasi-regular force deployed along the front lines and in fortified positions was supplemented by the militia operating inside the refugee camps. Further, the force was bolstered by volunteers from various Arab and Moslem countries, including hundreds of men from Bangladesh, Pakistan, even India and Sri Lanka. Most of these volunteers served in administrative posts, although some were assigned to field units.

The Palestinians didn't stand a chance against the Israeli juggernaut that bore down on them—and they knew it. The only question was how long they would be able to delay the IDF's thrust through the south, and the cost in casualties. Three divisional forces closed in on the Palestinian units from every side. On the western axis Brigadier General Yitzhak Mordechai's brigades began to barrel up the coast, while to the rear of the Palestinian deployment, between Sidon and Beirut, Amos Yaron's men landed at the estuary of the Awali River. At the same time the Israeli Navy shelled and blockaded the Lebanese coast to prevent the flight of Palestinian forces or the transfer of reinforcements by sea. To the east Brigadier General Avigdor Kahalani's division climbed up the Nabatiye highland and then cut northwest to the coastal city of Sidon.

Moving over a number of different axes, these armored and mechanized forces surrounded south Lebanon and its Palestinian defenders. The skies over the area were exclusively Israeli controlled and air support from both helicopters and combat planes was generously provided. Finally, from the moment the war broke out, it was painfully obvious that the Palestinians were on their own. The Arab states made do with hollow declarations of support, and if they bothered to send equipment at all, it never got past Syrian or Syrian-controlled territory. Even the Shiites and the Druze whom the Palestinians had counted on as allies in the event of an Israeli invasion, chose to hold their fire; in only two places did a handful of armed Shiites fight alongside the Palestinians.

The prime weakness of the Palestinian force in south Lebanon was not a shortage of arms but the pitiful performance of its senior command. Most of the high-ranking officers fled during the war, and many of their subordinates in the quasi-regular units stripped off their uniforms as soon as they saw that their commanders had run. The plan for holding off the Israelis was never implemented. The Palestinians neglected to blow up the bridges over the area's main rivers and hardly even mined the roads or passes.

And yet many Palestinians were undaunted by the approach of an armored war machine so capable of enormous fire power, and they fought with uncommon valor. The fact is that the most tenacious battles were fought not by the semi-regulars but by the scantily trained militiamen in the refugee camps—undoubtedly because they were defending their own homes and families. The proof of their perseverance was that the IDF failed to keep to its timetable for advancing up the coast. It took several days for the Israelis to break through the Palestinian defenses in Sidon, and the linkup with Amos Yaron's force waiting at the Awali River did not take place until some seventy hours into the war. And even though the distance from the Israeli border to Beirut is a mere ninety kilometers, Israeli forces did not join up with the Phalangists until noon on Sunday June 13, the eighth day of the war.

In the opening phase of the advance the Israeli armored forces were to skirt the refugee camps and continue quickly northward. Colonel Eli Geva's brigade, which led the thrust up the coast, managed to cross the Kasmiye Bridge over the Litani without incident and reached the town of Sarafand at the close of the first day. On the following day Geva was surprised to find that the Palestinians likewise had failed to blow up the bridge over the second river on his route—the Zaharani south of Sidon. Geva's force did suffer one serious hitch, though, when a battalion of paratroops attached to the brigade took a wrong turn on the outskirts of Tyre and, instead of circumventing the city and the el-Bas refugee camp, drove into a defended crossroads. In addition to losing a number of tanks and vehicles the battalion lost its commander, Uri Geiger, who fell prisoner to the Palestinians and was murdered a few days later.

In the eastern sector, meanwhile, a fierce battle was fought between Israeli and Palestinian forces on the first day of the war in the ruined fortress of Beaufort (dating from the time of the Crusades), which over the years had become something of a symbol to both sides. To the Israelis the towering ruin dominating the skyline and commanding the Upper Galilee from a height of over 2,300 feet was a constant reminder of the vulnerability of the Galilean settlements to the PLO's artillery; to the Palestinians this fortress, which had been wrested back from the Crusaders by Saladin, symbolized their ability to stand up to the IDF's formidable war machine. The PLO even printed up posters showing armed Palestinians standing on its ramparts.

An elite unit was assigned to capture Beaufort. Actually it was not even necessary to storm the fortress because within a day it would have been far to the rear of the swiftly advancing Israeli forces, and its defenders would surely have had to withdraw or surrender. In fact this is precisely what the front command assumed, so that the Chief of Staff ordered the attack held in abeyance. Yet due to an oversight somewhere down the chain of command his order never reached the unit in question, and the assault was mounted anyway. The Palestinians who remained in the fortress fought heroically until they were overcome; six members of the Golani Commando Unit lost their lives in the action.

The battle for the refugee camps in the west was slow, protracted, and equally bloody. The IDF could have sent the air force in to reduce the camps to rubble and saved on Israeli casualties, but neither the commander of the ground troops in the western sector nor the commanders of the air force were prepared to risk the heavy civilian losses that such bombing would entail. Consequently the battle was conducted more cautiously and took much longer. The camps were organized for defense by sectors, each well endowed with bunkers. The narrow alleyways and dense construction made it difficult for armored vehicles to penetrate the camps without becoming easy targets for anti-tank fire and grenades tossed from windows and rooftops. It took several days to subdue the camps around Tyre; Rashidiye did not fall until the fourth day of the war.

The most difficult battle of all, however, was in the Ein Hilweh camp on the southern edge of Sidon. The defenders turned the camp's residents into hostages by preventing their flight, but more to the point they succeeded in blocking the movement of Israeli forces up the coast for two days. Even after the Israelis broke throught the obstacle in Sidon proper and streamed toward the Awali linkup and Beirut, the battle for the beleagured camp continued. By then, however, it had become a suicidal last stand by a desperate group that refused repeated opportunities to surrender with honor, even rebuffing the pleas of successive delegations of civilians from Sidon. The battle for Ein Hilweh raged on street by street until Monday June 14, when the last bunker in the camp was destroyed.

On Sunday afternoon, June 13, the Israeli paratroops finally linked up with the Phalange force awaiting them in a suburb of Beirut. The paratroops had reached East Beirut by taking a circuitous mountain road to avoid the obstacles on the coastal road leading to Beirut Airport, and even Begin was surprised to learn that Israeli armored cars were driving throught the streets of Beirut. Finally it was clear to all involved that the IDF had outstripped the Israeli government.

The IDF's arrival in Beirut marked the turning point in the war. From a military vantage, the imposition of a siege on the city that hosted the headquarters of the PLO's constituent organizations was an impressive achievement. But it soon transpired that the siege was costing Israel the support of world public opinion. Even those who had applauded the effort to push the PLO's guns out of the range of the population in the Galilee could no longer endorse Israel's cause once her own guns began to shell the city that was home to hundreds of thousands of Lebanese.

At first Israel argued that one of her motives for invading Lebanon was to free the Lebanese from the grip of the Palestinian terrorists; yet it soon emerged that Israeli fire was being released indiscriminately on both the terrorists and their presumed hostages. The ruthless bombing and shelling of Beirut had a telling effect on public opinion in Israel as well—to say nothing of the mood of the

IDF itself. Eli Geva, commander of the armored brigade laying siege to the city, asked to be relieved of his command rather than face the prospect of having to order his men to storm West Beirut and cause untold civilian casualties.

Back in Israel the demonstrations against the war and sharp criticism of the way it was being conducted grew in proportion to the savagery of the Israeli bombings. Yet as the siege of the city dragged on and the leaders of the PLO stood firm in their refusal to evacuate Beirut, the option of ordering Israeli ground forces into West Beirut became an increasingly pressing one. Without question the attempt to combat guerrilla forces in a built-up area covered with rubble would exact a high casualty toll among the attackers. Yet by then a number of Cabinet ministers were united in their opposition to Sharon's resolve to take the city regardless of the cost, and even senior IDF officers balked at the prospect of fighting in the streets of Beirut.

The solution to the impasse came through American mediation: after weeks of fruitless negotiatons with both sides, Philip Habib finally hammered out an agreement whereby the PLO's troops and command would evacuate the city. First the Syrian brigade, which likewise had been trapped in Beirut, would withdraw overland to Syria; then American, French, and Italian forces would assume responsibility for the evacuation of the Palestinians over land and by sea. To secure the PLO's willingness to leave, the United States guaranteed that no harm would come to the Palestinian civilians remaining in Beirut and that the IDF would not enter the western half of the city. At about the same time President Reagan published the essence of a new political initiative to solve the Middle East conflict, but it was promptly rejected by the Israeli government and the PLO.

As the evacuation got under way, the Lebanese Parliament convened and elected Bashir Gemayel as the country's new President. This was ostensibly another achievement for Israel, which had definitely had an interest as well as a hand in getting Bashir elected. Yet this victory proved to be no more than an illusion: just as he had held his men back from fighting alongside the IDF as originally promised, upon being elected President Gemayel informed Begin that he would not sign a peace treaty with Israel. In fact he was not prepared to commit himself to anything beyond the maintenance of informal ties with Israel because—or so he explained—he intended to serve as President for the entire Lebanese population, not just the Christian Phalangists. This reversal was of little avail, for despite his reneging on the issue of full relations with his partners to the war, Gemayel remained a prime target to his enemies, and to none more than the Syrians. It had long been clear that they would not rest until they had disposed of him—as indeed one of their agents did very effectively on September 14.

In the wake of Gemayel's assassination, and despite Israel's pledge (as a condition for the PLO's evacuation) that her forces would not enter the predominantly Moslem half of the city, the IDF was ordered to move into West Beirut. However, it was decided that Israeli forces would not enter the large refugee camps of Sabra and Shatila; instead this task was left to the Phalangists. When the Americans protested the IDF's move they were told that Israel felt obliged to enter West Beirut to maintain order and protect the population against outbursts of revenge over Gemayal's murder. It had long been common knowledge that hundreds of Palestinians stopped at Phalangist roadblocks in Beirut had subsequently vanished. Quite independent of Gemayel's murder the Phalangists had a long list of scores with the Palestinians and were perennially out to settle them.

When the killing was over and the truth came to light the only surprise was the harrowing extent of the carnage. Men, women, and children—entire families—were indiscriminately slaughtered. Needless to say the massacre in Sabra and Shatila marked a new shift in the war, for the defensibility of Israel's position in West Beirut had been demolished. The IDF's presence in Beirut—once regarded as a military victory—had been deteriorated into an intolerable burden to Israel's morale and a stain on her image as a moral society. Within days hundreds of thousands of Israelis came out to demonstrate in Tel Aviv, demanding both the IDF's unconditional withdrawal from Lebanon and the appointment of an official commission of inquiry to investigate Israel's implication in the Beirut massacre. The IDF was forced to pull out of West Beirut immediately and was replaced by the return of the multinational force that had presided over the PLO's evacuation.

In February 1983 the inquiry commission headed by Supreme Court Justice Yitzhak Kahan published its finding that Israel was indirectly responsible for what had happened in Sabra and Shatila. Ariel Sharon was forced to resign as Defense Minister and the head of Military Intelligence was relieved of his duties. Yet the impact of the report, like the war itself, only seemed to deepen the rift in Israeli society.

Presumably Israel finally reaped the fruits of her runaway war in

May 1983 when she signed a political agreement with the Lebanese government. Although it fell considerably short of a formal peace treaty, the accord was supposed to enable the IDF to conduct a staged withdrawal from Lebanon. It also imposed certain limitations on the Lebanese, obliging their government to maintain commercial ties with Israel, and provided for the establishment of a permanent Israeli representation in Lebanon. What is more it forbade Lebanon from accepting in her harbors arms and equipment destined for any other Arab state. To the degree that this agreement was indeed a political achievement, it was a short-lived one. For the internal situation in Lebanon began to deteriorate sharply in the autumn of 1983, after the IDF's withdrawal from the Shouf Mountains where it had served in a policing role between the warring Druze and Phalangist camps. By the end of the winter Amin Gemayel's government, beset by a new outbreak of civil war and more susceptible than ever before to Syrian pressure, felt constrained to break the agreement with Israel, and shortly thereafter Israel recalled its representatives from Beirut.

Slowly but surely Israel scaled her objectives in Lebanon down to a more realistic scale. Following Sharon's ouster as Defense Minister in February 1983, and particularly after Begin's resignation the following summer (which evidently was influenced if not wholly precipitated by the outcome of the Lebanese escapade), their successors concluded that Israel could no longer guarantee the safety of the Christian community in Lebanon. Moreover Israel resigned herself to the Syrian military presence in Lebanon. Now her aim was to extricate the IDF from Lebanon while ensuring the security of settlements in the Galilee.

The Israeli position was further softened with the formation of a National Unity Government following the elections of July 1984. Israel was prepared not only to live with a Syrian military presence in Lebanon but to acknowledge that Syria played a focal and permanent role in Lebanon. All she asked for was assurances that the Syrians would not move their forces southward after the IDF withdrew from the Bekaa Valley, or permit armed Palestinians to operate against Israel from the territory under their control. Her position on UNIFIL also changed markedly, and Chief of Staff Moshe Levi asserted that UNIFIL could play a positive role in Lebanon. Still, Israel continued to insist that its forces not be deployed directly along the border but in a zone further north.

Despite the many concessions, however, Israel has not been able to reach an agreement with the Lebanese government—or indirectly with Damascus—on satisfactory security arrangements in south Lebanon. As the war reached the middle of its third year Israel was still unable to conclude it and bring her soldiers home.

The war in Lebanon has been a source of great disappointment in Israel. An interim assessment of its achievements and failures indicates that it has fallen considerably short of the expectations that attended it, and Israel has paid a very steep price for her meager gains. One important achievement of the war was the destruction of the PLO's military network in south Lebanon, which had posed a constant threat to settlements in northern Israel. Isolated Palestinian squads can, of course, occasionally position a Katyusha rocket launcher and fire at the Galilee, but such exceptions cannot be compared to the artillery grid that existed in south Lebanon before the war. On the other hand, although the PLO's network was destroyed, the demographic foundation of the Palestinian presence in south Lebanon has remained intact: no fewer than 90,000 Palestinians are to be found in refugee camps a short distance from the Israeli border.

The war's other much-touted achievement was the removal of the PLO's headquarters from Beirut—and effectively from Lebanon as a whole. Ironically, however, the final expulsion of Yasser Arafat and his men from Lebanon came courtesy of the Syrians. Israel indeed was responsible for the eviction of the PLO's command and thousands of its fighters from Beirut, but the Syrians and their supporters in the highly factionalized Palestinian national movement are to be credited with driving Arafat and his men out of Tripoli.

The strains within the PLO itself and between its leaders and Damascus, which began to show even before the war, were sorely exacerbated during the fighting. Arafat's readiness to mend his relations with King Hussein, who by then was mooting the notion of a compromise with Israel, ultimately led to a schism within the PLO. But although Arafat managed to overcome this split in the ranks and was reconfirmed as the organization's leader by the Palestinian National Council when it convened in Amman in the winter of 1984 the rift between his majority faction and the powers in Damascus grew even wider. Israel might have exploited this opportunity to break the Middle East deadlock by making a magnanimous political gesture to the Palestinians or to Jordan, but she failed to do so. The result was that the war in Lebanon ended in a stalemate between Israel and the Palestinians similar to the one that had caused the war in the first place.

And so the war that had been conceived as a means to achieve political ends wound up as no more than a grueling and corrosive military action. There was no reason for the Palestinian leaders in the West Bank and Gaza Strip to cooperate with Israel by opposing the PLO's official line; on the contrary, while their sense of frustration undoubtedly soared, their willingness to join in finding a political solution tailored to Jerusalem's dictates declined sharply.

The war also brought about another political setback for Israel in her relations with Egypt. The Egyptian ambassador was recalled following the massacre in the refugee camps and a marked deterioration in the contacts between the two countries ensued. Certain quarters in Egypt have even argued that by invading Lebanon Israel has shown herself to be a country whose foreign policy is based solely on the exercise of force, obliging Egypt to arm herself more conscientiously and prepare for the worst in her relations with the Jewish state. In this respect the war in Lebanon has proven highly damaging to the critically important Camp David process.

Israel has created a new enemy for herself to the north in the Shiite population of south Lebanon. Primarily ardent Moslems, the Shiites justly regard the IDF as an occupying army. At the beginning of the war many Shiites in the area welcomed the arrival of the Israeli Army because it was routing the Palestinian forces. But as the IDF's occupation of south Lebanon wore on the resistance of the Shiite population mounted—and with it came a seething hatred for Israel. The guerrilla war against the Israeli troops in Lebanon has in fact been conducted primarily by the Shiites, with the Palestinians relegated to second place in these operations. Thus while the IDF presence in Lebanon has prevented the shelling of Israeli settlements, the number of Israeli casualties—in this case soldiers—is many times higher than it was before the war. Whether the Shiites will pursue their guerrilla war and attempt to carry it over the border into Israel once the IDF withdraws from Lebanon remains to be seen.

Perhaps the most significant setback from Israel's point of view has occurred in Lebanon itself. In terms of its internal balance of power, Lebanon has become more of a Moslem Arab country than ever before. The standing of the Lebanese Christians, and especially the Phalangist militia, has eroded considerably, and they find themselves in far worse a position now than they were on the eve of the war. Of course Lebanon has not become a confrontation state in the full sense of the term; on the other hand there is no question that Syria calls the shots in Lebanon today.

The war was also responsible for upsetting the delicate military balance between Israel and Syria, for in its wake Syria has received an astounding infusion of arms. In fact the Syrians have almost doubled their military strength since 1982, with the Soviet Union supplying advanced weapons systems—including aircraft and surface-to-air missiles, to say nothing of the highly accurate SA-21 surface-to-surface missile—that were not made available before. At the same time the Soviets have insinuated themselves into the Syrian military infrastructure: SAM-5 missile batteries are manned by Russian teams, and the Syrian air-defense system is now set up to draw upon the network of Soviet surveillance satellites.

As Syria's military strength has grown, Israel has found herself drawn into a fierce arms race that places an ever greater strain on her chronically ailing economy. There is also no question that the war in Lebanon has contributed directly to the economic crisis in Israel, for in addition to the costs of the fighting and the maintenance of an occupation force, the Israeli government has spent huge sums in Lebanon building the defensive infrastructure needed to sustain its army there.

Finally, the sad but unavoidable fact at this writing is that the Israeli Army is stuck in Lebanon: routine maneuvers have been neglected; all attention is focused on a problem that is strategically marginal; and the long-term effect will be a weakening of its military prowess. What's more the war that led to this highly unsatisfactory situation exposed a number of failings in the IDF itself, so that certain military experts no longer hold the Israeli Army in quite the same professional regard as before. These failings are certainly reparable—on condition, of course, that the IDF attends to them. But as long as the army is tied down in Lebanon as an occupation army, it is difficult to see just how it will be able to do so.

Above and beyond facing these failings and setbacks, Israel must now bear the cost of its venture in Lebanon: hundreds of dead, thousands of wounded, and the shattering of a long-standing consensus on security that has produced an alarming rift within Israeli society. From the sobering consequences of Operation Peace for Galilee one may be forced to conclude that a country can be victorious on the battlefield but lose a war strategically; that a small nation whose leaders fail to appreciate the limits of military power is doomed to pay dearly for their arrogance; and that a democracy like Israel, whose defense is based on a militia army, cannot possibly win a war that lacks not only broad public support but even the slimmest national consensus regarding its very necessity. If these are the lessons learned from the war, the IDF is sure to return to its true character as the defense army of Israel.

Index